Sons of Ishmael

UNIVERSITY PRESS OF FLORIDA

Florida A&M University, Tallahassee
Florida Atlantic University, Boca Raton
Florida Gulf Coast University, Ft. Myers
Florida International University, Miami
Florida State University, Tallahassee
New College of Florida, Sarasota
University of Central Florida, Orlando
University of Florida, Gainesville
University of North Florida, Jacksonville
University of South Florida, Tampa
University of West Florida, Pensacola

Sons of Ishmael

Muslims through European Eyes in the Middle Ages

John V. Tolan

University Press of Florida
Gainesville Tallahassee Tampa Boca Raton Pensacola
Orlando Miami Jacksonville Ft. Myers Sarasota

Printed in the United States of America on acid-free paper

First cloth printing, 2008
First paperback printing, 2013

Library of Congress Cataloging-in-Publication Data
Tolan, John Victor, 1959–
Sons of Ishmael: Muslims through European eyes in the Middle Ages/John Tolan.
p. cm.
Includes bibliographical references and index.
ISBN 978-0-8130-3222-1 (cloth: alk. paper)
ISBN 978-0-8130-4467-5 (pbk.)
1. Islam—Relations—Christianity. 2. Christianity and other religions—Islam.
3. Religious thought—Europe. 4. Religious thought—Middle Ages, 600–1500.
5. Middle East—Relations—Europe. 6. Europe—Relations—Middle East. 7. Middle Ages—Historiography. 8. Islam—Controversial literature. I. Title.
BP172.T63 2008
261.2'709409029–dc22 2007042547

The University Press of Florida is the scholarly publishing agency for the State University System of Florida, comprising Florida A&M University, Florida Atlantic University, Florida Gulf Coast University, Florida International University, Florida State University, New College of Florida, University of Central Florida, University of Florida, University of North Florida, University of South Florida, and University of West Florida.

University Press of Florida
15 Northwest 15th Street
Gainesville, FL 32611-2079
http://www.upf.com

For Marie and Paraska

Contents

Introduction

The snows had been heavy in the Alps during the winter of 1215–16. That at least was what Jacques de Vitry thought as he prepared to ford a swollen river in the north of Italy in April 1216. Jacques was on his way to Rome, his mule loaded with two chests of personal effects, in particular books, in order to be ordained bishop of Acre, de facto capital of the crusader Kingdom of Jerusalem since the loss of the holy city to Saladin in 1187. Jacques, closely associated with the movements of intellectual and spiritual renewal in Flanders and Paris, was renowned as an ardent reformer and brilliant preacher; he had preached the crusade against the Cathar heretics of Languedoc and against the Muslims in order to recapture Jerusalem. Tireless advocate of ecclesiastical reform, enthralling orator, zealous proponent of crusade, he was a natural choice for the bishopric of Acre. Yet he had a formidable adversary—the devil. As Jacques explained in a letter to friends in Paris and Flanders:

> As I entered Lombardy, the devil cast into a river my arms, that is to say my books, with which I had undertaken to combat him, along with other things necessary for my sustenance. He pulled them down into the deep and tempestuous torrents. Because of the melting snow, the river was unusually violent; it had swept away bridges and large stones. It carried off one of my chests, full of books. The other chest, in which the finger of my [spiritual] mother Marie d'Oignies rested, held up my mule and prevented him from sinking. Against all odds, my mule, with the chest, arrived safely on the opposite bank. The other chest was miraculously found downstream, held back by the roots

> of some trees. What was particularly miraculous was that, although the water darkened the pages of my books a bit, all of them remained perfectly legible.[1]

Jacques sees himself as a soldier of Christ, fighting with spiritual and intellectual weapons against the great Enemy, the devil, and all his minions, be they Cathar heretics, Muslims, or bad Christians. It is only natural that the devil should attack him and seek to disarm him. Jacques could count on the aid of God and his saints—in this instance, in particular of Marie d'Oignies, the Beguine whom Jacques had served as confessor until her death in 1213 and whose *Life* Jacques subsequently wrote. Jacques carried her finger with him as a relic ever after; in the Holy Land, he would wear it, housed in a silver casket, on a chain around his neck.[2] Here he credits it with saving him and his mule, buoying up the chest in which it rested and guiding the mule safely to the far bank of the river.

In this spiritual combat with the devil, Jacques's arms are his books. He deploys them in order to preach the crusade, to dispute with heretics in Milan or Acre, and to attempt to convert Muslims to Christianity. Jacques is also a forger of arms—author of letters, sermons, and chronicles. He is not the only medieval author to describe books and knowledge in military metaphors. Petrus Alfonsi, in his *Dialogue against the Jews* (1110), affirms to his Jewish adversary, "I desire greatly to slay you with your own sword"—the "sword" being the Torah, with which he hopes to prove the falsity of Judaism.[3] In the same vein, Dominican Riccoldo da Montecroce, in his *Against the Law of the Saracens* (c. 1300), affirms that he can use the Qur'ân to confound the "perfidious law of the Saracens," just as David slew Goliath with the latter's own sword.[4] Such imagery is not limited to interreligious polemics: Peter Abelard describes his rivalry with Parisian master William of Champeaux as a siege, and Bernard of Clairvaux presents his own confrontation with Abelard as that of a pious David against an intellectual Goliath.[5] The very titles of medieval religious polemics, by Christians or by Muslims, evoke military struggle: the *Pugio fidei (Dagger of the Faith)* by Ramon Martí (1278), the *Maqâmi' al-Sulbân fi-l-radd 'alâ 'abadat al-awthân* (*Bludgeons for the Suppression of Crosses in the Refutation of the Idolaters*) by the Muslim al-Khazrajî (late 12th century), *The Sharpened Sword: A Response to the Coran*, by the Damascene Christian al-Mu'taman Ibn al-'Assâl,[6] *Al-Sârim al-maslûl 'alâ shâtim al-Rasûl (The Sword Unsheathed against He Who Insults the Messenger of God)* by the Muslim Ibn Taymiyya (1293), etc.

Judaism, Christianity, and Islam are religions of the book, and it should perhaps not surprise us that medieval authors of the three faiths see books as both targets and weapons in interreligious conflict. Jacques de Vitry's Parisian education was very much an initiation into oral performance—intellectual disputes carried out before masters and students, or sermons preached before different audiences. Yet these highly structured oral performances were centered on the explication of texts: texts of logic, theology, and of course the Bible.

This book is an exploration of how various Christian European authors, from the ninth century to the fourteenth, direct their pens against Islam. In some cases, these medieval authors composed polemical treatises, designed to attack or refute the doctrines and practices of Islam, or apologetical treatises, seeking to defend Christianity against (real or potential) Muslim arguments; many treatises combine both polemical and apologetical elements. Such texts were only rarely addressed to readers of the rival faith: more commonly, they were meant to persuade vacillating Christians of the superiority of their religion to Islam, in order to prevent them from converting to Islam or in order to convince them of the justice and necessity of wars against Muslims.

Other texts analyzed in these pages are not polemical, but rather eschatological or historical. Their authors grapple with the challenge that the success of Islam posed to their Christian worldview. Ever since the conversion of the Roman Empire to Christianity in the fourth century, Christian authors had proclaimed that the new Christian Empire was destined to triumph over its heathen enemies. This vision was shaken by the invasions of Germanic and other "barbarian" peoples in the following centuries, but the conversion of many of the invaders to Christianity brought new hope. The Muslims, in contrast, conquered the wealthiest and most populous parts of the old Roman Empire, made them part of a rich and flourishing civilization, and gradually persuaded most descendants of the conquered inhabitants to convert to Islam. The challenge for many authors was to explain these tremendous changes in ways that would reassure Christians that God still preferred them and that He destined them for an ultimate triumph.

I have explored these issues in a previous book, *Saracens: Islam in the Medieval European Imagination,* tracing the development of European images and perceptions of Islam through the first six Muslim centuries. The roots of these images are found in the defensive ruminations of Christian *dhimmis,* minorities whose rights to practice their religion were scrupulously guaranteed, but who were second-class citizens, subjects of a vigorous new Muslim empire. The earliest Christian authors to describe the Muslim conquest and dominion of the Christian Roman Empire reiterated the standard *topoi* used since the Hebrew prophets to explain their subjugation: the Muslim invader was a scourge sent by God to punish his wayward flock. As Christians got to know Islam better, and as they saw with growing alarm that their coreligionists were converting to Islam, they portrayed the rival faith as a Christological heresy, a worldly religion cleverly crafted by the cunning heresiarch Muhammad to dupe an uncouth and lascivious people into following him.

Far from these communities of *dhimmis,* Christians of northern Europe and of Byzantium imagined their Saracen enemies as idolaters who practiced the discredited and colorful rites of the ancient pagans, devoting sacrifices and prayers to a pantheon of idols that included Jupiter, Apollo, and their special god Muhammad. This image of Saracen idolatry provided a useful caricature with which the Christian author could justify and glorify war against Muslims. By creating a largely imaginary enemy outside the bounds of Christian Europe, the chansons de geste could revel in the knightly violence that was in reality more often directed at internal Christian enemies.

This caricature of Saracen paganism was untenable for those with even a rudimentary familiarity with Islam, many of whom portrayed Islam as a heresy—that is to say, as a deviant form of Christianity. For Guibert de Nogent, who in 1109 composed a chronicle of the first crusade, Muhammad was merely the latest and most nefarious of a long line of Oriental heresiarchs: the success of Islam was proof of the Oriental penchant for heresy, calling for the intervention of vigorous and stolid Latins. The image of Islam as heresy, forged by *dhimmis* in the Near East and Spain, came to northern Europe at a time when Latin Christians came into frequent contact with Muslims and when they were increasingly preoccupied with the supposedly nefarious influence of other non-Christians: Jews and heretics. The association between these various enemies of the faith is crucial for understanding the Christian perceptions of Muslims (or, for that matter, of Jews or heretics) in the following centuries. Petrus Alfonsi included an anti-Muslim chapter in his *Dialogues against the Jews;* Peter of Cluny composed a polemical triptych against Jews, Muslims, and Petrobrusian heretics; Alain de Lille wrote a treatise against Cathars, Waldensians, Jews, and Muslims.

The development of scholastic theology in the twelfth and thirteenth centuries went hand in hand with the new forms of argumentation used against infidels. If Catholic doctrine was based on reason, it should be possible to prove it to Jews, heretics, and Muslims through logical exposition and argumentation. For various Christian writers, from Petrus Alfonsi to Roger Bacon and Ramon Llull, logical "necessary reasons" (*rationes necessariae*) could prove the faith to the infidel. Others did not go so far: Thomas Aquinas affirmed that the faith could be shown not to be contradicted by reason but could not be proven by rational arguments. Fellow Dominicans such as Ramon Martí and Riccoldo da Montecroce accordingly used rational argumentation and textual criticism to attack the beliefs, rites, and sacred writings of Jews, heretics, and Muslims but did not try to prove the articles of the Christian faith to them. By the fourteenth century, European Christian authors increasingly came to realize that these intellectual combats with Islam had failed as miserably as had their military struggles with Mamluks in the eastern Mediterranean and (increasingly) with the Ottomans in eastern Europe. In the following centuries, many Europeans would depend on the works of authors of the twelfth and thirteenth centuries for their knowledge (or at times disinformation) concerning Islam.

This book explores in greater depth some of the issues raised in *Saracens.* It brings together ten previously published essays. Christian polemics against Islam need to be understood in the broader context of interreligious polemics in the medieval Mediterranean world. The first chapters look in detail at specific themes in Christian anti-Muslim polemics. Embrico of Mainz's *Life of Muhammad,* in Latin verse, the object of chapter 1, depicts the prophet of Islam as a trickster and scoundrel, not an Antichrist but rather an anti-saint: an errant preacher who feigns holiness and performs bogus miracles through magic and sleight-of-hand, hoodwinking the gullible Arab masses into deeming him holy. Embrico's portrayal comes at a time when European contacts with Islam are on the rise, but also when churchmen feel threatened by wandering preachers closer to home, many of whom are denounced as charlatans or heretics. By portraying Muhammad in the familiar and despised role of mountebank preacher, Embrico seeks no doubt to kill two birds with one stone, discrediting both those who follow the prophet of Islam and those who follow itinerant visionaries closer to home.

Embrico's polemical biography concludes with a strange legend involving Muhammad's death and burial: God strikes Muhammad dead as punishment for his sins, and pigs begin to devour his corpse, the remains of which are subsequently placed in an iron coffin, suspended in midair by magnets. This trick successfully convinces the gullible "Saracen" masses that Muhammad had been a holy man and prophet. Chapter 2 examines this story of Muhammad's death and burial along with similar accounts by other Christian authors, showing how, according to long established literary and hagiographic *topoi,* the supposed desecration of the corpse of an enemy is meant to show his disfavor in the eyes of God, while the bogus miracle of his floating tomb is meant to help explain why he is revered as a holy man.

Chapter 3 compares several accounts of Muhammad's life written in the Iberian peninsula during the second half of the thirteenth century by Ramon Martí, King Alfonso X of Castile and León, and Pedro Pascual. Earlier historians, notably Norman Daniel, had taken the latter two authors to task for indiscriminately mixing bona fide Muslim sources and scurrilous Christian legends to concoct strangely hybrid and derogatory accounts of Muhammad's life; for Daniel, this shows the authors' lack of critical acumen in distinguishing accurate from inaccurate information. My reading of these authors, on the contrary, sees them carefully constructing an image of the Muslim prophet which could be both recognizable in its partial accuracy and effective in denying legitimacy to Muhammad and his followers. Rather than presenting an inept hodge-podge, these authors forge clever and coherent—although inaccurate—polemics.

Peter the Venerable, abbot of the rich and powerful Burgundian monastery of Cluny, in the 1140s commissioned a team of scholars to translate the Qur'ân and other texts concerning Islam from Arabic into Latin. Robert of Ketton's translation of the Qur'ân became an essential tool for Europeans of the following five centuries who wished to study Islam. Yet, as chapter 4 shows, the goal of Peter of Cluny in commissioning these translations and in writing two texts about the "law of Muhammad," was not the dispassionate study of a rival religion but the refutation of what he qualifies as the "diabolical heresy of the Saracens." Peter's intellectual combat is all the more necessary because it comes at a time when Europeans have become painfully aware of the cultural and intellectual gap with the Arab world. Among other things, Peter hopes to show potential doubters among his Latin readers that Christianity is indeed the superior religion, despite the higher level of learning and wealth of the Muslim world.

The following chapters explore different ideological purposes of the portrayals—positive and negative—of Muslims. Why do medieval crusade epics and chronicles paint Muslim adversaries as pagan idolaters? Chapter

5 examines the legends surrounding Kurbqa, Atabeg of Mosul, whom the troops of the First Crusade routed outside of Antioch in June 1098. Western chroniclers present him as Corbaran, a pagan king who curses his idols for failing to secure victory for him. A thirteenth-century *Chanson de Croisade* (Crusading epic), the *Chrétienté Corbaran*, goes further: it has him convert to Christianity, destroy the idols he once worshiped, and fight his former suzerain, the "Caliph of Paganism." At the end of the thirteenth century, in spite of the failure of the crusades, the anonymous poet dreams of converting a powerful enemy. History, it seems, repeats itself: Muslim rulers are cast in the familiar guise of pagan kings who (as potential new Constantines) might convert and come to the aid of an embattled Christendom.

Similar legends circulated regarding Salâh al-Dîn, better known in Europe as Saladin, the sultan of Egypt and Syria who captured Jerusalem in 1187, to the great shock and consternation of Latin Europe. In the immediate aftermath of 1187, as we see in chapter 6, some Latin writers portrayed Saladin stereotypically as a cruel scourge, sent by God to punish Christian sins. Yet more often, over the course of the Middle Ages, European authors saw him as an embodiment of chivalric virtues, a model knight and a just prince. In the increasingly elaborate and colorful legends surrounding him, a tension develops between two tendencies: some writers present him as living proof that one need not be Christian or European to be a near-perfect knight and prince; others forge bogus genealogies that make him the direct descendant of French knights and affirm that he secretly converted to Christianity. In the latter cases, Saladin, like the legendary Corbaran, converted to Christianity, offers new and illusory hope of a redoubtable Saracen enemy becoming a powerful ally.

In 1175 (as we shall see in chapter 7), Emperor Frederick I Barbarossa sent his chaplain Burchard of Strasbourg to Cairo and Damascus to negotiate an alliance with Saladin. We know nothing of the political negotiations that followed; we do know that twelve years later Saladin wrested Jerusalem from the Latins and that Frederick set out to fight him on the third crusade, dying on the way in 1190. But in 1175, Burchard was sent to negotiate peace; he subsequently wrote an account of his travels: how he sailed from Genoa to Alexandria, sailed up the Nile to Cairo, and crossed the desert to Damascus. He describes cities and countryside, the heat of the desert, crocodiles, the pyramids, the habits and dress of the locals. He makes note of numerous communities of Christians that thrive everywhere in the sultan's domains. He pays particular attention to the rites and practices of the "Saracens," in a manner remarkably free of polemical Christian prejudices. In particular, he narrates his pilgrimage to two holy sites devoted to the Virgin Mary: Matariyya, near Cairo, and Saydnâyâ, near Damascus. To each of these sanctuaries Christians and Muslims come to venerate the mother of Jesus. Burchard explains that Muslims believe that Mary was a holy virgin who miraculously gave birth to Jesus, a great prophet. This, he says, is why they show such devotion to her, and why they extend respect to Christians living throughout their land. And the Virgin rewards her devotees, both Christian and Muslim, by according them miracles, according to Burchard, for whom fundamental similarities between Muslims and Christians far outweigh their differences.

If Burchard testifies to what Maxime Rodinson has called "The Allure of Islam," some medieval writers saw this allure as perilous. This problem presented itself forcefully in the thirteenth century to a number of Latin writers on Islam, as we shall see in chapter 8. Thirteenth-century mendicant missionaries deployed rationalistic arguments in an attempt to prove the irrationality of Islam. Yet at the same time the works of Muslim scientists and philosophers became an integral part of the curriculum of European universities. How could the authors of such sophisticated works of erudition adhere to the supposedly irrational teachings of Muhammad? The answer, given in various forms by different authors, particularly Ramon Martí, Roger Bacon, Ramon Llull, and Riccoldo da Montecroce, was that they did not. These authors claimed that learned Saracens did not in fact believe in the doctrines of the Qur'ân and that only fear of physical punishment made them publicly proclaim their adherence to Islam. All four Christian polemicists were well read in Arabic philosophy and based their claims on key texts, notably those involving the disputes between Avicenna, al-Ghazâlî, and Averroes. The philosophical and theological disagreements between Muslim thinkers are distorted to make them "proofs" of the "irrationality" of Islam.

Chapter 9 examines the anti-Muslim polemics of Pedro Pascual, bishop of Jaén, who was captured by Grenadine raiders and spent the rest of his life in a prison in Granada. There he composed his *Sobre la seta Mahometana*, a virulent polemical work meant to discourage his fellow Christian prisoners from apostatizing. Pedro Pascual read Arabic and was familiar with Qur'ân and Hadith and conversant with Muslim practice; he affirms that he had debated with Muslims on questions of the faith. Pedro deploys his knowledge of Islam selectively and strategically in his tract, seeking to instruct his

Christian readers in the art of defending their faith through argumentation. But perhaps more than anything else, Pedro in his desperation paints Islam as an irrational cult of violence and licentiousness, in order to instill in his readers a contempt for Islam sufficient to prevent them from crossing the line and converting.

Some polemicists tried to use basic cultural differences between Christians and Muslims as a wedge to drive between the two, to accentuate the "otherness" of the adherents of the rival faith. An example of this is seen in chapter 10, "A Dreadful Racket: The Clanging of Bells and the Yowling of Muezzins in Iberian Interconfessional Polemics." Some Christian polemicists in ninth-century Muslim Spain depicted the muezzin's call for prayer as a diabolically inspired animalistic yelping; the same authors complained that Muslims mocked the sound of church bells. Both Muslim and Christian rulers at times restricted the rights of their minority subjects to ring bells or perform the call to prayer. Moreover, when conquering a rival city, one of the first symbolic acts of the victorious Christian ruler was often to transform the principal mosque into a church and hang bells in the minaret, while the victorious Muslims would transform the belfries into minarets and silence the bells.

In bringing together these essays, all of which were first published between 1996 and 2005 in journals or conference acts, I have added (mostly minor) corrections and revisions and have updated the bibliography. Six of the articles were originally published in French and one in Spanish; these appear for the first time in English.

These chapters were researched and written over the last decade; earlier forms of these chapters were presented to conferences and seminars from Cairo to Seattle. It would be a pleasure here to enumerate all the intellectual debts I have incurred in exchanges with colleagues whispered in the manuscript room of the Bibliothèque Nationale in Paris, ruminated at breakfast in the Casa Velazquez in Madrid, argued over beer in Houston, discussed while exploring the crusader castle of Tripoli, or mused in a car between Hammamet and Sousse. I will resist the temptation to reproduce—and amplify—the long list of acknowledgments I produced in the beginning of *Saracens,* to colleagues on both sides of the Atlantic and all sides of the Mediterranean. The attentive reader will find my debt to many of them acknowledged in the endnotes in the pages that follow.

∴ 1 ∴

Antihagiography

Embrico of Mainz's *Vita Mahumeti*

In the late eleventh and early twelfth centuries, the spiritual and intellectual landscape of northwestern Europe experienced tremendous changes: the reform movements associated with Gregory VII and with new monastic orders; the rapid spread of heresy for the first time since the sixth century; the Crusades; increasing intellectual and cultural contact with the Mediterranean (especially Muslim) world. Robert I. Moore and other scholars have argued that the first two of these phenomena were closely related: the more the new orthodoxy defined itself, the more deviant doctrine and practice were labeled heretical.[1]

How does Islam—or more exactly, Christians' perceptions of Islam—fit into this picture? In earlier texts, "Saracen" religion was portrayed (if at all) as pagan idolatry; in the *Song of Roland*, for example, the Saracens worship a trinity of golden idols: Apollo, Tervagant, and Mahomet.[2] In the twelfth century it became more frequently portrayed as Christian heresy.[3] The most common explanation for this change is that as Latin Christian writers and their readers grew more familiar with Islam (through trade, crusade, and translations of Arabic texts into Latin), the pagan paradigm became untenable. Clearly Muslims were not polytheists, and Muhammad was not a golden idol; it was more plausible to portray him as a charlatan who led Christians astray through a clever mix of Christianity and diabolical error.

Yet this only explains part of the story. For Christians of northern Europe before the eleventh century, paganism—rather than heresy—was the common face of error. Wars were fought against pagan nations and missionaries were sent unto them. It was natural to imagine the distant Saracens in the guise of more familiar enemies of Christendom. By the late eleventh century, paganism had faded and heresy and reform had become the two great preoccupations of northern European prelates. Now Islam was seen as one of the great Christian heresies and Muhammad as that familiar and dangerous figure: the scheming, power-hungry, lustful, demonically driven heresiarch, so dangerous because he feigns holiness so skillfully. For these twelfth-century writers, Islam was not paganism; still less was it a belief system distinct from Christianity. Rather, it was part of the great enemy: heresy.

Sometime in the early twelfth century, Embrico of Mainz composed a life of Muhammad in 1,149 rhymed leonine hexameters. This is perhaps the earliest and certainly the most elaborate twelfth-century portrayal of Muhammad. It is also the first coherent theological response to Islam by a Latin writer. Embrico presented Muhammad in the guise of a fourth-century Libyan heresiarch driven by lust and worldly ambition to lead his people into a depraved cult. This portrayal enabled him to denigrate Islam while at the same time explaining its tremendous temporal success.

As proponents of Gregorian reform attempted to gain tighter papal control over appointment to church office, maintenance of church lands and monies, and liturgical practice, increasing numbers of Christians were labeled heretics: bishops jealous of their prerogatives so labeled proponents of papal reforms, proponents of reform so labeled recalcitrant clerics, and those who believed that the reforms did not go far enough were branded as heretics by both parties. For the first time since the conversion of the Arians in the fifth and sixth centuries, heresy had become a problem in northern Europe. Often, "heretic" and "reformer" were attacking the same traditional sources of authority and spouting very similar arguments; there was much anxiety over whom to believe and how to distinguish truth from error.[4]

The heresiarch Henry of Lausanne (or Henry the Monk) provides an apt example. A monk and then a preacher in Lausanne, he sent word in 1116 to Hildebert of Lavardin, bishop of Le Mans, that he wished to come to preach reform. Hildebert replied that he was welcome to come. When Henry arrived and began to preach, Hildebert was away in Rome. When Hildebert returned, he found the local count vainly attempting to crush an anticlerical uprising fomented by Henry. With some difficulty Hildebert was able to regain control of the city, expel Henry, and calm the passions of his people.[5]

Henry was a wolf in sheep's clothing: welcomed as a reformer, he turned out to be a dangerous heresiarch.

In the same way, Embrico's Muhammad (or Mammutius, as he calls him) is a heretic who poses as holy man. Embrico indeed was not the first Christian writer to portray Muhammad in such terms: Arab, Byzantine and Spanish anti-Muslim polemicists had already written prose biographies presenting Muhammad as a heresiarch and forerunner of Antichrist. Embrico uses these traditions, though it is unclear how—or in what form—he has access to them.[6] Embrico deftly weaves together these strands of legend to form a hostile biography of Islam's prophet.

No Latin author before Embrico had written a biography of Muhammad in verse. Yet Embrico had a model close at hand: hagiography. His contemporaries were writing saints' lives in Leonine Hexameters; Embrico took these as a model for his new brand of antihagiography: using the standard hagiographical topoi that fill saints' lives, he created the supreme antisaint.

Just as hagiography provides archetypes of pure Christian lives, Embrico used the various topoi of hagiography to provide an archetype of a sinful, heretical life. These topoi, or signs of sanctity, are so well known, indeed so standardized, that as Benedicta Ward has said, "The life of a saint whose history was unknown could be entirely reconstructed from hagiographic models."[7] Embrico uses these topoi in two distinct ways: at times, Muhammad and his mentor (the nameless Magus) deliberately feign these signs of sanctity to trick people into following them. Like Simon Magus or Antichrist, they are magicians who perform bogus miracles and mimic pious behavior in order to lead their people astray.[8] In other instances, the opposite of a hagiographical topos occurs to them, showing that they do not have God's favor.

Embrico also used classical Latin poetry for inspiration.[9] Indeed, Latin hagiography was inspired by classical poetry and was in a way a response to classical epic. In the earliest hagiographical texts, such as the *Vitae patrum*, ascetic saints are described as athletes who engage in epic battles with demons. Many earlier hagiographical texts—in Greek and Latin—are written in prose, taking as models the classical traditions of history and biography. But early on, some Latin hagiographers wrote in hexameters (often rhymed leonine hexameters), taking as their models the epics of antiquity and the early Middle Ages.[10] Such, for example, is Fortunatus's sixth-century *Vita Sancti Martini*, in hexameters—a rewriting of the prose life by Sepulcius

Severus.[11] These were new Christian epics that presented new Christian heroes: ascetics and martyrs.

These two parallel hagiographical traditions—in prose and in verse—were widely practiced in Latin Europe during the eleventh and twelfth centuries. In general, lives of contemporary or recent saints were written in prose; leonine hexameters were employed for recasting Latin prose biographies of the ascetics and martyrs of the early church.[12]

The lives of the ascetic saints (or *vitae* as opposed to the *passiones* of the martyrs) tend to follow a similar plot structure.[13] The saint moves gradually from the concerns of the world into greater and greater isolation: for example, a rich man gives away his money to become a monk, picks a particularly isolated cell, and then goes off to live alone in the desert. There, perhaps, he is miraculously fed or saved from danger, showing God's favor. At the end, the saint—alive or dead—is reintegrated into the community, but as its model: he returns to become a bishop or abbot, or perhaps people flock to him to found a new monastic community, or perhaps it is his relics that become a new focus of devotion.

Given the twelfth century's interest in both reform and heresy, these ascetic heroes naturally evoked both adulation and uneasiness: just as it was difficult (in the case of someone like Henry of Lausanne) to tell the live holy man from the live heretic, it was at times difficult to tell the dead saint from the dead heresiarch. The Latin texts about heresiarchs—like the *vitae* of ascetic saints—tended to follow typological models. Like the saint, the heresiarch follows his own spiritual path, distinguishing himself from his peers, developing a reputation for sanctity, and attracting a following apart from (and at times in conflict with) the existing church structure. This series of disquieting parallels is perhaps what leads these authors to stress the heresiarch's moral depravity lying under the veneer of piety. Jerome, for example, describes the lewd orgies performed by Simon Magus, Nicolas of Antioch, and Priscillian.[14] Moral depravity shows the true nature of heretics. Yet in order to explain their successes, these heresiarchs are often portrayed feigning the signs of sanctity familiar from the lives of the saints. Embrico makes this parallel all the more striking by modeling his life of Muhammad on the hagiographical *vitae*, with their rhymed hexameters, so popular among early twelfth-century writers.

The early twelfth century's most skilled and prolific verse hagiographers were those of the poetic school surrounding Hildebert of Lavardin—most notably Hildebert himself and Marbod of Rennes, two bishops active both in reform and in the suppression of heresy.[15] These authors wrote saints' lives both in prose and in leonine hexameters. Again, their verse hagiography is reserved for the saints of the early church, including largely legendary figures such as Theophilus and Mary the Egyptian.

The *Vita Beatae Mariae Aegyptiacae (Life of Saint Mary the Egyptian)* is the longest of Hildebert's hagiographical poems. The legend of Mary the Egyptian enjoyed tremendous popularity in the Middle Ages; several versions—in Greek and Latin—precede Hildebert's text, and numerous later authors composed verse lives of Mary: in Latin, German, Dutch, French, and Spanish.[16] Hildebert's *Vita* is in fact the story of two people: Mary, a converted prostitute, and Zosimas, a pious monk. These two embody two standard types of saints: Mary, the reformed sinner, Zosimas, pure and saintly from birth. Hildebert begins with Zosimas, telling us of his youth and of his entrance into an idealized monastic community on the banks of the Jordan. Zosimas and others of this community frequently cross the Jordan to live in the desert as hermits. On one such occasion, Mary comes to Zosimas in the desert and asks for his prayers. She narrates at length her debauched life as a prostitute, her subsequent conversion, and her forty-seven years spent as a hermit in the desert.[17] She asks Zosimas to return to his monastery and bring back the Eucharist so that she can take communion; he does this. A year later, when Zosimas next sets out into the desert, he finds Mary dead. He weeps over her body and performs funeral rites. He tries to dig a grave for her, but finds himself too old and frail for the task. A lion comes along, shows reverence for Mary's body, and—at Zosimas's bidding—digs her grave.

Embrico's *Vita Mahumeti* is a work in the same tradition of verse hagiography as of Hildebert's *Life of Saint Mary the Egyptian*. Embrico's poem, however, is antihagiography; it portrays two scurrilous characters by exploiting the topoi of the hagiographical tradition. Moreover, it is written in leonine hexameters—the same verse that Hildebert and his contemporaries used in their hagiographical poems.

These similarities, perhaps, led the copyist of one manuscript to attribute the *Vita Mahumeti* to Hildebert himself and led scholars to accept this attribution until the twentieth century.[18] Later scholars found that the verse style of the *Vita Mahumeti* was inferior to that of Hildebert's work.[19] They also discovered a poetic *Vita auctori*, which refers to the author of the *Vita Mahumeti*, saying that his name was Embrico and mentioning that he was from Mainz.[20] This poem, full of praise for Embrico's piety, learning, and poetic skill, tells us very little about who Embrico was. Records from Mainz have presented us with several possible candidates, the most likely being the treasurer of Mainz from 1090 until 1112.[21] The comparisons I will make between Embrico's *Vita Mahumeti* and Hildebert's *Life of Saint Mary the Egyptian* serve two purposes. First, I will show that Embrico knew of the work of Hildebert and his school and modeled his antihagiographical poem on their verse hagiography—indeed, he may be familiar with Hildebert's *Life of Saint Mary the Egyptian*. Second, I wish to show that throughout his work, Embrico is consciously using standard hagiographic topoi familiar to his readers: the life of St. Mary provides good examples of many of these topoi.

As we have seen, with Embrico's *Vita Mahumeti,* Muhammad the heresiarch begins to replace Muhammad the golden idol in the European imagination. Embrico makes this break clear near the beginning of the *Vita*, explaining that Muslims (whom he refers to as "pagans") worship neither the gods of classical antiquity nor any other idols; he catalogues the Roman gods whom Muslims spurn. Moreover, Embrico explains, these pagans claim that they worship the One true God, while Jews and Christians are in error.

Here one may ask whom they so venerate:

His name is Mahumet; having confided in this leader, they
    are puffed up with pride.
The worship of all the other gods has given way to him,
    He who holds the very reign of perfidy.
This new error expelled the old errors
    And to Mahumet alone are given the kingdoms of deception.

Hic si queratur qui sit quem sic ueneratur:
    Nomen habet Mahumet; quo duce fisa tumet.
Illi cunctorum cessit cultura deorum
    Qui tenet ut proprium perfidie solium.
Expulit errores error nouus iste priores
    Et Mahumet soli sunt data regna doli. (ll. 67–72)

Embrico knows enough to show that these modern "pagans" spurn the idols of ancient Rome and that they are monotheists. But he seems to imply that their God is Mahumet or at least that they worship Mahumet.[22] (When he later discusses the Prophet, he uses the name Mammutius; whether Embrico means to make a distinction between the two names is unclear.)

When we turn to geography and chronology, Embrico's knowledge is even weaker. He places Muhammad in Libya.[23] It is unclear what Libya's political status is meant to be: it has both a *rex* (king) and a *consul* (Roman provincial governor). Embrico's one hint on chronology places Muhammad in the fourth century, over two hundred years too early, making him a contemporary of Theodosius and Ambrose.[24] Guy Cambier has traced the possible sources of this chronological confusion,[25] but perhaps the sources of this error are less crucial than its effect. The mention of Theodosius and Ambrose, along with a vaguely defined "Libya," places Embrico's narrative in a milieu that I shall call the "Early Christian East." The Early Christian East, familiar to Latin readers of the Middle Ages, is where the blood of the Martyrs was spilt, where many of the adventures of the Apostles occurred, and where the desert fathers performed their ascetic athletics. It was known to these readers through the Acts (and apocryphal Acts) of the Apostles, through the *Vitae Patrum*, through martyrologies, and through hagiographical narrations like the various *Lives* of Saint Mary the Egyptian. Embrico does not elaborate on the setting of his poem, on his "Early Christian East," but it is there. He merely needs to suggest Jerusalem, the desert, Libya—and to mention that this is the epoch of Ambrose and Theodosius.

The fourth century was also a time of Christian heresy. To explain both Islam's similarities to Christianity and its differences, Embrico envisages Islam as a heretical deviation from Christianity. The prophet Mammutius is not the most important figure in the *Vita Mahumeti*; Embrico instead focuses on a nameless Christian "Magus," a scheming heretic who leads Mammutius astray, puts him in political power, and provides him with a new law. The Magus is the real villain of the *Vita Mahumeti*; Mammutius himself is not as clever or as important as his evil teacher. The two aid and abet each other in their evil schemes, just as Zosimas and Mary the Egyptian, in Hildebert's life, aid each other in attaining sanctity. This perspective helps Embrico denigrate Islam by making it derivative of heretical Christianity and by eliminating any creative role for Muhammad and his Arab (or "Libyan") compatriots.

This heretical Magus is not entirely Embrico's invention. Several passages in the Qur'ân speak of Christians who prophesy Muhammad's coming or who recognize him as the new prophet; particular importance is given to a monk named Bahîra and to Waraqah, the first cousin of Muhammad's wife Khadija. In eastern Christian polemic against Islam, the importance of these Qur'ânic Christians was greatly inflated; they were made into Muhammad's teachers (or sometimes one single teacher), and they were generally made out to be heretics.[26]

But nowhere is the character of this heretical Christian teacher as fully developed—or as important—as in Embrico. By calling him simply "magus" Embrico shrouds him in anonymity and gives him a sinister, descriptive name. "Magus"—poorly translated in English as "magician"—had very negative connotations to the medieval reader. It evoked necromancy, blood rituals, sexual depravity, and traffic with demons. Embrico's readers would particular think of Simon Magus, often described as the spiritual father of heresy.[27] Other characters called "magus" (with the notable exception of the three Magi of the Gospels) are almost all nefarious: Ham and Theophilus are two prominent examples.[28] The legend of Theophilus's conversion from magic and devil worship through the good graces of the Virgin was extremely popular in Embrico's day; it, too, had been translated from Greek into Latin by Paul the Deacon, and Marbod of Rennes composed a verse adaptation.[29]

Heresiarch, sex maniac, magus: these are the elements that make up this most dangerous of characters. Here, again, Embrico is following the standard typology of the heresiarch.[30] Embrico's Magus is uncompromisingly evil, but he is a wolf in sheep's clothing. He is dangerous because he is a hypocrite: oozing piety and humility, he easily leads the impressionable masses astray. Here is how Embrico introduces him:

For a certain man, evilly pious, cleansed through baptism,
  Full of perfidy lived in the Church.
He sought the praises of men by means of magic fraud,
  So that through his zeal he might corrupt the Church.
Because while he concealed and carefully dissimulated
  He sat in the Church just as a wolf sits in ambush
With sweet speech and with feigned piety
  He flattered the populace under the guise of faith.
This false man arrived with horrid clothes as witnesses to this [faith]
  His withered flesh rarely indulged in food.
Fleeing far from games, he walked barefoot,
  Ritually bowing his head when he said anything.
As he proceeded in front of them, he moved his lips
  So that anyone seeing him would think he were a saint.
He came then in this way, sighing,

Lowering his eyes, so that he would rouse the people
Then he turned up his palms and raised up his voice,
Not for his own merit but for the misery of the people.

Nam male deuotus quidam, baptismate lotus,
Plenus perfidia uixit in Ecclesia.
Per magicas fraudes querens hominum sibi laudes
Vt sua per studia corruat Ecclesia.
Quod dum celabat et caute dissimulabat,
Ceu lupus Ecclesiis sedit in insidiis.
Dulci sermone, ficta quoque religione
Blanditur populo sub fidei titulo.
Falsus ad hoc testis accesserat horrida uestis,
Fota cibis raro marcida pene caro.
Qui procul a ludo fugiens ibat pede nudo,
Obstipo rite cuncta loquens capite.
Quando pergebat coram, sua labra mouebat
Vt sanctum teneat, quisquis eum uideat.
Sed suspirando si tolleret hic aliquando
summissos oculos, concitet ut populos,
Tunc exaltabat palmas uocemque leuabat
Non pro se merens sed populi miserens. (ll. 87–104)

Embrico describes him here in a series of striking oxymorons: *male deuotus, per studia corruat, ficta religio.* This *ficta religio* (feigned piety) is the Magus's most potent weapon. Indeed, in outward appearance he resembles the pious Zosimas, whom Hildebert describes thus:

His witness was his moderate sleep, his simple clothes,
His food and lodging, once in glory, now crucified.
Witness was the monk's color, and his flesh, unaware of Bacchus
Not flesh, but a meager hide, pallid, scored by whips,
Taught to resist itself, to serve the spirit.
In these torments, the melody of a holy mind
Sung Psalms to Christ, if ever the tongue was silent.

Huius erat testis modicus sopor, aspera vestis,
Et cibus et stratus, modo gloria, tunc cruciatus.
Testis erat monachi color, et caro nescia Bacchi:

Non caro, sed pellis macra, pallida, trita flagellis,
Docta reluctari sibi, spiritui famulari.
His in tormentis, sacrae modulatio mentis
Christo psallebat, si quando lingua tacebat. (PL 171:1323a)

Embrico's description is based on the same hagiographical topoi employed here by Hildebert: in each case, the author refers to these attributes as witnesses (*testes*) to the man's sanctity. The difference is that the Magus deliberately contrives false witnesses. His *religio* is *ficta*; it disguises his real motives, which are evil. It is not only in the lives of saints (and anti-saints) that Christians of Embrico's day were confronted with this kind of potentially ambivalent display of ascetic zeal. Marbod of Rennes describes Robert of Arbrissel, who had been sent by Urban II to preach against simony and clerical unchastity, in similar terms: "Marching barefoot through the crowds, having cast off the habit of a regular, his flesh covered by a hair-shirt, wearing a thin and torn cloak, bare-legged, beard tangled, offering a new spectacle to the onlookers since only a club was missing from the outfit of a lunatic."[31] His followers, Marbod continues, are dressed in a similar fashion; they wear shoes in the countryside but walk barefoot through the towns. Thus, Marbod insinuates, they are hypocrites: their outward display of piety is, to use Embrico's words, *ficta religio*. Marbod's description betrays a good deal of uneasiness about the potential effectiveness of their zeal; the fact that the preachers whom he dismisses in these terms were licensed by a pope to preach reform shows how potentially explosive the situation was. Embrico, painting his lurid picture of a hypocritical heresiarch, may have contemporary models (such as Henry of Lausanne) in mind.

The differences between Zosimas and Embrico's Magus are apparent in their itineraries: Zosimas, like any ascetic worth his salt, moves from civilization to the wilderness: fleeing from worldly wealth, he goes first to a monastery, then to the desert. The Magus, moving in search of power and renown, has the opposite itinerary.

When we first meet the Magus he is coming to Jerusalem, where he finds that the "father of the city" has just died. The magus delights over the death of this pious man, hoping to become father of the city himself. The identity of this *pater urbis* is uncertain—Embrico elsewhere refers to him as *pontifex*,[32] a term which, in Embrico's day, can mean either pope or bishop.[33] Embrico confuses things further by suggesting that the king of Jerusalem will decide who will become *pontifex*. A king of Jerusalem, under the Emperor Theodosius? Here again, we err if we expect Embrico to be precise about such things. A king in Jerusalem, who appoints a *pontifex*: these fit well into Embrico's vision of the Early Christian East, shrouded in a mist of geographical and chronological vagueness. Similar vagueness surrounded some of the contemporary *Vitae* of Antichrist, who also was supposed to attempt to take power in Jerusalem—although *he* was supposed to succeed.[34]

Embrico tells us that the Magus himself wishes to *pontificari*, and that he so electrifies the crowd that they flock to his cause. Just as the people are clamoring to their king that he make the Magus the new *pontifex*, a host of demons stream in, making horrifying screams. The Magus himself passes out. When he comes to, the people, who have finally seen his true nature, reject him. He calls to his demons, who snatch him up and take him away to Libya; there, he vows, he will corrupt the Church. This seems to be another echo of the Simon Magus legend; he too was supposed to have flown with the aid of demons.[35]

In Libya he meets Mammutius, a slave to the local governor. Tellingly, nothing is said of Mammutius's birth or youth; he is an insignificant slave until he meets the evil Magus. The two make a pact to work together to bring Mammutius power and glory. Through some sort of magic ("prestigia mouit," l. 255), the Magus makes the governor ill; then at night, he and Mammutius sneak into his house and suffocate him in his bed. The next day the governor is found dead, and there is general mourning. No one seems sadder than the Magus himself,

> Who, wet from crying and falling down with grief
> Was made an example of weeping and grieving
> Whereby no one imagined that he was guilty.
>
> Qui lacrimando madens inque dolendo cadens
> Exemplum flendi factus fuit atque dolendi:
> Quare nullus eum credidit esse reum. (ll. 292–94)

The Magus consoles the governor's widow, urging her to remarry. When she asks whom she should marry, the Magus recommends Mammutius; hence Mammutius marries into wealth and power, becoming governor through marriage.

Muhammad, Muslim sources tell us, married the wealthy widow Khadija, whom he had served as a merchant for several years. Christian polemicists tried to make this marriage seem scandalous, either by painting Muhammad as a cynical youth marrying solely to obtain wealth or by implying that there was something unnatural in a marriage between the young prophet and an older woman.[36] Here Embrico adds a new twist, implicating Muhammad in the murder of his new wife's former husband; not only is he a cynical climber who marries into wealth and power but he will kill to make such a marriage possible.

Embrico next introduces us to a diabolical beast: a calf that the Magus and Mammutius have raised in secret, far from the gaze of the Libyan people.[37] They excavate a cave, almost down to the depth of Hell. There they rear the calf, which becomes a hideous and powerful bull; Embrico describes it in these terms:

> For its form was not that of a bull, but a foreign
> Form of a new monster; nor did it resemble a cow.
> Horrible with its horns, more fearful than a rhinoceros;
> The fiery light from its eyes was the terror of the people,
> The form of its very cheeks horrified: they bristled as if with thorns;
> No beast has ever had a nose like this one.
> Horrible snorting, the cleft of his mouth was huge
> And his gaping, black gullet had the form of the abyss.
>
> Nam non taurina fuit illi sed peregrina
> Monstri forma noui, nec simulanda boui.
> Cornibus horrendus, plus rinocerote timendus;
> Ignea lux oculi terror erat populi,
> Horruit ipsarum quasi spinis forma genarum;
> Huic habuit nares bestia nulla pares.
> Terribilis flatus, patulus fuit oris hiatus
> Et rictus atri forma fuit baratri. (371–78)

The purpose of rearing this hideous beast soon is made clear. News arrives that the king of Libya has died (somehow Libya had both a *consul* and a *rex*). The people begin debating whom they should choose as his successor. The Magus arrives, reeking of piety, and the people ask him for advice; he humbly refuses. They insist, and finally he tells them that God will send a powerful bull to them; the man who can yoke this bull will be their next king. The bull appears, and a young Libyan man dies trying to tame it. Finally Mammutius arrives. Since the bull knows him and is obedient to him, he yokes it easily and the people proclaim him as their new king.

The submission of wild beasts is another hagiographical topos: from St. George's dragon to St. Patrick's ridding Ireland of snakes.[38] Having wild animals submit and serve the saint is a more emphatic form of the same topos: the *Historia monachorum in Aegypto* describes how Abba Helle rides across the Nile on the back of a submissive crocodile;[39] various early saints' biographies have eagles or beasts protecting saints or bringing them food.[40] The apostle Peter tames Simon Magus's ravenous dogs, turns them against Simon, and has one dog speak to him in accusation.[41] In Hildebert's narrative, as we have seen, a lion shows reverence for the body of the deceased Mary and actually digs her grave. Here again, the signs of sanctity are deliberately feigned by the Magus in another manifestation of his *ficta religio*. The animal is raised for the purpose of this deception, and its horrendous, diabolical aspect contrasts starkly with the nobility of Mary's lion.

This episode, moreover, allowed the Magus to feign another attribute of sanctity: prophetic power. He predicted, to the gullible Libyans, the imminent arrival of the beast. Prophetic power is also commonplace in saints' lives.[42] Mary divines Zosimas's status as monk, priest, and presbyter; Zosimas acknowledges that this information must have been given to her directly by God.[43] She also shows herself to be a prophet (*vates* is the term that Hildebert uses)[44] when she predicts that Zosimas will fall ill (but recover)[45] and when she warns him of trouble among his monks.[46] Again, Embrico's Magus uses clever subterfuge to appear holy.

Through the submission of the beast, then, Mammutius obtains kingship over Libya. But this is not enough; the Magus has greater things in mind for his protégé. He bids Mammutius replace the law of the Gospels with a new Law, one that will be both easier and more pleasurable to obey. He enjoins Mammutius:

> The Gospels must be changed; their law is difficult,
> It deems us void of sense and foolish
> Since it prohibits us from adultery and wantonness
> And it destroys marriage between blood relatives
> It forbids or enjoins many things through its inept rules

Which you will condemn when you give more appropriate ones.
For adultery and making love you will establish by law;
Let food abound and let love be set free!
But you should close your decree with this ending:
That whatever was prohibited should now be permitted.

Lex mutandorum grauis est Euangeliorum,
Que sensu uacuos nos putat et fatuos
Dum nos mechari prohibet uel luxuriari
Et cognatorum destruit ipsa thorum
Multaque preceptis uetat aut confirmat ineptis,
Que tu dampnabis dum magis apta dabis;
Nam tu mechandum statues uenerique vacandum;
Luxuriet penus sitque soluta uenus!
Sed tua decreta debes hac claudere meta
Vt modo sit licitum, quicquid erat uetitum. (711–20)

Muslim law is a travesty of Christian law: "Let everything be now permitted that was before prohibited." The reasons for the instigation of this new law are the Magus's diabolical anti-Christianity and Mammutius' desire for power and sex. Here Embrico is playing a common chord in Christian anti-Muslim polemic: Muhammad's polygamy and his political and military might are turned against him; he is implicitly compared to Christ, chaste and powerless.[47] Moreover, Muhammad's compatriots are painted as a particularly lecherous people; this image is based perhaps on Islam's legalized polygamy and on the promise of *houris* (beautiful virgins) to be enjoyed in Paradise. Moreover, accusations of sexual debauchery were often made against heresiarchs; Jerome, as we have seen, makes such charges against Simon Magus, Nicolas of Antioch, and Priscillian. Le Mans chroniclers charged that Henry of Lausanne seduced boys and women, performing obscene acts that are described in detail.[47] Sexual depravity was also often associated with the figure of the magus.[49]

Mammutius then preaches his new law, resulting in a wave of conversions and in lechery and incest:

Then, against custom, a brother grasps his sister,
The married sister becomes the victim of her brother's greedy maw
A son defiles his mother, a daughter her father:
Thus whatever they wished, the new law permitted.

Mox contra morem frater premit ipse sororem,
 Nupta soror fratri uictima fit baratri;
Incestat matrem sua proles, filia patrem:
 Sic quicquid libuit, lege noua licuit. (805–8)

In the midst of this orgy, there are, Embrico tells us, a few Christians who attempt, by word and example, to oppose this new law. These suffer torture and martyrdom: they are stoned, put to the sword, and thrown to the tigers.

These orgies are similar to those of the prostitute Mary, as described by Hildebert (although she never speaks of incest). But Mary narrated past sins; she had moved from a life of godless lechery to that of piety. Once distant from God, she now was close to Him. Mammutius had the opposite itinerary: into lechery and ever further from God. To Mammutius's lechery, too, is added a heretical element absent from Mary's: he claims that God ordered it, and he puts to death pious Christians who refuse to participate in it.

Muslims, of course, did not throw Christians to tigers. Rather, the martyrdoms show, again, that Embrico's narrative takes place in the Early Christian East: in this context, religious conflict naturally conjures up images of amphitheaters where Christians are thrown to tigers and slain by gladiators.

As punishment for instigating this new law, Embrico continues, God racks Mammutius with epilepsy; his people stand horrified, watching him writhe on the ground. But the Magus remains cool and deceptive. As Mammutius contorts, the Magus loudly praises God for showing the king such favor. He then explains to the astonished onlookers that angels have spirited Mammutius' soul out of his body, are whisking him up to see God, and will then return him to his body. When Mammutius comes to, the Magus takes him aside and explains his ruse. Mammutius then addresses his people, recounting in glowing terms his voyage to heaven and his communion with God. He goes as far as to say that God promised that, upon his return to heaven, Mammutius would hold the scepter of the heavens (sceptra poli), and that with God "only I will rule all that is to be ruled" (solus ego queque regenda rego, 954–56). This is a parody of the Muslim legend of Muhammad's *Mi'râj,* his celestial ascent from Jerusalem into heaven. Not only is the voyage discredited by being dismissed as the improvised explanation for an epileptic fit, but Mammutius heretically boasts that he shares (or will share) in God's power.[50]

Divine punishment for impiety (in this case in the form of epilepsy) is of course a common theme in both the Bible and in hagiographical literature. God punishes a sinner. The sinner either repents and changes his ways (moving toward God) or obstinately persists in his error, increasing his crimes against God. Mary, a worldly, irreligious prostitute, was barred entrance to the Temple at Jerusalem, repulsed three times by Heavenly Force.[51] Mary responded to the divine chastisement, prayed for assistance from the Virgin Mary, and converted to a life of asceticism.[52] Mammutius, far from recognizing the chastisement, makes it the pretense for more heretical lies, moving further from God.

Mammutius says that during his celestial voyage God had revealed to him a new law: "after sinning anyone is washed clean with water" ("post peccata quisque lavatur aqua," 966). Muslims' ritual ablutions are a favorite target for Christian polemicists; Muslims are accused of confusing physical and spiritual uncleanliness.[53] Here Embrico makes the charge even harsher; ablutions are a blanket license to sin, as long as one carefully washes oneself after sinning. Again, the outward semblance of piety (in this case, ritual washing) is used to camouflage impiety.

Shortly thereafter, God strikes Mammutius dead for his sins, and pigs begin to devour his body. The Magus comes along, finds Mammutius dead, drives off the pigs, and takes the corpse away. He dresses and perfumes the body and comes to the people to make a funeral oration, in which he bids the people not to eat pork, since pigs have devoured the dead Mammutius. Pigs provide a vivid contrast with Mary's lion. Mammutius' corpse is desecrated by dirty, ignoble beasts; Mary's is honored by a noble one.

Embrico closes with a description of Mammutius' tomb, designed by the Magus. His gilded sarcophagus is held aloft by a system of magnets; hence it appears to the credulous masses that God is miraculously holding Mammutius in midair.[54] This floating coffin embodies another hagiographical topos: levitation as a sign of sanctity. During her first encounter with Zosimas, at one point Mary, praying fervently, rises into the air and stays there throughout her prayers. The monk's first reaction is terror:

> Zosimas was terrified by such things, and he thought this an evil omen.

Talibus expauit Zosimas, monstrumque putauit. (PL 171:1327d)

He flees, to be called back by Mary as she finishes her prayers. She eventually brings him to recognize that her levitation is a sign of true sanctity. But, Hildebert implies, Zosimas's caution was well founded: such signs are ambiguous; they can signify either divine favor or magical, diabolical art.[55] Simon Magus, as we have seen, used flight to deceive the people into thinking he was holy. Zosimas is wiser than the credulous followers of Mammutius, who are easily duped by the Magus's magical manipulation of magnets.

Embrico's *Vita Mahumeti* is an original work. It imaginatively fuses two traditions: the anti-Islamic polemics of Spain and Byzantium and the hagiographic poetry of Hildebert and his circle. It is unique in two particularly interesting ways: it is the first instance of an antihagiographical poem in Latin, and it is the first coherent response to Islam by a Latin writer north of the Pyrenees.

Coherent does not mean fair or accurate. What little modern scholarship there is on Embrico tends to find fault with him because of his lack of accuracy: how is it that one biased and erroneous portrayal of Islam (that Muhammad is a golden idol) is replaced by another one (that Muhammad is a heresiarch)?[56] This is, of course, anachronistic: that Embrico's treatment of Muhammad is hostile rather than objective should surprise no one. The *Vita Mahumeti* explains Islam to a Latin Europe that has just begun to confront Islam seriously. By narrating Muhammad's life and making him a heresiarch of the fourth century, Embrico presents Islam as something knowable, something familiar. Instead of a young, vigorous rival to Christianity, Islam is reduced to an old and particularly corrupt species of heresy—to something which can be easily understood and utterly dismissed.

The twelfth-century writers saw Islam as heresy because they perceived heresy to be the great menace. Embrico is concerned as much with the threat posed by itinerant preachers like Henry of Lausanne as he is with the threat of Islam itself. Within his *Vita Mahumeti* lies a tension: how can one tell the heretic from the holy man? The typology of the heresiarch, as we have seen, is in many ways the mirror image of the typology of the saint. Both appear pious to the masses, but one leads them to God while the other leads them to perdition. Like Simon Magus, like Antichrist, like Henry of Lausanne, Embrico's Mammutius is a disquieting figure. From the omniscient standpoint of the narrator (and reader) one knows how to distinguish the man of God from the man of Satan. But the next time an itinerant preacher arrives, will we be able to tell what side he is on?

Other twelfth-century authors (such as Petrus Alfonsi and Peter the Venerable of Cluny) will approach the task of denigrating Islam differently. As theologians and scholars, they will attack Islam in more ponderous works of prose. They will know more about Islam than Embrico, and they will take it more seriously as a rival creed. They will provide their readers with an explanation of key Muslim beliefs and with attempts to refute those beliefs. Embrico, through his lively rhymed hexameters, gave his readers something more tangible and more appealing: Mammutius, an enemy that they would love to hate and whose followers they could hold in contempt.[57]

2

A Mangled Corpse

The Polemical Dismemberment of Muhammad

"The Greeks and Latins," wrote Edward Gibbon, "have invented and propagated the vulgar and ridiculous story, that Mahomet's iron tomb is suspended in the air at Mecca, by the action of equal and potent lodestones. Without any philosophical inquiries, it may suffice, that, 1. the prophet was not buried at Mecca; and. 2, That his tomb at Medina, which has been visited by millions, is placed on the ground."[1]

That Gibbon takes such pains to refute this strange legend implies that it was given some credence in 1776. Where did it come from? Why was it believed? I intend in this article to look at the origins of this peculiar story in the twelfth century and its development until Gibbon rejects it in 1776. In particular, I want to examine the purpose this legend served in the construction of an image of the Saracen other. Muhammad's floating coffin at Mecca becomes, for certain Christian authors, the fictive center of the Muslim world, imbued with a terrifying magical power, an object of fear and loathing.

Muhammad's death and what happened to his corpse preoccupied many of the polemical Christian biographers of Muhammad. Their biographies denigrate Islam (and hence attempt to assure their readers of the superiority of Christianity) by portraying Muhammad as a scoundrel. He is variously shown to be a pervert, drunkard, epileptic, magician, heretic, swindler, murderer, Machiavellian political schemer, and intimate of Satan. These biographies originated in the work of Christians of the eighth and ninth centuries, who—appalled to see their brethren converting to Islam in droves—tried to paint the Muslim prophet in the most negative terms possible in order to stem the tides of conversion. These biographies—written in Arabic, Greek, or Syriac—often formed parts of larger polemical texts aimed at convincing Christians that Islam was but a twisted caricature of the true faith, Christianity. Similar hostile biographies of Muhammad (most of them quite brief) were written into polemical texts and chronicles of ninth- and tenth-century Spain by Christians writing in both Latin and Arabic.[2]

Hostile and inaccurate as these texts are, none of them contain the strange story about Muhammad's floating coffin; that particular legend is a product of the Rhineland in the twelfth century, as we shall see presently. It is in the twelfth century that northern Europe begins to take an interest in Islam, due to its expanding contact with the Muslim world, through crusade, increased trade, and a growing influx of philosophical and scientific texts translated from Arabic into Latin. More distant from Islam than their eastern and Spanish brethren, northern European authors could take these hostile legends about Muhammad and twist them at times beyond recognition. Seeking to explain Islam's role in the divine plan and unhampered by any real knowledge of Islam, they could make of Muhammad what they wanted: an incarnation of error and evil, an inverted image of Christ and the saints.

An ignominious death for Muhammad, followed by the desecration of his corpse, was usually part of these polemics. These legends become widespread in texts about Islam written in Latin and the European vernaculars from the twelfth century to the eighteenth, texts as various as religious polemics, crusader chronicles, travelogues, etc. In the following pages I will examine the various purposes these stories about Muhammad's death served and how they helped both explain and denigrate Islam to a Christian audience. Rather than moving in strictly chronological order and tracing the sources of each permutation of these legends (an impossible and perhaps not very interesting task), I will look at them typologically. First I will look at texts that merely assert that Muhammad met an ignominious end, then at texts that try to place his demise into a Christian eschatology, and finally at how the legend of Muhammad's floating coffin (or in some versions, a floating idol of Muhammad), usually believed to be in Mecca, comes to provide not only an eschatological explanation of Islam but a concrete (if entirely fictional) locus of Muslim power and an objective for Christian hatred: an object of both fear and hope, for various texts assert that the destruction of Muhammad's floating coffin in Mecca will result in the end of Islam itself. Finally, we will see that the demise of the legend of Muhammad's floating coffin is due to the receding of the Muslim threat to Europe, as much as it is to the historical method of Gibbon and his ilk.

First, then, are the texts which merely ascribe a vile and shameful death to Muhammad in order to discredit him. Several of these lives have him killed and subsequently dismembered by dogs or pigs. Guibert de Nogent, for example, inserts a brief biography of Muhammad in his Latin chronicle of the First Crusade (composed in the twelfth century); its purpose is to help justify the crusade by discrediting Muhammad and his followers. He says that Muhammad was in the midst of an epileptic fit when he was killed by pigs.[3] Thirteenth-century chronicler Matthew Paris (who, like many medieval chroniclers, inserts material from diverse and often contradictory sources into his *Chronica maior*) has him killed by pigs on a dung heap.[4]

As if this were not enough, other authors connect his death with his supposedly debauched morals. Two fourteenth-century texts have him murdered in the wake of illicit sexual encounters.[5] One commentator to Matthew Paris said that he had been punished with a triple death: struck with epilepsy because he sinned against the father, poisoned because he sinned against the son, drunk because he sinned against the Holy Spirit.[6]

These polemicists implicitly contrast Muhammad's death (as well as his life) with that of Christ and the saints: they portray him as an Antichrist or an anti-saint. Our second group of sources makes these contrasts more explicit, saying that Muhammad claimed that he, like Christ, would rise again; a failed resurrection thus becomes part of the death scene, and Muhammad becomes an Antichrist. Already in eighth- or ninth-century Spain, an anonymous Christian author[7] composed a brief life of Muhammad that shows real knowledge of Islam: he describes Muhammad's marriage to the older widow Khadija, the role of Gabriel in the revelation of the Qur'ân, the titles of various Qur'ânic Suras, and Muhammad's marriage to Zaynab, the divorced wife of his disciple Zayd. All of these events, however, are presented in the worst possible light, twisted almost beyond recognition by the hostile pen of the author. Muhammad's death is described in a manner that has nothing to do with Muslim tradition, but comes straight out of Christian traditions about Antichrist:

> Sensing his imminent destruction and knowing that he would in no way be resurrected on his own merit, he predicted that he would be revived on the third day by the angel Gabriel, who was in the habit of appearing to him in the guise of a vulture, as Muhammad himself said. When he gave up his soul to hell, they ordered his body to be guarded with an arduous vigil, anxious about the miracle which he had promised them. When on the third day they saw he was rotting, and determined that he would not by any means be rising, they said the angels did not come because they were frightened by their presence. Having found sound advice—or so they thought—they left his body unguarded, and immediately instead of angels, dogs followed his stench and devoured his flank. Learning of the deed, they surrendered the rest of his body to the soil. And in vindication of this injury, they ordered dogs to be slaughtered every year so that they, who on his behalf deserve a worthy martyrdom here, might share in his merit there. It was appropriate that a prophet of this kind fill the stomach of dogs, a prophet who committed not only his own soul, but those of many, to hell.[8]

Here we have a rotting corpse desecrated by beasts—a vicious and emphatic image. If one casts Muhammad in the role of Antichrist, one imagines that he occupies the same role in Islam that Christ occupies in Christianity. It seemed self-evident to many of these Christian polemicists that Muhammad had claimed to be the Messiah and that he had claimed he would be resurrected. A rotting or desecrated corpse was presented as evidence that he was *not* the Messiah. The fact that no Muslim ever affirmed that Muhammad was the Messiah or that he would be resurrected changes nothing: this image of Muhammad as Antichrist gives the Christian reader a coherent and comprehensible idea of Islam and helps him confront it.

The *Sobre la seta mahometana* (c. 1300), attributed to Pedro Pascual, bishop of Jaén, presents a particularly vicious mix of these legends in his anti-Muslim tract.[9] The same story, with slight variations, is found in a fourteenth-century manuscript now in Pisa. In both versions, Muhammad attempts to seduce a Jewish woman, who—afraid to refuse him—tells him to come to her in secret. As night falls, her relatives ambush and kill Muhammad, cut up his corpse, and throw everything but his left foot to the pigs. When Muhammad's angry and armed followers come looking for him, the woman offers this defense, according to the Pisan manuscript:

> My lords, you will know that the lord king loved me and the other night came to me in secret and lay with me in my bed. When we had gone to sleep, angels came sent by God and taking [Muhammad] by the arm, began to raise him up. I, knowing that I would be accused about this, held onto his left foot. The angels pulled him up, and I pulled him down. And thus we fought all night, but about dawn the angels (who were stronger than I since there were so many of them) took his body and left me his foot, which came off of the body with great force. In your honor I have dressed it in aromatic herbs and have wrapped it in this precious cloth and devoutly placed it in my box. Go now, take this, which is yours. Accept it and guard it diligently.

The text subsequently tells us that the foot is reverently buried and pilgrims flock to it in droves.[10] In both texts, as in the others we have examined, Muhammad dies a despicable death and his corpse is profaned. It is because pigs devoured Muhammad's body, the reader is told, that his followers refuse to eat pork, and it is because the Jews killed Muhammad that Jews and Muslims hate each other. The principal reason for Muhammad's death is his supposed appetite for sexual debauchery, and having him killed through the ruses of a woman—and a Jewess to boot—is no doubt meant to aggravate the scurrilous nature of his death in the eyes of the Christian reader. Instead of a failed resurrection, here we have a caricature of the hagiographic topos of the saint carried off to heaven, as is supposed to have happened to Moses, Elijah, and the Virgin Mary. The authors are perhaps parodying the legends of Muhammad's *Mi'râj*, or celestial voyage, and combining them with a polemical presentation of his death.[11] The woman's lie is supposed to explain why the Saracens still follow Muhammad's law after his ignominious death: they know nothing about it, but believe he was carried off to heaven by angels. In their viciousness, the authors lose their logical coherence: if the Muslims know nothing about the murder of Muhammad at the hands of Jews and of the desecration of his corpse by pigs, why should they hate Jews and avoid pork?

Let us now look at the legend of the floating sarcophagus, first attested in the early twelfth-century *Vita Mahumeti* of Embrico of Mainz and subsequently used in a score of medieval texts. The essentials of this story, in its various versions, remain the same: Muhammad is buried in a metal sarcophagus and placed in a mosque (or temple) that has magnets set into the ceiling or arches. The sarcophagus floats in midair, and the credulous masses take this as a sign of God's favor.

What purpose do these vicious stories about Muhammad's corpse serve? How do they fit into the larger context of western perceptions of the world of Islam? We have seen that the legends of Muhammad's murder and the desecration of his corpse were meant to discredit his teachings, to reassure Christian readers that Islam was evil. Certain passages were meant to explain (and denigrate) Islamic practice. But what was the purpose of the more and more elaborate and fabulous legends of failed resurrection, of the cult of Muhammad's foot, of his floating sarcophagus?

Let us not forget that in the twelfth century, when these legends began to take their more extravagant forms, the contacts between Latin Europe and the Arab world were multiplying. While some authors did not hesitate to depict "Saracens" as pagans who worshiped golden idols,[12] others were familiar enough with Islam to realize that Muslims were no polytheists. Islam presented a dilemma. Muslims are monotheists, they respect the Torah and the Gospel, they recognize Jesus as a prophet, but they adhere to a sacred text, the Qur'ân, and to religious rites that are foreign to Christianity. Moreover, the Muslim world was wealthier and more learned than the Latin world—how could such people fall victim to a depraved and ridiculous cult? Hence the polemicists of the twelfth century and beyond had to explain not only why Islam was wrong but also why it was so successful—that is, from their perspective, why God had allowed a faith alien to Him to spread throughout much of the world and why He allowed its adherents to be wealthy, educated, and cultured.

While the doctrine and practice of Islam were difficult to refute, it was easy to invent slanderous tales about its founder. If Muhammad could no longer be portrayed as a golden idol, there were other roles that now seemed to fit: those of Heresiarch and Antichrist. For each of these types (which often overlapped) the polemicist had a wealth of information from the Bible, the writings of the Church fathers, and the various lives of Antichrist.[13] Preoccupied with heretics at home, several twelfth-century authors saw in Muhammad a heresiarch. We have seen that Embrico of Mainz portrayed Muhammad as an anti-saint (rather than Antichrist) through the use (or abuse) of the standard topoi of hagiography: at times Muhammad does exactly the opposite of what a saint would do (showing his true character); at other times he feigns the signs of sanctity in order to hoodwink his followers. These models in themselves provided enough for one to write a biography of Muhammad; any information about Muhammad from other sources

(Muslim texts or Byzantine polemics, for example) could be used to flesh out this biography (see chapter 1).

Such an approach was not unique to Christian polemics against Islam. The Hebrew *Toledot Yeshu* (Generations of Jesus), composed in the ninth century or earlier, describes Jesus as the illegitimate child of Mary and Joseph who sneaks into the temple at Jerusalem to learn the name of God, through the power of which he is able to perform miracles. After Jesus' execution and burial, a gardener steals his body and reburies it in his garden. Jesus' followers, finding the tomb empty, proclaim his resurrection. Subsequently, the gardener produces Jesus' corpse and "all Israel . . . bound cords to the feet of [Jesus], and dragged him round the streets of Jerusalem."[14]

The parallels with the Christian biographies of Muhammad are clear. Certain elements of Jesus' life are distorted and transformed by the hostile pen: the virgin birth becomes an illegitimate birth, just as Muhammad's trembling and ecstasy as the Qur'ân is revealed to him become epileptic fits in the Christian biographies. Jesus performs miracles, but by illegitimate, magical use of the divine name, just as Muhammad produces false miracles through a combination of magic and clever ruse.

The desecration of the corpse of Muhammad or Jesus is meant to show divine disfavor. Such desecration is, of course, an ancient topos: the best-known example is that of Achilles (in the *Iliad*) dragging Hector's body behind his chariot, abusing and mocking it. Just so, according to the *Toledot Yeshu,* did the Jews mock Jesus as they dragged his body through the streets of Jerusalem. The corollary of this topos is that those favored by God do not suffer such abuse—in particular, their bodies do not rot or stink. Hector's corpse, despite days of abuse by Achilles, was kept intact and sweet-smelling by Apollo. Christian hagiographers often described the sweet smell emanating from the corpses of saints. Animals, too, are overawed by the holiness of saints, alive or dead, and will not hurt them. According to her hagiographers, St. Mary the Egyptian was buried by a lion (the most noble of the beasts) who bowed down reverently before her corpse.[15] A rotting corpse, or one mangled by ignoble beasts such as dogs or pigs, shows God's disfavor.

If such stories can debase a rival religion, they can hardly make comprehensible the tremendous successes of Islam. Here the stories of false miracles and false resurrection are much more useful. Just as the *Toledot Yeshu* gives plausible explanations for the success of Christianity, twelfth-century polemicist Petrus Alfonsi uses the legend of Muhammad's failed resurrection to help explain the successes of Islam:

> After Muhammad's death, everyone wished to abandon his Law. He himself had said that on the third day his body would be borne up to heaven. When they realized that this was a lie and saw his corpse rotting, he was buried and the greater part [of his followers] abandoned [Islam]. ʿAlî, the son of Abû Tâlib, one of Muhammad's ten associates, took over the kingdom at Muhammad's death. He coolly predicted and hotly admonished the people to believe, and said that they had not properly understood Muhammad's words. "Muhammad," he said, "did not say that he would be resurrected before his burial or while men watched. He said rather, that after the burial of his body the angels would, with no one knowing, bear him up to heaven. Therefore, when they did not immediately bury him, he began to decompose, so that they might bury him immediately." By means of this argument [ʿAlî] kept the people for a while in their original error.[16]

This legend is essentially the same as that of the early life of Muhammad from Spain, which, as we saw, describes his death and failure to resurrect in terms that evoke Christian traditions of Antichrist. In the first text, however, none of the Muslims have reasonable cause to believe that Muhammad has indeed been resurrected; Alfonsi makes the success of Islam more plausible by adding an element of deception. Just as the *Toledot Yeshu* describes Jesus' tomb being found empty and rumors of his resurrection, Alfonsi narrates Muhammad's promises of resurrection and ʿAli's claim that he is to be buried so that the angels can take him up to heaven in secret. In both cases, we have numerous witnesses to the desecration of the corpse and plausible reasons that some people could believe in its resurrection.

This same purpose is more dramatically and more viciously served by the story of the Jewess who claims that Muhammad had ascended to heaven and left his foot in her hand. He dies as a result of his lust and his abuse of power, and it is difficult to imagine a more ignoble death than being murdered, dismembered, and devoured by pigs. The preposterous and profane relic of Muhammad's foot, perfumed, wrapped in precious cloth, and placed in what seems to be a reliquary, contrasts—or at least is meant to contrast—with the true relics of the saints.

The legend of the floating coffin lends further credibility to the success of Islam.[17] The story (as I mentioned) is first attested in the early twelfth-century verse life of Muhammad by Embrico of Mainz. As we have seen in chapter 1, Embrico does not present Muhammad as an Antichrist (his Muhammad makes no claims to divinity or resurrection); rather, he is a heresiarch and anti-saint. God punishes Muhammad with epilepsy and subsequently kills him. When pigs begin to devour his corpse, his mentor, the Magus, drives them away and tells the faithful that they should no longer eat pork.

Then the Magus has a glorious temple built (in Libya) of gold and marble, with magnets set into the arches. There Muhammad's gilded, gem-studded sarcophagus hangs in midair. "The prodigious tumult of rude people, when they see this, hold this thing as a sign; the miserable people believe that this is done through the agency of Mahumet. . . . when these stupid people see this, they worship Mahumet."[18] Above the entrance to the temple is inscribed, "Here whatever is asked shall be granted by Mahumet."[19] Through one final and perpetual false miracle, Muhammad—or rather the Magus—deceives the Muslim masses for generations to come. Just as the tombs of the saints and of Christ are thought to produce real miracles into the present, the tomb of Muhammad continues to produce a prodigious false miracle. Levitation is another common topos in saints' lives.[20] Embrico's anti-saint Muhammad feigns the signs of sanctity—again, through an ingenious ruse.

Gauthier de Compiègne, writing later in the twelfth century, describes Muhammad's floating sarcophagus in much the same terms but with one crucial difference: he places the tomb in *Mecha*, an appropriate name because Muhammad was an adulterer (*Mechus*, or *Moechus*, in classical spelling); others, Gauthier tells us, place his tomb in Babel, also appropriate because Muhammad's effrontery matched that of the builders of the tower of Babel.[21] Mecca-Babel here is the supreme center of a depraved cult, the opposite of Jerusalem. The choice of Babel (Babylon)—locus of iniquity and illegitimate might for the prophets and for John the Apocalypst—is particularly apt. This is why, in the *Song of Roland*, Baligant, the leader of the pagan forces ranged against Charlemagne, is the emir of Babylon.[22]

Other authors also placed Muhammad's tomb in Mecca, which thus became the supreme anti-Christian site (though not all of these authors have the tomb float). Since the supreme site of Christian pilgrimage was Jesus' tomb in Jerusalem, it seemed self-evident that the supreme focus of the Muslim pilgrimage to Mecca must be Muhammad's tomb.[23] So much so that when, for example, fourteenth-century polemicist Petrus de Pennis copied Petrus Alfonsi's largely accurate description of the Muslim pilgrimage rites, he adds after the word *Mecca* "where the body of Muhammad lies." Jacobo di Verona says that Mecca is "where the body of that vile pig lies."[24]

The legend of Muhammad's floating sarcophagus was well enough known by the fourteenth century that polemicist Raymond Llull goes to some length to explain that it is not true.[25] It was so well known, in fact, that even an author familiar enough with Islam to realize how improbable it was sought to transform it, in order to render it plausible, rather than to reject it outright. The anonymous author of the *Libro del conoscimiento de todos los reinos* places in Mecca "the law and the testament of Mahomat, which is in an iron ark in a house made of magnetic rock. And for this reason it floats in the air, neither descending nor rising. And know that this Mecca is the head of the empire of the Arabs."[26] In this hybrid version of the story, the author attempts to reconcile the legend of the floating coffin with his knowledge of Islam: aware that Muhammad's tomb is at Medina and that Muslims revere the Qur'ân more than the body of the prophet, he places the *Qur'ân* in the floating ark (if indeed it is the Qur'ân he means by "the law and the testament of Mahomat").

Muhammad's floating coffin at Mecca becomes enough a part of Europe's oneiric landscape that it finds its way into works that claim to be *récits de voyages*. Andrea da Barberino, in his early fourteenth-century epic *Guerrino il meschino*, describes the adventures of mercenary knight Guerrino, who at one point comes to Mecca and enters the mosque. Here is his description of Muhammad's tomb:

> In the middle of this cupola was an urn shaped in the fashion of an evenly formed iron casket—I estimated almost a *braccio* and a half in length, and a bit less on its other side—and it was suspended and not touching anything. Then I recognized the false Muhammad's deception, since I realized that that part of the false church was from the middle up made entirely of lodestone which is a marine rock that is between black and grey in color and has this property in it: that it pulls iron to it because of its coldness. . . . It's this reason that the ark of Muhammad (which is made of iron) stays suspended: because the magnetic rock holds it; and the obtuse Saracen people don't know what lodestone is: they believe that the ark stays up by a miracle.[27]

Andrea's description is precise and detailed; he describes the force of the lodestones as natural rather than magic. This realism demystifies Muhammad's tomb, stripping it of its frightening power. The narrator's cool, scientific description and his rapid comprehension of the magnetic properties involved (a perspective which the reader is invited to share) sharply contrast with the credulity of the Saracens. What amazes him is not so much the mosque or the floating coffin but the obtuseness of the Saracens in taking this for a miracle. We Europeans, Andrea da Barberino seems to suggest, are too intelligent to be duped by such a hoax, which deceives the Saracen "imbeciles."

Yet other texts emphasized the power of this floating coffin, seen as the center of the Muslim world. The fourteenth-century *Liber Nycholay* presents a mixture of some of the legends we have seen. The Arab Marczuces finds Muhammad trying to seduce his wife; together they kill him, cut up his body, and cast it to the pigs, except for the foot. They tell the (now familiar) story about angels coming to get Muhammad and leaving his foot in the woman's hand. The foot is placed in the floating iron coffin, and it is revered in Mecca, which the author also refers to as Baghdad (Baldacca and Bladacta). Conflating the spiritual and political centers of the Muslim world, the author makes Baghdad-Mecca the center of the imagined Muslim world; a locus of magic and anti-Christianity in contrast with Jerusalem and a place of frightening power.

From the fourteenth century to the eighteenth, various Christians dream of attacking this (fictive) citadel of Muslim power, of destroying the Mecca of their imagination. The final victory of Christendom, promised in the Apocalypse, becomes linked, for some authors, with the success of the Crusades and the destruction of Mecca. For the epic *Chanson d'Antioche*, it is an idol of Mahomet (rather than his coffin) that floats in midair; the anonymous poet has a Saracen predict the destruction of the temple of Mecca and of the idol of Mahomet. In the *Chanson de Jérusalem*, Godfrey of Bouillon himself promises to destroy Mecca.[28]

Pope Innocent III, in *Quia maior*, the encyclical calling for the Fifth Crusade, identifies Muhammad with the beast of the Apocalypse and, affirming that 600 of the 666 years allotted to the Beast in Revelation have elapsed, predicts the ultimate defeat of the Saracens.[29] Yet as the crusade foundered in Egypt, the ambitions described to earlier crusaders, to capture and destroy Mecca, the spiritual center of Islam, now seemed impossible. Oliver of Paderborn, describing the capture and subsequent loss of Damietta in the Fifth Crusade, placed his hopes not on the successes of the crusaders but on the aid of mysterious Christians from afar. Oliver tells of a book of ancient prophecy that was found in Damietta. It foretold, among other things, the successes of the First Crusade, the recapture of Jerusalem by Saladin, and even the capture of Damietta by the current crusade. It went on, says Oliver, to predict that

> a certain king of the Christian Nubians was to destroy the city of Mecca and cast out the scattered bones of Mohammed, the false prophet, and certain other things which have not yet come to pass. If they are brought about, however, they will lead to the exaltation of Christianity and the suppression of the Agarenes [i.e., Muslims].[30]

The capture of Mecca, and the scattering of Muhammad's bones, will mark, it is hoped, the decisive victory of Christianity over Islam. Oliver and others of the thirteenth century now realize that this is impossible for crusading forces, unable even to hold Damietta, but he pins his hopes on mysterious Christian allies from the East. These hopes, embodied in the legends of Prester John, reached their height in the later thirteenth century as Mongols invaded the heartlands of Islam. Reports of the fall of Baghdad, along with reports of Christians among the Mongols, fueled these apocalyptic hopes and fears.[31]

Matthew Paris's *Chronicle*, after recounting the devastating invasion of the Kingdom of Jerusalem by Khwarazmians, gives the following explanation:

> Knowing that a few years ago the image of Machomet in Mecca fell, as a great vengeance for this event—and to the great affront of Christ and Christians, who had insulted this ruined image—the Chorosmini [Khwarazmians] violently attacked Christians and their holy places, saying that by the Grace of their god Machomet this victory was granted to them.[32]

He here describes an image or idol of Muhammad falling, rather than a sarcophagus. This divine event seems a victory for the Christians, yet it leads to a fresh and devastating invasion, which in turn reaffirms the faith of the Saracens. Matthew places all of this in a frightening apocalyptic scenario: falling stars, eclipses, missionary friars reaching the ends of the earth and hence fulfilling biblical prophecies about the last days. The fate of Mecca has become part of the drama of the eschaton.

If neither crusader military prowess nor even that of distant and mysterious Christian allies could now stem the military might of Islam and destroy the magic center of Mecca, one could still hope for an act of God. Another passage in Matthew's *Chronicle* gives an even more dramatic and apocalyptic description of the destruction of Mecca. Matthew tells us that a priest from the Church of St. Thomas at Acre came to his monastery of St. Albans:

> He added to his narrations that a certain sort of infernal fire, which perhaps had descended from the ether, suddenly inflamed and destroyed the temple of Machomet along with his image, and what is more, another force similar to the first one submerged it into the earth, and a third one deeper into the earth, and, as it is believed, destroyed it in the Abyss. . . . And in this way the entire city of Mecca and the surrounding area have been consumed by an inextinguishable fire.[33]

This dramatic destruction by infernal fire suggests divine punishment and coming apocalypse. This connection is made explicitly in the St. Albans manuscript known as the Addimenta (i.e., additions to Matthew Paris's *Chronicle*). The story of the destruction of Mecca is paraphrased, and at the same time Baghdad is struck first by flood and then by the invading Tartars. The meaning of this is made clear:

> The Tartars, pouring out of their lands like a plague of locusts, brought massacres to men. This is the belief and principal proposition of their king: that there is one lord in heaven as on earth.[34] A schism broke out in Paris and Oxford between the universities of scholars and other evil and wondrous things occurred, auguring the end of the world with terrible portents.[35]

The last days are terrifying yet exciting: they are supposed to bring both destruction and an ultimate Christian victory. To the thirteenth-century observer, signs of the end seemed many, including news of the imminent destruction of Islam: the (false) stories of the destruction of Mecca, the (true) story of the Mongol sack of Baghdad, and the (true, but greatly exaggerated) accounts of Christians among the Mongol hordes. It seemed (to some at least) that the predictions of the destruction of Islam at the hands of eastern Christians were being fulfilled. Such hopes did not last long; soon the Mongols converted en masse to Islam; at the same time, the Ottomans began to take power in Anatolia, and the apocalyptic scenarios looked grimmer to European Christians.

Fantasies of Mecca's destruction, however, were still possible. Dominican Felix Fabri describes his pilgrimage to Jerusalem in the 1480s. He says that he was unable to enter the Dome of the Rock in Jerusalem, since entry to non-Muslims was forbidden. He tells us that "in the whole of this temple there is nothing whatever save only on the north side there is a likeness of the sepulcher of Mahomet, a raised marble tomb, representing the sepulcher of Mahomet at Mecca, which they so greatly revere that they worship its likeness in all mosques."[36] Felix Fabri describes Mecca, and the rites of pilgrimage there, in a derogatory passage that he has taken principally from Petrus Alfonsi. The focus of the pilgrimage, though, is the floating coffin, which not only confirms "the besotted people" in their error but even lures Christians into renouncing their faith. To this frightening notion he finds a comforting solution:

> But we have heard a truthful and certain tale, that in the year of our lord 1480, there came on a sudden and terrible storm, sent, doubtless, by Divine Providence. Lightning flashed, dread thunder resounded, fire came down from heaven, and great hailstones fell upon Mecca, and drove the temple and the tomb of that accursed seducer deep into the earth, or rather into hell, so that there after it could not by any means or pains be found again. A great part of the temple also fell, consumed by fire, and thus the Saracens have been deprived of the relics and body of their false prophet, and utterly put to confusion, had they but minds to understand it; but their foolish heart hath been hardened, and now they go on pilgrimages to the place as before.[37]

While this tale may have seemed comforting to Felix Fabri and his readers, it was soon apparent that the Muslim center was still strong, as Ottoman troops marched further west into the heart of Europe. When all else failed, Muslim magic could be opposed, it seems, by Christian magic. On at least two occasions in the early sixteenth century, the people of Buda attempted to combat through sorcery the Turkish might that they were unable to defeat in battle. They created an effigy of a mosque in which the Ottoman sultan and his followers stood before the floating coffin of Muhammad; again, we see a conflation of the spiritual power of Islam (Muhammad's coffin in the mosque) and the military-political power (the sultan and his men) in a imagined center that becomes the focus of fear and hatred. In the effigy was placed gunpowder and other explosives. As the cardinal passed in procession, carrying the Eucharist, the mosque was inflamed, and as the fireworks subsided, people attacked the burning edifice with sticks and stones until it was completely destroyed. German traveler Thomas Dainero, who asked for an explanation, was told that, according to prophecy, Islam would come to an end as soon as the sarcophagus of Muhammad was destroyed.[38]

The legend of Muhammad's floating coffin persists into the seventeenth and eighteenth centuries, although it generally is mentioned in order to be discredited, even by such stridently anti-Muslim works as Humphrey Prideaux's *The True Nature of the Imposture Fully Displayed in the Life of Mahomet*, published in 1697. Prideaux explains that Muhammad was buried in Medina, under what had been 'Â'isha's bed. "And there he lieth to this day, without *iron-coffin* or *lodestones* to hang him in the air, as the stories which go about him commonly relate."[39] It was not only writers on Islam who assumed that their audiences knew this story: Mary Wollstonecraft, in her *Vindication of the Rights of Woman* (1792), says that "women appear to be suspended by destiny, according to the vulgar tale of Mahomet's coffin."[40] She recognizes the tale as "vulgar," but apparently feels that it is well known enough for use as a metaphor. And Alexander Eckhardt found the image of Muhammad's floating coffin still in use in the late nineteenth and early twentieth centuries in Hungary and Sicily.[41]

Yet the legend is dying by the time Prideaux rejects it in 1697, and after Gibbon ridicules it in 1776 it is never again taken seriously by western writers on Islam. The legend's demise during the enlightenment in many ways fits the spirit of the age. The first genuinely sympathetic western biography of Muhammad was that of Henri, comte de Boulainvilliers, uncompleted at his death in 1722 and published in 1730.[42] Boulainvilliers portrays Muhammad as a shrewd political leader and reformer, maintaining that Muhammad was indeed inspired by God, since God would not want half the world to be led into error. He presents Islam as a virtuous (though slightly overzealous) reaction to the abuses of clerical power by the eastern Christian Church; Muhammad properly eliminated the privileges of the prelate and bishop and reestablished the direct link between man and God, unencumbered by sacraments and priests. All of this is a barely veiled attack on the French Catholic Church. Throughout, Boulainvilliers takes pains to dispel the hostile medieval legends about Muhammad. (Since Boulainvilliers did not finish *La vie de Mahomet,* he did not discuss Muhammad's death and burial.)

Edward Gibbon includes a short biography of Muhammad in his *Rise and Fall of the Roman Empire.*[43] Based to some extent on Boulainvilliers,[44] Gibbon's portrayal of Muhammad is sympathetic, though tinged with condescension. His Arabs and Muhammad are proud and simple people: fierce warriors, emotional, impulsive, lustful, not prone to reflection. Gibbon explains this character as the result of the influence of climate and environment. He goes to some length to dispel many of the elements of the polemical Christian biographies of Muhammad.

It would be easy to ascribe the demise of the legend of Muhammad's floating coffin to a victory of Enlightenment rationalism, a beam of light dispelling the shadows of superstition. But neither Boulainvilliers nor Gibbon was afraid to shape his portrayal of history to fit his own polemical purposes. Gibbon was eager to cast Antonine Rome as a moral and political model for the British Empire. Boulainvilliers's Muhammad was an anticlerical stick with which to beat the French Catholic Church; in many ways, his Muhammad is no more real than the Persian travelers of Montesquieu's *Persian Letters*.

Rather, to invert the prophecy of Thomas Dainero's Hungarian informant, the floating sarcophagus of Muhammad was destroyed as soon as the threat of Islam came to an end. In the wake of Jan Sobieski's victory over the Turkish forces besieging Vienna in 1683, as Istanbul gradually lost control over much of southeastern Europe, the Turk no longer seemed a threat to western European writers. The magic of the legend of Muhammad's floating sarcophagus—its ability to provide an origin and center for a frightening and vigorous enemy—was no longer needed.

For French writers of the eighteenth century, such as Boulainvilliers and Montesquieu, it was now possible to portray the Muslim as a sympathetic if benighted "other," rather than a threatening one.[45] Gibbon, citizen of what he saw as the new Rome, confident in the expanding powers of the Royal Navy, could portray Muhammad with an inimitable mix of praise and condescension. He was a law-giver, reformer, messenger, skilled ruler and general, but to a semibarbarous, lustful people who were no longer seen as a threat. European Christians, it seems, were finally willing to let Muhammad rest in peace in Medina.

∴ 3 ∴

Rhetoric, Polemics, and the Art of Hostile Biography

Portraying Muhammad in Thirteenth-Century Christian Spain

In 1298, the bishop of Jaén, Pedro Pascual, was captured by Muslim troops of the Nasrid emir Muhammad II of Granada, whose prisoner he remained until his death two years later.[1] While in prison, Pedro looked on as many fellow Christian captives converted to Islam.[2] In an attempt to discourage this apostasy, he composed an anti-Islamic tract in Castilian, *Sobre la seta Mahometana*.[3] He includes a hostile description of the life and teachings of Muhammad, a standard practice of anti-Muslim polemic. What is unusual, however, is that Pedro gives Muhammad's biography twice: he first explains according to Muslim sources, then according to Christian sources.

The first of these two biographical sections shows his knowledge of Arabic and his familiarity with the Qur'ân, Hadîth, and the *Mi'râj* (the celestial voyage of Muhammad), which he cites in Arabic, transliterated into Latin letters.[4] He explains his method in the following way: "I translated into romance the history of Muhammad as I found it written in our books. Beyond what is found in this history, I wrote some things that certain Moors told me as they attempted to praise their law, and [others] that I found written in the books of the Moors."[5] In addition to his frequent citation of the Qur'ân, Hadîth ("Alhadiz"), and the *Mi'râj*, he cites the Arab Christian apologetical work known as the *Risâlat al-Kindî*.[6] He also claims to have read (or at least to know about) Muslim works of polemic, but this knowledge seems limited. "And when I hear what some Moors say in their disputations, the praises of Jesus Christ that Muhammad pronounced bother them, because he clearly said them against the Moors."[7] It goes without saying that this is not a sentiment he would find in any Muslim polemic against Christianity.

When Pedro does present material from actual Muslim sources, he often interjects polemic into his narration. When he remarks that Muhammad was born at "Meca," he reminds his readers that *Meca* is Latin for adultery (*Obras,* 4:4). He berates "Adiga" (Khadija) for believing that Muhammad had seen the archangel Gabriel. "Don't you know," Pedro asks her, "that men lie?" (*Obras,* 4:8). Muhammad invented his visions of heaven, Pedro says, to stir his troops into battle; that God is not on the Muslims' side is made clear when one thousand Christian troops defeat two thousand Moors, as we see in the exploits of Alfonso VI and the Cid (*Obras,* 4:26–27). Pedro issues the standard enumeration and approbation of Muhammad's multiple marriages and in several places condemns him for being a diviner and interpreter of dreams (*Obras,* 4:30–37, 42). He describes contradictions or errors from the Qur'ân and Hadîth (*Obras,* 4:37–56).

Even in this section, supposedly on the Muslim version of the life of Muhammad, Pedro incorporates material both from the *Risâlat al-Kindî* and the polemical Latin biographies. He claims, for example, that the Christian Sergio—and his false miracle of finding water in the desert—are found in the Muslim sources (*Obras,* 4:29). In his section on "how Muhammad died according to the books of the Moors" ("como murió Mahomad según los libros de los moros"), he says (following earlier Christian polemics) that Muhammad tried to baptize himself on his death bed, and that he had declared that either he would ascend alive to heaven or his body would be taken up by angels (*Obras,* 4:56–62). He has nevertheless produced a biography that—while invariably hostile to the Prophet—is still largely based on Muslim sources.

Very different is Pedro's life of the Prophet according to, as he puts it, "those Christians *who saw* Muhammad and struggled to know the truth concerning his beginnings and his end."[8] The young Muhammad, Pedro tells us, is the protégé of a heretical Christian monk, from whom he learns the arts of necromancy and astrology. Muhammad becomes king of the Arabs by defeating a bull he has raised (but which the people believe to be sent by God); he passes himself off as prophet by having a trained dove eat in his ear and claiming that it is the Holy Spirit; he has another bull deliver the Qur'ân on its horns.[9] The most fantastic and vicious element in this Christian caricature of Muhammad is the account of his death. As

Muhammad goes off to sleep with a Jewess who dares not refuse him, her family ambushes him, kills him, and has his cadaver cut up and devoured by pigs—all but one foot, which they dress in myrrh and sweet-smelling unguents. When Muhammad's associates come looking for him, the woman claims that angels took Muhammad from her bed and that she held on to his foot, which came off in the subsequent tug of war.[10]

Apparently aware of the outrageousness of this tale, Pedro here inserts a disclaimer. I do not know, he says, if these stories are in fact true, but I found them in Latin and was asked to translate them, so I did. Anyway, he says, "it seems that the aforementioned writing is true."[11] In other words, Pedro refuses to choose between the Muslim and Christian biographies of Muhammad, but hints that the Christian sources, by "those Christians *who saw* Muhammad and struggled to know the truth," are more reliable.

Pedro's strange double biography of Muhammad challenges the commonly drawn distinction between "learned" and "popular" medieval traditions about Islam. The "learned" texts, according to Norman Daniel and other scholars, analyze (and attack) Islam on the basis of Muslim writings, in particular Qur'ân and Hadîth; they attempt to refute Islam on its own terms, as we see in Ramón Martí's *De Seta Machometi* (composed before 1257). The "popular" texts, by contrast (such as Embrico of Mainz's *Vita Mahumeti,* discussed in chapter 1), present Muhammad as an object of derision: magician, astrologer, and sex maniac who uses bogus miracles to hoodwink his people into cleaving to a depraved and ridiculous cult. The scholarly texts, it seems, are the products of minds that have known and studied Islam, while the popular texts spring from hearsay and malicious fancy.

Yet here is Pedro Pascual, well versed in Arabic, familiar with Qur'ân and Hadîth, who actually *prefers* the hostile and ridiculous Christian legends. Why? Norman Daniel has posited that it was animosity that drove Pedro (and many medieval authors) to prefer the most ludicrous and debasing of whatever they heard or read about Muhammad. Those (such as Ramón Martí) who steer clear of such legends are enlightened exceptions to this rather depressing rule.[12] Blinded by his hostility, Pedro was unable to distinguish between the true and false about Islam, instead producing a strange amalgam. The same charge could be leveled against Alfonso el Sabio, who creates a hybrid biography of Muhammad from "learned" and "popular" sources.

Yet Pedro and Alfonso construct their texts in anything but a haphazard manner. Recent scholarship has shown that Alfonso carefully crafted his *Estoria de España* to bolster his royal and imperial authority: the choice of subject and sources is more deliberate than it appears.[13] The same can be said of Pedro Pascual's *Sobre la seta:* the dual biography of Muhammad is calculated to dissuade his readers from converting to Islam. Perhaps we should turn the question around and ask why authors like Ramón Martí shun these Christian legends.

Dominican friar Ramon Martí, schooled in Arabic and Hebrew, in the Talmud and Arabic philosophy,[14] directed his missionary efforts against Muslims and especially Jews. He attempted to attack each religion at its base by showing how its own scriptures invalidate its precepts. This strategy is not new: Mozarab Christians attacked the Qur'ân and Hadîth as impious and silly, at the same time trying to find proof of Christian Truth in them.[15] Petrus Alfonsi in 1110 ridiculed the Qur'ân and the Talmud, showing supposed contradictions in both.[16] Yet the Dominican missionaries pursued this tactic with a zeal and perseverance never seen before: they schooled themselves in Hebrew, Aramaic, and Arabic, pored over the Talmud and Qur'ân, produced massive tracts for the use of their missionaries, and (with the aid of King James I of Aragon) forced Jewish and Muslim scholars to debate with them. The best known of these disputations was that between Dominican Pablo Cristiá and Rabbi Moses ben Nachman (Nachmanides), at the king's court in Barcelona in 1263.[17] The Dominicans staged other such confrontations with Muslims and with Jews.

Martí meant his *De Seta Machometi*, like his anti-Jewish *Pugio fidei*, to be a practical guide for Christians in theological disputes.[18] But while the *Pugio fidei* was an immense encyclopedia of anti-Jewish argument, *De Seta* is a brief text in two parts: an attack on the life and deeds of Muhammad followed by a defense of Christianity from the charge of falsification of the scriptures. This sequence is calculated: the attack on Muhammad must prove that Islam is false, while the defense of Christian scriptures—based on the Qur'ân—is meant to prove to the Muslim that Christianity is the true religion. This strategy had been commonly used by Mozarab Christian polemicists against Islam; Martí and other Dominicans were to deploy it not only against the Qur'ân but also against the Talmud: the missionaries attacked it to show that Jews hold an irrational document as sacred, but they mined it for "proofs" that the Messiah had come in the person of Jesus.

Muhammad is not a true prophet, Martí claims; rather, he is one of the false prophets that Jesus announced in Matthew 7:15–16: "Beware of false prophets, which come to you in sheep's clothing, but inwardly they are ravening wolves. Ye shall know them by their fruits." Martí organizes his tract around this central premise. The "fruits" mentioned in Matthew, Martí expounds, are the four signs of prophethood: truthfulness, holiness, miracles, and a true Law. Martí's "Quadruplex refutatio" aims to show that Muhammad meets none of these four tests. His strategy is to make the Prophet a scapegoat: it is the Prophet and his false law that he attacks, not the wisdom of subsequent Muslims. He will try to bring the Arab philosophers into the Christian camp by using their philosophical arguments against Muhammad: he cites Averroes to prove that a true prophet must produce miracles (*De seta,* 16). Muhammad becomes Martí's sole (if formidable) adversary: reason, natural law, philosophy, and even much of Muslim doctrine, he will try to show, are on the Christians' side.

While Martí sticks scrupulously to Arab (and principally Muslim) sources, he at times fails to distinguish between essential Muslim doctrine and pious legend: he attacks with equal force the precepts of the Qur'ân and the sayings attributed to Muhammad in the Hadîth collections of al-Bukhârî and Muslim ibn al-Hajjaj. This is a problem that the Dominicans faced in their polemics against Judaism as well: in the 1263 Barcelona disputation, Nachmanides takes Friar Pablo Cristiá to task for presenting Talmudic Aggadah as if they were canonical.[19]

Martí has scoured the vast traditional literature for anything that will seem immoral, impious, or absurd. A good example is his presentation of the following piece of advice attributed to Muhammad in al-Bukhârî's *Sahih*: "When a fly falls in a dish, submerge it there, for if it has poison in one wing and antidote in the other, put first the wing which has the poison and then the other."[20] The choice of passages clearly shows the polemical purpose. By pouncing on whatever he finds to be shocking or ridiculous, he can conclude, "All these things seem more the words of an idiot or a scoffer than of a prophet or messenger of God."[21] The purpose is not to understand Islam but to vilify it. While this could no doubt evoke nods of approbation from fellow Dominican missionaries, it is hard to imagine Muslims being convinced through such an arbitrary and hostile selection of Hadîth passages.

But the brunt of Martí's attack is against the sexual foibles of Muhammad and his followers; here he attacks Hadîth and especially the Qur'ân. Martí presents the Muslim paradise, full of the pleasures of eating and love-making, and contrasts it with the pure and austere heaven of Paul and the Gospels (*De seta,* 30). A recitation of the wives and concubines of Muhammad is enough, for Martí, to prove that he did not lead a holy life. Since holiness is the second "fruit of prophecy," this helps prove that Muhammad was not a true prophet but a false one (*De seta,* 34–36).

Martí's fourth fruit of prophecy is a good and holy law. He tries to show that the law brought by Muhammad goes against both divine law (as mandated by scripture) and natural law (as mandated by reason). Of the eleven Muslim laws that Martí here assails, seven involve sex and marriage. He derides polygamy as "manifestly against divine law, against natural law and against reason."[22] He similarly condemns what he presents as Muslim law regarding divorce, nonvaginal intercourse, concubinage, coitus interruptus, and homosexuality (*De seta,* 44–48). Acknowledging that homosexuality is in fact illegal in Islam, he nonetheless claims that since four witnesses are needed to convict homosexuals, Muhammad thus "gave cause and occasion to his followers to perpetrate this crime almost without shame and fear."[23]

For Ramón Martí, a missionary friar under a vow of celibacy, the most false and shocking thing about Muhammad and his followers is their sex life: polygamy, homosexuality, even sex in heaven! This obsession flavors Martí's description of Muhammad's death. Martí, unlike Pedro Pascual, eschews the horrendous tales of murder and dismemberment in favor of the Muslim story of his death, which shows the Prophet surrounded by his loved ones, peacefully dying with his head in the lap of his beloved wife 'Â'isha. For Muslims, this touching scene emphasizes the Prophet's human frailty and the love which his family and followers held for him. Yet Martí is unable to see anything but filth in this scene: "When he died he had his head between 'Â'isha's breast and her chin, and she mixed her saliva with that of Muhammad. In this way the death or end of Muhammad was vile, unclean, and abominable. And such a death is in no way appropriate for a prophet or a messenger of God" (*De seta,* 52). In a standard Christian deathbed scene, an attentive priest would hear confession and administer communion and extreme unction, and the dying man would prepare his soul to meet its Maker. Instead of the Body of Christ, Martí seems to be implying, Muhammad's last solace was the saliva of profane kisses; instead of the anointing hand of a priest, he is caressed by the breasts of a woman; instead of confessing and turning away from sin, he is clinging desperately to it.[24]

Martí, unlike most earlier Latin polemicists, has sketched a biography of Muhammad that Muslims would recognize as true in most of its details, gleaned as they are from Arab (and principally Muslim) sources. Yet the selection and presentation of these sources show an unshakable hostility: from the wide range of material in the Qur'ân, ibn Ishaq, al-Bukhârî, and Muslim ibn al-Hajjaj, Martí focuses on what will shock a Christian clerical audience: the sex life of the Muslim prophet and Muslim laws regarding sex and marriage.

If we turn back to the "learned-popular" distinction with which we started, Martí does not look quite as "learned" as he did at first glance. Granted, he peruses authentic Muslim texts in Arabic, but he does so with an invariably hostile eye, looking for what will condemn Islam and support conversion to Christianity. Well schooled in Arabic philosophy, he shows surprisingly little theological sophistication in his attack, failing to distinguish between essential and incidental in Muslim doctrine.

When we turn to Alfonso el Sabio's *Estoria de España,* we find a different picture of Muhammad's life—and particularly of his death. Here is not the place to plunge into the scholarly debates surrounding the composition of this Castilian chronicle and the nature of the king's role in it.[25] Suffice it to say that Alfonso seems to have closely supervised the creation of this sweeping history, which was originally supposed to narrate the history of Spain from the arrival of Hercules to the accession of Alfonso himself. Most of the text (or of that part of it that was actually composed under Alfonso) deals with Roman and Visigothic history. Alfonso apparently meant it to bolster his claim to the Imperial crown; it is probably no coincidence that he abandons the *Estoria* at the same time as he gives up his claim to the title of Roman emperor.[26] Alfonso's scriptorium also produced translations from Arabic of scientific texts, the *Mi'râj*, and possibly the Qur'ân.[27] For the *Estoria*'s biographical sketch of Muhammad, Alfonso relied primarily on the Latin *Historia Arabum* of Rodrigo Jiménez de Rada, archbishop of Toledo (1208–47).[28] Rodrigo's portrayal of Muhammad is similar to Martí's: hostile, but based to a large extent on Arab Muslim sources.[29]

Yet when recounting Muhammad's death, Alfonso deliberately rejects Rodrigo's account in favor of a more flamboyant (and far less reliable) legend from Lucas de Tuy. He tells us that Muhammad had predicted that he would die after reigning over the Arabs ten years and that three days after his death he would rise from the dead. (Alfonso earlier recounted—following Lucas rather than Rodrigo—that Muhammad had claimed to be the Messiah.)[30] One of his disciples, Albimor, wishing to put Muhammad to the test, poisons him. At his death his disciples watch his body closely for three days; seeing that he will not rise, and repulsed by the stench of his rotting corpse, they leave him. Albimor later returns to find the body devoured by dogs. He takes the bones and has them buried in Medina.

Why does Alfonso deliberately choose Lucas's dramatic legend over the sober, terse account given by Rodrigo, whom he usually prefers? Rodrigo, like Martí and other Christian polemicists, had focused his biography of Muhammad on the implicit contrast between Muhammad and Jesus: Christ, shunning sex and worldly power; Muhammad, eagerly pursuing both. Alfonso wanted to carry this contrast farther, to their deaths: Christ's, the supreme sacrifice and glorious victory; Muhammad's, the death of an Antichrist, complete with a failed resurrection and a rotting, dog-defiled corpse. The death story, gleaned from Lucas, made dramatic and theological sense. It also made sense in the broader sweep of Alfonso's narrative, in which he describes the various groups that had ruled Spain. He privileges two groups, the Romans and the Goths: their rule is legitimate and celebrated. Alfonso sees himself, of course, as the incarnation of both: Roman emperor and Gothic king. The Arabs, by contrast, he portrays as interlopers, never as legitimate rulers.[31] Just as Alfonso glorifies the origins of Roman and Gothic rule, he must denigrate the origins of Arab rule. What better way than by presenting their prophet and first statesman as a liar, scoundrel, and Antichrist? Thus, to return to Norman Daniel's dilemma, the failure of Alfonso and his team of scholars to stick with good, reliable Arabic texts does not mean that they are unable to distinguish between their sources. On the contrary, it shows a consummate historiographical skill (if one that most of us like to think we avoid): the ability to shape the past to fit a political agenda.

This brings us back to Pedro Pascual and to the question of why *he* prefers his dubious Christian sources to his impeccable Muslim ones. Pedro, like Ramón Martí, we have seen, knew Arabic and Hebrew; like Martí, he composed polemics against both Judaism and Islam.[32] Yet the purpose, nature, and audience of the two authors' texts could not be more different. Ramón Martí wrote in Latin for a highly educated cadre of missionary friars, whose task was offensive: to convert Jews and Muslims to Christianity through preaching and disputation. Pedro Pascual wrote in the vernacular—Valencian and Castilian—for a less educated audience to whom he presented edifying religious stories and clearly defined boundaries between true religion and error. If Martí has dreams of converting Muslims through his *De seta Machometi*, Pedro Pascual in apprehension watches Christians converting to Islam; his *Sobre la seta Mahometana* is an attempt to stem that tide of conversion. It is defensive where Martí's work was offensive. Pedro tells his readers, "You will find in it [his book] the material with which you can defend yourself against the enemies of our law."[33]

This is why Pedro can include—and prefer—the Christian polemical legends about Muhammad's life and death. While such material would only be ridiculed by the Muslims whom Martí wished to convert, it will prove useful to explain and vilify Islam to Pedro's "amigos," to whom he addresses his tract by recommending that they read it rather than "fables of romances of love or other vanities," which is apparently their more usual fare.[34]

That Pedro knows what he is doing is clear in the organization of his tract. He intends his first chapter (which includes the dual biography of Muhammad) to discredit Islam in the eyes of his Christian readers. In chapters 2–16, by contrast, the beleaguered Christian can find arguments in support of the Trinity, the cult of images, noncircumcision, the Eucharist, the incarnation and divinity of Christ, etc.—in short, for the basic Christian doctrines that Muslims find most shocking or perplexing. He tells his readers which specific arguments they can use against Muslims.[35] Significantly, it is only innocuous, defensive arguments that he urges upon his flock, not offensive attacks on Islam or its prophet.

Pedro very carefully modifies his message to fit the purpose to which his readers are meant to put it. Let us look at a small but telling example. In his anti-*Jewish* polemic, the *Disputa contra los Jueus,* he describes the differing interpretations of Isaiah 7:14: "Behold, an *'alma* shall conceive, and bear a son, and shall call his name Immanuel." The key, controversial Hebrew word, *'alma,* means merely "young girl" according to Jewish scholars, while Christians claim it means "virgin." For the Christian exegete, this is a clear and incontrovertible prophecy of the Virgin Birth, while for Jews it deals with a mere teenage pregnancy. In his discussion of this passage in the *Disputa contra los Jueus,* Pedro gives both sides of the argument, preferring, of course, the Christian side.[36] When Pedro discusses the same passage from Isaiah in *Sobre la seta Mahometana*, he does not even acknowledge that there might be controversy about its interpretation. Muslims, after all, believe in the Virgin Birth, so there is no need to trouble his readers with Jewish objections (*Obras,* 4:169). In other words, he gave his readers exactly the information he thought they would need in view of the specific religious adversary, Jew or Muslim.

Christians and Muslims in thirteenth-century Spain spoke to each other about their respective creeds. Pedro himself refers several times to such discussions he had with Muslims.[37] There is also evidence that Christians, Muslims, and Jews participated together in practices and beliefs that we today might consider on the borders of "religion": weddings, burials, festivals, magical and astrological practice. Pedro condemns Muslims' involvement in magical and divinatory practice, and blames Muslim influence for Christians' participation in such practices. He condemns, for example, a ritual that seems to have been practiced by Muslims around him. In order to appease the fates, who come to visit a child seven days after its birth, Pedro tells us, the Moors shave part of its scalp, give it a name, set the table with a white sheet, and leave various treats for the fates: bread, water, and figs (for girls) or dates (for boys). He condemns this as a "vile heresy" and says that it contradicts Muslim fatalism as expressed in the *Mi'râj*. Pedro says that he himself questioned Moors about this practice, which seems to have been current in Spain in his day (*Obras*, 4:97–98); indeed, he seems to be eager to discourage his Christian readers from participating in such "heretical" rituals, which probably shocked Muslim *'ulama* as much as it did Pedro and which may well have crossed confessional lines. Pedro felt that such practices and such fraternization with Muslims were dangerous. They could lead down the slippery slope toward apostasy. He needed to give Christians arguments to deploy against Muslims and particularly to instill in them a sense of difference from Muslims, to construct a wall of antipathy that would prevent his readers from converting. Whereas Christian missionaries to Islam at times emphasized the similarity between Islam and Christianity in order to attract Muslim converts (or to argue to a Christian audience that conversion of Muslims should not be difficult), Pedro Pascual had to convince his readers that the similarities between Islam and Christianity were illusory, that the two religions were diametrically opposed.

While theological distinctions may be enough to instill a feeling of difference in the friars who deployed Ramón Martí's missionary tracts, they were unlikely to impress Pedro's vernacular audience. Martí, we recall, dwelled on the sexual foibles of Muhammad and Muslims, which were enough to shock any good Dominican who had taken his vow of celibacy. But perhaps polygamy and sex in heaven would not have repulsed Pedro's readers as much as it would have intrigued them; remember that stories of love and adventure are their more usual fare. Instead, violence and destiny must be seen to separate the two communities and to make them inevitably opposed.

Having already inspired in his Christian readers contempt toward Muslims, in his seventh chapter (ostensibly a defense of the Christian notion of martyrdom) Pedro tries to inspire hatred. Like a wartime propagandist, he seeks to stir righteous ire by describing what "they" have done to "us." By projecting this violent hostility into the past as well as the present, he tries to present it as eternal, inevitable: the wall of violence cannot be crossed. Martyrdom is the great separator: he tells of Christians killed by Muslims, among others Pelayo, martyred in Cordoba in the tenth century (*Obras,* 4:202). He dwells on the story of Friar Daniel, who (along with fellow Franciscan missionaries) went to preach to the moors of Ceuta and was brought before the Muslim king and sentenced to death by decapitation. The Infante Don Pedro of Portugal was in Ceuta at the time. According to Pedro, he witnessed the martyrdom, saw miracles subsequently performed by the martyrs, and brought their heads back to the monastery of Sancta Cruz de Coimbra. Pedro himself saw the heads there, which miraculously looked as fresh as if they had been recently lopped off (*Obras,* 4:201–2). The willingness to suffer martyrdom for the faith is, for Pedro, an imperative; he condemns those who refuse martyrdom and claim to be Christians in their hearts, referring, it seems, to some of his fellow prisoners (*Obras,* 4:202–3).

In this context, Pedro's strange double biography of Muhammad makes sense: he needs to give his readers an idea of what Muslims say about Muhammad, yet to inspire in them so much contempt for Islam that they are ready to prefer death to apostasy. Neither Pedro Pascual nor Alfonso el Sabio is any less shrewd than Ramón Martí; on the contrary, they manipulate their sources with skill and seem to know their audiences better than does Martí. If anything, it is the scholarly Martí who now seems ingenuous, with his dreams of converting Muslims through argumentation. Alfonso and Pedro, nervously watching the interaction of Christian and Muslim Spaniards, forge clever lies in order to prevent apostasy and to keep the boundaries clear between truth and error. Not a flattering picture, perhaps, but let us not call them naïve.[38]

∴ 4 ∴

Peter of Cluny on the "Diabolical Heresy of the Saracens"

Peter the Venerable, abbot of Cluny, traveled to Spain in 1142–43. There he assembled a team of translators whom he enticed to produce a full, annotated Latin version of the Qur'ân, along with translations of other Muslim texts and of an Arab-Christian polemical work, the *Risâlat al-Kindî.* Using this collection of texts, Peter himself composed two anti-Islamic tracts: the first, his *Summa totius haeresis Saracenorum,* describes and vilifies Islam to a Christian readership, and the second, the *Contra sectam siue haeresim Saracenorum,* attempts to refute Islam on its own terms and enjoins its Muslim readers to convert to Christianity.[1]

Why did Peter of Cluny undertake, at great cost and considerable effort, this ambitious venture? James Kritzeck rightly emphasizes the uniqueness of this endeavor and the zeal with which Peter and his associates brought it to completion. Yet if Kritzeck characterizes it as a "project to study, comprehensively and from original sources, the religion of Islam,"[2] these are not the terms that Peter of Cluny himself employs. For Peter, the point is not to "study" a "religion" but to refute a particularly vile form of heresy. Previous scholars have shown that Kritzeck's vision of Peter as a tolerant, irenic student of Islam is wide of the mark; yet these same scholars, seeming to accept Peter's own claim that no one before him had refuted the "heretic" Muhammad, ignore Peter's use of earlier anti-Muslim polemic.[3]

This chapter is an attempt to rectify this picture, to place Peter of Cluny's important initiative in context, or rather in two contexts: first, Peter's selective use of an earlier Christian Arabic tradition of anti-Muslim polemic and, second, Peter's own very particular concerns and outlook, which shape his views of Islam. Peter (like other twelfth-century authors on Islam) understood and portrayed this "Saracen heresy" according to the fears and hopes of twelfth-century Europe. Peter uses previous polemical works: the *Risâlat al-Kindî* (by a ninth- or tenth-century Arab Christian author) and the *Dialogi contra Iudeos* of Andalusian Petrus Alfonsi. He nevertheless portrays Islam in a very different light, reflecting the preoccupation with heretics close to home, the ambivalence toward philosophical and scientific study, and a need to intellectually justify Christianity in the face of a wave of texts and ideas flowing in from the Arab world. He strove to explain Islam in ways that would account for the erudition and opulence of its adherents while reassuring the Christian reader that he was right to remain true to his ancestral faith.

Peter of Cluny was poised at the confluence of various tides of change surging across Europe: monastic reform, new heretical movements, new applications of logic to theology (including attempts to prove the fundamental doctrines of Christianity by rational arguments). Peter wrote to condemn the heretic Peter of Bruys, he mediated between Abelard and Bernard of Clairvaux, welcoming Abelard as one of his monks, he read Petrus Alfonsi's *Dialogi contra Iudeos,* reusing its anti-Talmudic arguments in his own *Adversus Iudeorum inveteratam duritiem,* and he traveled to Spain where he hired translators—taking them away from their study of philosophy and astronomy—to translate the series of texts on Islam often (and rather misleadingly) called the *Collectio Toletana,* despite the fact that nothing links them with Toledo. Throughout Peter's polemics, we see hopes and worries of the abbot, fighter of heresies, and interested spectator of the new developments in knowledge.

What intellectual baggage did Peter bring along on his encounter with Islam? He did not confront it *tabula rasa.* How then did his previous experiences and ideas affect the way he read and reacted to the Qur'ân and the other works that had been translated? My aim is not to narrate Peter's biography; that has been amply done.[4] Rather, I want to highlight the elements in his life that will shape his understanding of Islam, the intellectual frame of reference that was constructed before he confronted the law of Muhammad and through which he read the Qur'ân and other texts on Islam.

The first and broadest influence is his monastic education and his experience as a monk and abbot. As a child oblate virtually weaned on the

Bible and Church fathers, he was bound to find the Qur'ânic stories of (say) Potiphar's wife and Joseph, or of Abraham and his son Ishmael, to be strange and deviant. Even more shocking, of course, would be the Qur'ânic Jesus: born of the Virgin Mary, yet uncrucified and undivine. Yet this would not have been completely unfamiliar to a reader of the Church Fathers—Augustine and others—who often wielded their pens against deviant Christologies. Peter places himself proudly in their tradition as he writes to combat what he can only see as the latest and most virulent Christological heresy.

As abbot, Peter piloted Cluny through what Lester Little has called "the critical phase of the crisis of monasticism."[5] Cluny found itself under increasing criticism from advocates of reform, notably the Cistercians. Much has been written about the "feud" between Cluny and Cîteaux and about the friendly if at times strained exchanges of letters between Peter and Bernard of Clairvaux.[6] At the heart of the issue, perhaps, was the Cistercian accusation that the Cluniacs slavishly followed the *letter* of the Benedictine Rule, while the Cistercians followed the Rule in *spirit*. Intentionality, or inward purity, is what matters, according to many twelfth-century thinkers, rather than slavish obedience to ritual; this formed the basis for Abelard's (and Heloise's) critique of monastic formalism.[7] It may thus have struck a chord in Peter to read in Petrus Alfonsi's *Dialogi* and in the *Risâlat al-Kindî* that Muslims clung to formal, ritualistic purity (e.g., in ablution before prayer) rather than true purity (sinlessness and contrition).[8]

In the twelfth century, the line was often thin between reform and heresy—or, to use the terminology of Lester Little, between "moderate" and "radical" reform.[9] If the role of faith and intentionality in monastic discipline could be a source of friendly debate between Peter and Bernard, it could also be incendiary, as was shown several times during the twelfth century—quite literally so for Peter of Bruys, who,in order to burn crucifixes,built a bonfire at Saint Gilles les Boucheries, only to end up immolated on his own fire by the angry inhabitants. Almost all of what little we know about this heresy comes from the *Contra Petrobrusianos,* in which Peter of Cluny enumerates five principal heretical doctrines of Peter of Bruys: the heresiarch was against infant baptism, against the building and use of churches (since all places are equally holy to God), against the veneration of crucifixes (which should be destroyed rather than revered), against the sacrament of the Eucharist, and against the prayers and offerings for the souls of the dead. Why write a tract against a man who already has been burned for his errors? Because, Peter says, these errors are now spreading to Gascony: "that stupid and impious heresy is killing many, like some pestilence."[10] He addresses his tract as a letter to the bishops of Die, Embrun, and Gap, whom he enjoins to extirpate the heresy through preaching, resorting if necessary to the arms of laymen:

> Your task is to drive them out of those places, in which their dens are found, by preaching and also—if it should prove necessary, by the armed force of laymen. But because it is a greater service to convert them than to exterminate them, it is proper to employ Christian charity. Let authority be proffered to them and let reason be employed, so that if they wish to remain Christians they may be compelled to desist by authority and if they wish to remain humans, they may be compelled by reason. (*Contra Petrobrusianos,* 3)

This is the same attitude that he will show toward Islam: it is best to convert the infidels by preaching to them in the spirit of Christian love, but failing that, the force of arms should be used.[11] Christians can be brought back to the fold through arguments based on authority (*auctoritas*); non-Christians, since they are human and ergo rational, can be brought to Christian truth through reason (*ratio*). This strategy underlies not only his polemics against the Petrobrusians but also those against Judaism and Islam: while he bitterly condemns Jews who refuse to listen to Christian "reason," he hopes that rational argumentation might convince Muslims to embrace Christianity.

Parallel to his anti-Islamic strategy, too, are the two purposes he ascribes to his *Contra Petrobrusianos:* first, to try to convince the heretics to abandon their stupidity (*stulticia*); failing that, he hopes he may at least warn his Christian readers away from the errors of the heretics (*Contra Petrobrusianos,* 6). Moreover, he says that he should not pass over any heresy in silence, but,in the tradition of the Church fathers, fight them with the twin weapons of reason (*ratio*) and authority (*auctoritas*). To this end, he organizes his tract into five parts (one for each of the principal errors of Peter of Bruys); he marshals a large array of scriptural citations to refute each point. While Robert I. Moore is certainly right to characterize the *Contra Petrobrusianos* as "by far the most powerful and sophisticated rebuttal of popular heresy in this period," Jean Châtillon has noted the cultural and social gap between such learned, exegetically based polemics and the popular heresy it was meant to combat.[12] It is doubtful that this strategy would have had much impact on the practice of heresy, but Peter was writing the kind of polemics he knew how to write, in the tradition of such learned rebuttals of heresy. It is the same tradition he will perpetuate in his polemics against Islam, with the same results. Peter was aware that some of Peter of Bruys's errors were shared by Catholics: the questioning of the efficacy of prayers and masses for the dead, for example. Such doubts would have seemed especially troubling to the abbot of Cluny, whose monks continually said masses for the souls of dead lay benefactors: he specifically addresses such "secret thoughts of certain Catholics."[13]

The enthusiastic embrace of *ratio* as a means to spiritual truth characterizes Peter's polemics against Jews, Petrobrusians, and Muslims, and marks him off from contemporaries such as Bernard of Clairvaux. Learned study and speculation, far from leading one into dangerous error, lead toward Christian truth. This attitude may have induced Peter to welcome to Cluny Peter Abelard, recently condemned as a heretic, and to help orchestrate his reconciliation with Bernard, the repeal of his excommunication, and his acceptance as a monk at Cluny. The episode is well known enough to need no retelling here.[14]

Several scholars have speculated on the influence Abelard may have had on Peter of Cluny's anti-Jewish and anti-Islamic polemics, in particular through his *Dialogue between a Philosopher, a Jew, and a Christian.*[15] While Peter did not directly use Abelard's *Dialogue,* it, like Peter's own apologetical work, reflects the same spirit of rationalistic debate, the same hope of proving Christian truth to Jews through exegetical argument based on the Old Testament and to "Pagans" (a term which probably embraces both ancient paganism and Islam) using only rational argumentation. It is also clear that Abelard is continuing Anselm's tradition of *fides quaerens intellectum:* the Christian seeking rational confirmation of his faith. Even if the exercise serves no missionary purpose, it can be useful in dispelling the doubts of the Christian reader.

Peter's own anti-Jewish polemic is a far cry from Abelard's irenic tract. He composed his *Against the Inveterate Stubbornness of the Jews* in 1144, revising and expanding it in 1146–47.[16] The first four chapters of his work include the standard topoi of anti-Jewish polemic since Augustine; they comprise an attack based on a Christian exegesis of the Old Testament. Peter's fifth chapter, however, is a direct assault on the Talmud. Here he makes use of Petrus Alfonsi's *Dialogi Contra Iudeos* and the *Alphabet of Ben Sira,*[17] although claiming that Christ alone gave him knowledge of the Talmud.[18] But where Petrus Alfonsi's repudiation of Talmudic legends is replete with rational and scientific counterarguments, Peter merely responds to these Talmudic legends with this invective addressed, significantly, to his Christian reader:

> What do you hope for, reader? What do you expect? Do you think that I will take some action against the Jews about these things? Nay, let me not act against them in these things, let me not respond to impudent dogs and vile pigs as if they were capable of reason and hence show them to be worthy of any response in these matters.[19]

If Peter needs to refute Judaism, he expresses little hope that his refutation will result in the conversion of Jews. Aware that they have withstood centuries of such argumentation, he prefers to impute this to their lack of human reason, to their "bovine intellect," than to any lack of rational basis for Christian truth.[20] He will approach the Muslims with more confidence that his rationalistic apologetics may win converts.

Peter of Cluny seems to have decided upon his polemical enterprise against Islam during a trip to Castile and León in 1142–43.[21] He went to visit Cluniac houses in Spain and to receive a donation from King Alfonso VII. At Nájera he assembled his team of translators, whose efforts were apparently to be coordinated by his personal secretary, Peter of Poitiers.

One of Peter of Cluny's letters has largely escaped the attention of earlier scholars. It is the *Letter to Peter of Poitiers against those who claim that Christ never openly called himself God in the Gospels.*[22] The issue addressed evokes the Muslim claim that Jesus was a mere human prophet and that the Gospel that he revealed said nothing of his divinity. Yet here Peter is addressing a community of Christians, apparently clerics, for he recalls to Peter of Poitiers that the latter had told him of a conversation with "certain brothers" who asserted that nowhere in the Gospel did the Savior clearly say that he was God. Although Peter of Poitiers had not mentioned the names of these brothers, Peter of Cluny says that he believes he knows who they are and that he believed that their question sprang "not from weakness of faith, but from love and zeal to know things of which they were ignorant before" (PL 189:487). He describes them as learned, erudite, religious men. Peter says that he will respond to them and show them that Christ did indeed claim to be God, lest doubt should rise up in the hearts of such men.

Who are these learned Christian brothers who voice a very Muslim-sounding objection to one of the most basic principles of Christian biblical exegesis? It is tempting to identify them with some of the translators working in Spain: perhaps the exposure to the Muslim view of Christianity led these Christians to question their own exegetical traditions. Perhaps the doubts were in fact those of Peter of Poitiers, who attributed them to nameless "brothers." Yet these doubts could have been expressed by other philosophically inclined Christians of the twelfth century, and the text is undated. Abelard's Trinitarian speculations got him into trouble without any help from the Muslims; certainly a thoughtful student of the Bible could raise these objections.

If Peter of Cluny does not specifically say that Muslim views inspired these learned brothers, he certainly implies it. He describes how after the Church's victory over paganism, Satan created heretical errors to lead the faithful astray: Manicheism and Arianism both deny the true divinity of Christ. But worse, for Peter, is Satan's deception of the Saracens:

> Since Satan has occupied almost half the earth with his Saracens, he teaches them to preach that Christ is better than all men and the best, so that they nevertheless deny he is God. . . . For there is no doubt that it would not be religious, but rather sacrilegious to place any hope of salvation in him who, not divine, could neither be called savior nor would be able to save anyone. The Corruptor of human nature with this poison tainted and infected those whom I mentioned, the Saracens of modern times. He taught them to preach that Christ was born from the Virgin, and sent by God, and that He is the Word of God and the Spirit of God (as he understood it); but he persuaded them that He was not God and had not died. Thus the infidel notices that it is useless to believe anything, useless to preach anything, since the faith in the divinity and death of Christ is extinguished in human hearts and no salvation survives for humans who can neither be saved by Christ's divinity nor redeemed through his incarnation. (PL 189:489–90)

Peter goes on at some length to show that Jesus did indeed claim to be God, explaining why he usually did so indirectly. He does not lack grist to bring to this mill: he provides abundant scriptural citations to back up his quite standard exegesis. What is interesting in this text for our purposes is that he has clearly defined Islam as a heresy devised by Satan, a heresy centered on the denial of Christ's divinity. Moreover, this heretical "poison" can apparently corrupt the mind of learned Christians and perhaps not only the "brothers" mentioned in Peter of Poitiers's letter. Peter may have in mind philosophically inclined theologians or perhaps translators of Arabic texts into Latin, who would be more directly exposed to this Muslim source of "infection"; indeed, the two groups overlapped. His little tract makes no pretensions of trying to convince Muslims or other unbelievers of the divinity of Christ; he merely hopes to prevent the same error from taking root in the hearts of good Christians.

This fear of contamination of learned Christians imbued a sense of urgency to his translation project; he needed to make Muslim texts available to learned Christians and needed to show them the errors of their "perverse heresy." If the Arabic studies of such scholars were dangerous, the way to combat the danger was through more study. Full knowledge of the "Saracen errors," he thought, would encourage the Christian to remain steadfast in his faith. This sense of purpose pervades not only the two polemical tracts of Peter of Cluny but also the work of the translators of the collection.

The translation of the Qur'ân was the centerpiece of the collection, and Peter is quite aware of its importance. Robert of Ketton produced not a literal rendering of the Muslim sacred text but a Latin adaptation in which difficult and obscure passages are explained; it is generally impossible for the reader to distinguish between the actual text of the Qur'ân and the explicative material inserted by Robert. While scholars have long criticized Robert for this, current scholarship on medieval translation has shown that this was a common practice. Moreover, as Thomas Burman has recently shown, Robert scrupulously studied Muslim Qur'ânic commentaries in order to understand the standard Muslim interpretations of difficult and important passages; indeed, much of his interpolated material is adapted from such Muslim commentaries.[23] Robert has gone to great lengths to provide an accurate and comprehensible Latin version of the Qur'ân.

Yet Peter of Cluny's copy of Robert's translation was heavily annotated, and these annotations certainly guided Peter's reading of the text.[24] Much has been written about these annotations, which seem to date from the twelfth century and to have been made soon after the different works in the codex were bound together. They appear in different parts of the codex, and the reader is at times referred to another work in the collection.[25] It is unclear who wrote these annotations, although nominees include Robert himself, Peter of Toledo, and Peter of Poitiers. The annotations seem in fact to have been the result of at least two people: some of them show a basic ignorance of key Muslim beliefs and practices while others show good knowledge of Islam.[26]

Whoever and however many their authors, the annotations clearly show the polemical intent of the translation. They guide the reader of the "diabolical Qur'ân" (83r) by pointing out (through innumerable "Nota") passages that would seem particularly shocking to the Christian (and especially monastic) reader. The reader is constantly told to note the "insanity," "impiety," "ridiculousness," "stupidity," "superstition," "lying," and "blasphemy" of what he is reading. The very rubrics added at the opening of many Suras make this clear: "A stupid, vain, and impious Sura" (119v); "Sura of stupidity and lies, like the previous ones" (128v); "Vain and impious Sura" (128v); "Diabolical Sura, like the previous ones" (129r); "Repeating the habitual ditties endlessly and ineptly" (72r).

Wherever Qur'ânic stories differ from their biblical counterparts, the annotator brands them as heretical or ridiculous: the Qur'ânic version of the Cain and Abel story is a "stupid fable" (46r); the story of Joseph and Potiphar's wife he calls "insane lies and lying insanity" (69v). When the Qur'ân describes prophets not mentioned in the Bible, the comments of the annotator are no less caustic: "Note the unheard of names of prophets. Who ever heard of such prophets other than this diabolical one [meaning Muhammad]. . . . I think that these were not men but demons: they possessed this Satan, and in this way he concocted his ravings [presumably the Qur'ân]" (67v).

Especially ridiculed is Muslim Christology, dubbed "stupid and heretical sayings about Christ" (32v). The annotations qualify Muslim traditions on Jesus and the Virgin as "monstrous and unheard-of fables" (33v). The origins of this Christology are diabolical: "Note how inconsistent! how changeable! What vain and contradictory things are brought together in this diabolical spirit!" (32v). "Note how he everywhere says that Christ is the son of Mary, but against the Christians and the faith says that the son of Mary is not the son of God—which is the sum of all this diabolical heresy" (35r).

For the annotators, the devil and his follower Muhammad are the authors of this heresy. Numerous annotations accuse Muhammad of being too fond of women and of playing on the Saracens' lust by promising them houris in heaven (33v, 92r, 92v, 110r, 126r, 127v). He threatens his followers with hellfire in order to get them to follow his law and to conquer Christian lands (29v). All of this is in line with earlier heresies: "Note that he everywhere promises such a paradise of carnal delights, as other heresies had done before" (26r).

At several places the annotators reveal a penchant for rationalistic argument against the Qur'ân. One remarks that knowledge of the form of human and animal uteruses may have been given to Muhammad by a physician (112r). Another opposes the Qur'ânic notion of miracle with a twelfth-century Christian definition: if the Qur'ân ascribes to God the "miracle" of holding up the birds that fly in the air and the fish that swim in the sea, the annotator retorts that this is not miraculous, but part of the natural order that God instituted at creation. This misunderstanding of natural phenomena shows "the ignorance of an insane man" (77r). Such attacks on the "irrationality" of the Qur'ân are the stock and trade of Spanish Christian polemics against Islam in the twelfth century, seen, for example, in Petrus Alfonsi's *Dialogi*.

When Peter of Cluny opened the Arsenal manuscript of Robert of Ketton's Qur'ân, he found a text whose rubrics and marginal annotations guided his understanding of what he was reading. He was told where to be shocked and what to find ridiculous, irrational, etc. The annotations initiated him into a Mozarabic polemical view of Islam.

Yet while his reading of *Risâlat al-Kindî,* Petrus Alfonsi, and the annotations will teach him to see Islam through Mozarabic eyes, the polemical strategy that he produces in his two apologetical works is different: it reflects his own peculiar concerns. In his *Summa totius haeresis ac diabolicae sectae Saracenorum siue Hismahelitarum,* Peter will try to explain Islam to the readers of his corpus of translations: to Christian readers who wish to understand the nature of the "heresy of the Saracens." In his *Contra sectam siue haeresim Saracenorum,* on the other hand, he will try to refute Islam on its own terms, creating his own polemical strategy.

The continuity of Peter's approach with that of Mozarabic Christians and the novelty of Peter's approach become apparent when we compare Peter's two polemical works with two works that he used: the Latin translation of the *Risâlat al-Kindî* and Petrus Alfonsi's *Dialogi.* His use of the former has already been noted by Kritzeck, whose detailed analysis of the *Summa* I intend neither to replicate nor to replace.[27] Peter addresses his *Summa totius haeresis ac diabolicae sectae Saracenorum siue Hismahelitarum* to a Christian audience, as a preface to the translations; he probably composed it shortly after his return from Spain. Peter describes the purpose of his brief tract:

> It ought to be told what sort of a bird Muhammad was, and what he taught, so that those who will read that book [the Qur'ân] may better understand what they read and know how detestable were his life and his teachings.[28]

Peter wants to dispel the false opinions that many hold about the Saracens and Muhammad, whom some wrongly identify with the heresiarch

Nicholas, whose followers are condemned in Revelation (2:6 and 15). The only source of information that he explicitly cites on Muhammad's life is Anastasius Bibliothecarius' Latin translation of Theophanes' *Chronographia* (of which Cluny possessed a manuscript in the twelfth century).[29] That he should use Anastasius (and cite him) is natural: none of the texts translated in this collection provides a straightforward biography of Muhammad for the uninitiated reader. Peter will fill in Anastasius' account with information gleaned from *Risâlat al-Kindî* and Petrus Alfonsi's *Dialogi* (it is not always clear which, since Petrus Alfonsi himself relies heavily on the Arabic text of the *Risâlat al-Kindî*). Peter's account of Muhammad's life and teachings is much briefer than those of either of these sources, but he adds a clear sense of where the prophet and his followers fit in the history of error: the devil works behind and through Muhammad, leading a third of the world's population into error. Historically, Peter places Muhammad in the history of heresy, as a particularly loathsome and dangerous heresiarch.

Peter describes Muhammad as a poor, vile, unlettered Arab who achieved wealth and power through bloodshed, thievery, and intrigue. Finally realizing that a feigned religious vocation would serve his ambitions, he claimed that he was a prophet and usurped the authority of king. Then, at the bidding of Satan, a heretical Nestorian monk named Sergius came and joined Muhammad. Together with several Jews, they forged a new heretical doctrine.

> Muhammad, schooled in this way by the finest teachers—Jews and heretics—composed his Qur'ân. He wove together, in his barbarous fashion, nefarious scripture from the fables of the Jews and the ditties of the heretics.

All of this corresponds closely to Petrus Alfonsi's description.[30] Peter goes on to describe what the Qur'ân says about Moses and Jesus, about the torments of hell and the carnal pleasures of paradise. This mixture of truth and error inextricably woven together shows Muhammad to be the consummate heresiarch; here Peter compares Muhammad to earlier heresiarchs (not something done by either of his sources):

> Vomiting forth almost all of the excrement of the old heresies (which he had drunk up as the devil poured it out), he denies the trinity with Sabellius, with his Nestorius he rejects the divinity of Christ, with

> Mani he disavows the death of the Lord, though he does not deny that He returned to heaven. (*Summa*, §9)

Peter holds Muhammad's life—in particular his polygamy—up to opprobrium. Mixing good and evil, sublime and ridiculous, Muhammad created a monstrous cult, similar to the animal described by Horace as having a human head, a horse's neck, and feathers.[31]

The intention of this diabolic heresy, Peter continues, is to present Christ as a holy man, loved by God, a great prophet—but wholly human and in no way son of God.

> Indeed [this heresy], long ago conceived by the plotting of the devil, first spread by Arius, then promoted by this Satan, namely Muhammad, will be completed by Antichrist, in complete accordance with the intentions of the devil. (*Summa*, §13)

Peter sees three great adversaries whom the devil uses to lead Christians astray: Arius, Muhammad, and Antichrist. Each manages to trick his followers into denying Christ's divinity. In order to better elucidate this anti-Christian doctrine, Peter also compares Muhammad to the philosopher Porphyry, who (Peter erroneously claims) was an apostate from Christianity.[32] Having asked the oracles of his gods about Christ, Porphyry was told by the demon Hecate that Jesus had been a virtuous man, but that his followers sinned gravely in attributing divinity to him. Porphyry's views are repudiated, Peter tells us, by Augustine. Indeed, in *De ciuitate Dei* xix.23, Augustine describes an utterance of the oracle Hecate, reported by Porphyry in his εκ λογίων φιλοσοφίας; for Augustine, this shows the clever hostility of the demons, who, wishing to appear objective, praise Jesus at the same time that they condemn the central truth of Christianity. Yet Muhammad is worse than the apostate philosopher, says Peter, for whereas God did not permit Porphyry to seduce Christians with his errors, Muhammad has led countless people into eternal perdition. It is for this reason, Peter tells us, that he composed his *Summa* and that he had the Qur'ân and other texts translated: "I translated from Arabic into Latin the whole of this sect, along with the execrable life of its evil inventor, and exposed it to the scrutiny of our people, so that it be known what a filthy and frivolous heresy it is" (*Summa*, §18).

While Peter uses the works of earlier anti-Islamic polemicists, he clearly felt that they were inadequate. He sets aside much of their material, apparently deeming it useless: for example, the names of Muhammad's associates or the polemical descriptions of ʿAli's teachings and the birth of Shiʿism (Peter did not know enough about Islam to appreciate the importance of the latter). On the other hand, Peter finds that these earlier polemics lack a proper taxonomy of error, a lack of the sense of Islam's place in the divine plan. The devil inspired heresiarchs to lead the faithful into error; only through careful comparison with the teachings of other heresiarchs and the perusal of antiheretical works of the Church fathers could this new and dangerous heresy be combated.[33]

Peter is aware that his *Summa* is merely an introduction to the "Saracen heresy" for the Christian reader, not a refutation of it. The man whom he deemed most appropriate to refute Islam was Bernard of Clairvaux, to whom he sent a letter along with the Latin translation of the *Risâlat al-Kindî* in 1144. He tells Bernard that he is aware that the *Risâla* has not proved useful to the Saracens in their own language and will not become more useful to them by virtue of being translated into Latin. "Yet perhaps it will be useful to some Latins, to whom it will teach things of which they were ignorant and will show what a damnable heresy it is. It will show them that they must defend themselves against it and attack it, should they ever come across it."[34] Indeed, this description of the defensive purpose of the translation of the *Risâlat al-Kindî* could characterize the whole of the translation enterprise, including Peter's own *Summa*. For an offensive tract against Islam, a real rational refutation of the Saracen heresy, the *Risâlat al-Kindî* apparently would not do. Who better to compose such a refutation than Bernard: theologian, fighter of heresies, and preacher of crusade?

Bernard, however, failed to respond to that summons, and Peter himself undertook the task of refuting Islam, probably in 1155–56.[35] The work as it survives is composed of a long prologue and two books; it may be that Peter wrote more that was subsequently lost or that he left it incomplete at his death on Christmas Day in 1156.[36]

Both the structure and the strategy of the *Contra sectam siue haeresim Saracenorum* are quite different from those of the *Summa*. In the *Summa* he lambasted Muhammad from a Christian perspective; in the *Contra sectam* (after a prologue in which he justifies his polemics to Christian readers) he (in book one) enjoins his Muslim readers to listen impartially to his arguments and tries to convince them that according to the Qur'ân they should accept Christian scripture. In book two, he tries to prove that

Muhammad is not a prophet by contrasting his life with those of Old Testament prophets.

In the long prologue to the *Contra sectam,* Peter justifies his enterprise by placing himself in the company of the church fathers who refuted earlier heretical doctrines, following the rule that "every error should be refuted."[37] He lists the names of ancient heresiarchs, "names monstrous to Christians," and then those of the holy men who rebutted their heresies. The need to refute Muhammad's sect is particularly urgent; its acolytes are the "worst adversaries" of the Church (§1), for they dominate Asia and Africa and are present even in Europe (in Spain).

Peter then gives a rhetorical objection to this line of argument: one could say that the Saracens were pagans (*ethnici* or *pagani*) rather than heretics. Didn't John define the "many Antichrists" (which, for Peter, means heresiarchs) as those who "went out from us, but they were not of us" (I John 2:19), in other words, as those who had been part of the Church and had broken away from it? Peter notes that, like heretics, the followers of Muhammad adopt parts of the Christian faith and reject other parts, while they also follow some rites that seem to Peter "pagan." Like certain heretics, Peter says, Muhammad "wrote in his impious Qur'ân" that Christ was born of the Virgin Mary, lived without sin, and performed miracles; like the Manicheans, the Saracens deny His death. Like the pagans, on the other hand, they reject baptism, the mass, and the other sacraments. Heretics or pagans, "choose whichever you like" (*Contra sectam,* §14). He asserts that pagans should also be opposed by written polemic; here, too, he lists the names of illustrious church fathers who attacked paganism in their writings. Peter himself generally prefers to view the "Mahometan error" as a heresy.

Peter addresses one final rhetorical objection to his tract: why compose for Muhammad's followers a treatise in Latin, a language they do not understand? Here Peter has two responses. First of all, he hopes that someone may undertake to translate his tract into Arabic; after all, the fathers frequently translated works useful to the church from Hebrew to Greek, Greek to Latin, Latin to Greek, etc. Second, Peter says that his tract may prove useful to Christian readers, even if it stays untranslated (which it did). If there are any Christians who have the slightest tendency to respect or admire Islam, Peter hopes his work will quickly dissuade them.

> Perhaps this tract will cure the hidden cogitations of some of our people, thoughts by which they could be led into evil if they think that

> there is some piety in those impious people and think that some truth is to be found with the ministers of lies. (*Contra sectam*, §20)

Who are these Latin Christians who in their "hidden cogitations" might think that the Saracens were pious? Peter does not say, but certainly the most likely candidates were the translators and students of Arabic science and philosophy. One such scholar, Adelard of Bath, proclaimed, "I learnt from my masters, the Arabs, to follow the light of reason, while you are led by the bridle of authority; for what other word than *bridle* can I use to describe authority?"[38] Might such preference for "Arabic reason" over "Latin Authority" lead such Christian scholars into doubt, even apostasy? As he had shown in his *Epistola ad Petrum Ioannem* and his *Contra Petrobrusianos*, Peter is concerned about the doubts that the devil might sow in the minds of Christians in order to lead them into heretical error. In this light his polemics look more like a defense of Christianity than an offensive missionary effort.

While the prologue to the *Contra sectam* is a defense of his tract to possible Christian detractors, the text itself is addressed to "the Arabs, sons of Ishmael, who serve the law of him who is called Muhammad" (*Contra sectam*, §23). He tells his readers that it is love that bids him write to them, love that Christian law enjoins on him. "I love you; loving you, I write to you; writing, I invite you to salvation" (*Contra sectam*, §26). Peter realizes, he says, that the first reaction of his Arab readers will be that they would never abandon the law given them by their prophet. He also is aware that the Qur'ân enjoins death on those who dispute the Muslim law.[39] This, he says, astounds him because his Arab readers are "not only rational [*rationales*] by nature, but logical in temperament and training [*ingenio et arte rationabiles*]"; they are, moreover "learned in worldly knowledge [*scientiam secularem*]" (*Contra sectam*, §30). The injunction against debating religion flies in the face of the Arabs' propensity for learning: no rational man should accept something as true without first verifying its truth for himself.

These Arab philosophers use their reason to comprehend nature. Do they not know that this nature, the highest object of the search for truth, the uncreated creator, the ultimate substance or essence, is God?[40] Should they not use their reason to investigate the truth concerning God? The law prohibiting religious dispute is an "infernal counsel," a law fit for irrational sheep, not rational men. Instead of reaching for your swords or stones when a Christian comes to preach the gospel, Peter says, follow rather the example of Christians who dispute with Jews, listening patiently to their arguments and responding wisely. (This hardly characterizes the rancor of Peter's own anti-Jewish tract.) Or follow the example of King Ethelbert of Kent, who received Christian missionaries with honor and heard them out.

Peter has emphasized the rationality and learning of his Muslim audience. This is all the more striking when contrasted with his descriptions of the enemies of his *Aduersus Iudaeorum inveteratam duritiem*, whom he brands as beasts without reason. There he contents himself with lambasting irrational Jewish beliefs for a Christian audience, showing no hope of converting Jews. Here, on the contrary, he pleads with his learned Muslim readers to hear him out, invoking the pagan king Ethelbert. Muslims, it seems, should be predisposed to recognize Christian reason; in order to prevent this, Muhammad had forbidden them under pain of death to debate matters of the faith.

Having crossed this first theoretical hurdle to gain a hearing from his rational, philosophical Muslim readership, his first and fundamental argument in favor of Christianity is not rationalistic or scientific but scriptural. While earlier polemics (including both the *Risâlat al-Kindî* and Petrus Alfonsi's *Dialogi*) often tried to prove the Trinity using various triads of philosophical concepts, Peter makes no such attempt.[41] Such argumentation is foreign to him. Since exegetical argumentation is his forte, his most pressing need is to establish the validity of the Bible to his Muslim audience so he can then comfortably deploy the scriptural weapons he handles so well.

In order to prove the validity of the Jewish and Christian scriptures, Peter starts from the normal Christian viewpoint that Qur'ânic stories of, say, Abraham or Noah are corrupted versions of their biblical counterparts. We have seen that the marginal notations in Robert's translation of the Qur'ân reflected this notion. Peter says that he was amazed to find that Muhammad, in the Qur'ân, had mixed elements from Christian and Jewish scriptures and moreover had praised those scriptures. Assuming, rather than arguing for, the primacy of Judeo-Christian scripture, he argues that if these scriptures are divine, they should be accepted wholly, not in part; if they are not divine, they should be rejected wholly, not in part (*Contra sectam*, §57).

He knows that the Muslim objection to this argument will be the charge that the God-given scriptures of Jews and Christians have been corrupted and that only the Qur'ân represents the uncorrupted word of God. Here he refers to Muslim stories, gleaned from a marginal annotation to the Qur'ân,[4] according to which the Jews lost the Torah on their way back to Israel after the Babylonian captivity. Here Peter is quite capable of ridiculing this story using his scriptural arsenal. In particular, he employs the logical arguments gleaned from the *Risâlat al-Kindî* showing how difficult it would be for Jews and Christians, dispersed over half the world, to connive together to corrupt the Torah.[43] He argues similarly against charges that Christians have corrupted the Gospel. He then concludes book one with the assertion that he has proved that the Bible is divine, that it is superior to the Qur'ân, and that its authority should be accepted by all Muslims (*Contra sectam*, §88).

In book two, Peter attempts to prove that Muhammad is not a prophet, for a prophet by definition foresees the future, whereas Muhammad did not. Here Peter is unaware that the Muslim concept of *rasul* is quite different from the Christian notion of *propheta*. In showing that Muhammad does not correspond to Peter's notion of prophethood, he is scoring a point that would carry little weight with a Muslim audience.[44] Peter uses material from the *Risâlat al-Kindî*, reshaping it to fit into his more coherent, theologically based structure. Peter narrates only the details of Muhammad's life that are necessary to show that he is not a prophet, especially his inability to foresee his military defeats and his failure to produce miracles.[45]

Peter asserts that the last of the prophets was John the Baptist. Yet Paul foretold of the errors of false prophets: "For the time will come when they will not endure sound doctrine . . . and they shall turn away their ears from the truth, and shall be turned unto fables."[46] Just so, says Peter, were the Saracens converted to the fables of Muhammad and Jews to the fables of the Talmud. He describes the prophecies and virtuous lives of various Hebrew prophets and challenges his readers to produce anything analogous in order to prove that Muhammad is a prophet. This brings him back to his initial argument on the Qur'ân: the Saracens should accept Christian scripture, reject Muhammad, and convert to Christianity (*Contra sectam*, §147–54).

Whether Peter considered his polemical work complete or whether he intended to write further, his polemical strategy, while indebted to that of his Arab and Spanish predecessors, is clearly distinct from it. While effusively expressing his admiration and respect for philosophy and *ratio*, Peter is clearly not adept in the scientific-rational forms of argumentation common in the *Risâlat al-Kindî*, Petrus Alfonsi's *Dialogi*, and other such works. He is much more at home when he can marshal his formidable knowledge of scripture to refute Saracen errors.

This difference is clearly seen in the organization of the *Contra sectam*. The *Risâlat al-Kindî* opens with a defense of the Trinity based on a triad of divine attributes, an argument which apparently failed to impress Peter, since he does not reproduce it. Petrus Alfonsi opens his attack on Islam by attacking Muhammad. Because his anti-Islamic chapter is part of a debate between a Christian and a Jew, this is an understandable ploy to discredit Islam in the eyes of his Jewish interlocutor (indeed, this is the same strategy that Peter adapts in his *Summa*). Peter realized that to open the *Contra sectam* by directly attacking Muhammad would only provoke the hostility of his Muslim audience. Instead, Peter uses a few well chosen Qur'ânic citations to try to prove that Muslims should accept Christian scriptures. Once he has done that, he can return to the exegetically based polemical method that he had employed in the *Contra Petrobrusianos* and the *Aduersus Iudaeorum inveteratam duritiem*.

In this enterprise, as we have seen, Peter saw himself as continuing the tradition of the Church fathers, of scripturally based explication and refutation of heresy, just as he saw his *De miraculis* as a continuation of the traditions embodied in the writings of Gregory the Great.[47] His dissatisfaction with the earlier works of polemic that he used seems to stem from the fact that they do not resemble the works of the fathers with which Peter was so familiar. This, perhaps, explained why these had failed to convert the Muslims: they were not proper theological tracts.

If Peter thought that his polemics would be more likely to convert Muslims, he was badly mistaken. Peter had only a superficial bookish knowledge of Islam, nothing to compare with the more direct knowledge of Petrus Alfonsi or (especially) of the author of the *Risâlat al-Kindî.* We might offer Peter's anti-Muslim polemics the same reproach that Châtillon leveled against his *Contra Petrobrusianos:* Peter's elaborate, scripturally based arguments seem ill-equipped to convert his readers.

Yet in both works, Peter attempted to offer a defensive campaign against diabolical error: such polemics could quash the doubts of catholic readers. Torrell and Bouthillier have shown how, for Peter, Cluny was God's citadel constantly besieged by demons.[48] As Cluny's spiritual head, Peter was particularly well placed to repulse demonic incursions through pastoral care of his monks, through doctrinal works such as his *De miraculis,* and through his trilogy of theological polemics against Jews, Petrobrusians, and Saracens. If Muslims, Jews, and heretics could not be brought into the fold, at least their satanically inspired errors could be dispelled from the minds of Christians.[49]

The baptism of Corbaran from the *Chrétienté Corbaran* (Paris, Bibliothèque de l'Arsenal, MS 3139, f 235r). Reproduced with permission of the Bibliothèque Nationale de France.

~: 5 :~

The Dream of Conversion

Baptizing Pagan Kings in the Crusade Epics

In a manuscript of the *Chrétienté Corbaran*, a thirteenth-century epic, is an illumination of the baptism of the pagan king Corbaran. On the left Godfrey, king of Jerusalem, and a bishop raise Corbaran from the baptismal font; they are surrounded by clerics and knights. On the right, the newly Christian king rides off with his men, ready to fight against the pagans. In the *Chrétienté Corbaran* ("Baptism of Corbaran"), Corbaran, king of Oliferne, who had been the crusaders' principal enemy, decides to convert to Christianity. He arrives in Jerusalem, commends himself to King Godfrey, and accepts baptism. Upon his return to Oliferne, he gives his subjects the choice between conversion and death and orders the destruction of the idols he once worshiped. The poem then narrates a series of battles between the Christian armies and those of the Persian sultan and the "caliph of Paganism."

Although some of the characters in the *Chrétienté Corbaran* are connected with historical participants in the First Crusade, this is a fictive conversion. Corbaran's imaginary life is recounted in three branches of what specialists have dubbed "the first epic cycle of the Crusades," a series of poems composed by several authors over the course of the twelfth and thirteenth centuries. Corbaran, sworn enemy of the Christians, qualified as a "felon" in the *Chanson d'Antioche*, became a protagonist of *Les Chétifs*, and finally converted to Christianity in the *Chrétienté Corbaran*.[1]

In the third quarter of the thirteenth century, as each crusade ended in failure, epic poets dreamed of the conversion of a powerful enemy who would become the ally of the Christians. Yet this "Saracen" king is anything but Muslim: before his conversion, Corbaran worshiped idols of Mahomet and Tervagant. If this fictive conversion of a stereotypical pagan enemy teaches us nothing about Islam, it speaks eloquently of how medieval Christian Europeans imagined their "Saracen" adversaries and of the hopes they placed in their conversions, which would replay those of previous "pagan" rulers.

Many Christian authors, from the eighth century to the sixteenth, depicted the Saracens as idolatrous pagans. This image, familiar to us through the *Chanson de Roland* and other chansons de geste, is, according to some critics (in particular Norman Daniel), a mere literary convention, born of ignorance, which does not reflect the way that educated Europeans viewed Muslims and Islam.[2] Yet recent studies have shown to what extent this portrait of the Saracen Other could be used to justify and glorify the violence of the warrior class; the Saracen Other reinforces the ideology of Christian knighthood.[3] The story of Corbaran's conversion celebrates the crusaders' exploits and anchors them in Christian history and eschatology. They become events in the perennial struggle between Christians and pagans, a struggle that is destined to end in Christian victory.

This image of Saracen idolatry is not simply a convention of the chansons de geste. In many of the Latin chronicles of the First Crusade, the supposed paganism of the Saracen enemies justifies the holy war against them. For chroniclers Petrus Tudebodus and Raymond of Aguilers, the crusade plays an important role in the fight against paganism. The "pilgrims," new apostles and martyrs, beat back paganism and move toward the glory of the final days. Since these chroniclers present the crusaders as the reincarnation of figures well established and familiar to medieval readers (the army of the God of Israel, the apostles, the martyrs), they need to portray the crusaders' enemies in the garb of the traditional enemies of these figures: pagans, odious in the eyes of God, persecutors of the True Church.[4]

It is in this same ideological context that we can understand the baptism of the pagan king in the *Chrétienté Corbaran*. While this epic bears little relation to the historical events of the Crusades, it exposes an important and familiar medieval topos: the conversion of a pagan king, of which the best-known examples are Constantine and Clovis. The pagan king, enemy and persecutor of Christians, through conversion becomes their defender. He attacks and defeats the pagan armies and destroys the idols he once worshiped. The illumination of Corbaran's baptism is iconographically similar to representations of the baptism of other pagan kings. The archetype for such conversion is of course Constantine.

It is in the thirteenth century that European artists elaborate the iconography of Constantine's conversion. In the wake of the investiture controversy, Constantine's baptism was extremely useful for the popes and their apologists. The emperor is shown humbly receiving baptism from the hands of Pope Sylvester. In the frescoes of the Basilica dei Quattro Coronati (c. 1250), for example, the position and the size of the two protagonists indicate the superiority of the pope over the baptized emperor.[5] The emperor, enemy and persecutor of Christians, becomes a humble catechumen under the pope's watchful eye before becoming a powerful ally and protector of the Church.

This image of Constantine, which corresponds so well to the polemical needs of thirteenth-century popes and their apologists, is found in earlier texts. Gregory of Tours alludes to it when he describes the baptism of Clovis:

> Like some new Constantine he stepped forward to the baptismal pool, ready to wash away the sores of his old leprosy and to be cleansed in the flowing water from the sordid stains which he had borne so long. As he advanced for his baptism, the holy man of God [Remigius, bishop of Reims] addressed him in these pregnant words: "Put away your necklaces, Sicamber. Worship what you have burnt, burn what you have been wont to worship."[6]

This image of Clovis, pagan king and persecutor of the Church transformed into a meek Christian humbly accepting his bishop's reprimands, does not correspond to the historical Clovis.[7] No matter: Gregory wished to make Clovis into the Constantine of the Franks by dramatizing this transformation of a ravenous wolf into a meek lamb. Gregory may have found this comparison in the work of an earlier author, perhaps Bishop Remigius himself. For Gregory, as for other early medieval authors (such as Jerome or Isidore), Constantine is an ambivalent figure: the first Christian emperor, yet one who received baptism at the hands of Arian heretics.[8] The iconography of Clovis's baptism, like that of other Germanic kings supposedly converted from paganism, also corresponds to the Constantinian model: the bishop is invariably in a position of superiority vis-à-vis the baptized monarch.[9]

For some medieval authors, the paradigm of the converted pagan king should inspire new missions to the infidels. Peter of Cluny, in his *Liber con-*

tra sectam siue haeresim Sarracenorum, invokes the example of Ethelred, English pagan king converted by the missionaries sent by Pope Gregory the Great.[10] One of the *Cantigas de Santa María* of King Alfonso X of Castile and León describes the miraculous conversion of a "Moorish" sultan who was besieging Constantinople at the head of a "pagan" army.[11] The illumination shows the king, naked, in the baptismal fonts of the Church of San German. European Christians recalled the conversions of pagan kings of old and imagined that their new Saracen enemies could also be transformed into allies through a few dramatic and exemplary conversions.

While monastic authors often evoked the stories of illustrious converts (Paul, Augustine, Benedict) in order to glorify clerical or monastic life, the epic poets of the thirteenth and fourteenth centuries use the archetype of the converted pagan king to extol the deeds of the soldiers of Christ, the crusaders. Spreading the Word with the sword, eschewing theological disputation by decapitating those who refused baptism, these stalwart Christian soldiers sought by the force of their arms to convince their adversaries of the superiority of Christianity.

Constantine's name does not appear in the *Chrétienté Corbaran*, but the paradigm of the converted pagan king is central. The poet offers the hope that the problem posed by the Saracens, the new "pagan" enemies, can find a quick and dramatic solution. The transformation of a historical Muslim emir into a stereotypical converted king provides an interesting example of the sort of cultural filter that European writers used to understand and explain the events of the Crusades.

Corbaran corresponds to a historical person, Kurbuqa or Kerbôgha, emir and atabeg of Mosul, whom the crusaders defeated at Antioch—and who never converted to Christianity. It is the author of the *Chrétienté Corbaran* who first imagines, in the second half of the thirteenth century, that Corbaran converted, yet earlier poets had already made Kurbuqa into an epic hero.

Yaghi-Siyân, emir of Antioch, besieged by the crusaders, called upon Kurbuqa, who arrived at the head of a large army on June 6, 1098. But the crusaders had already captured the city three days earlier. Now Kurbuqa besieged the crusaders. Rivalries split the Muslim camp: Duqâq, emir of Damascus, fearing lest Kurbuqa attack Damascus after a victory over the crusaders at Antioch, decided that the real enemy was the atabeg of Mosul and not the Franks; he rallied other emirs to his opinion. When the crusaders issued forth from the besieged city to wage battle against Kurbuqa's far superior forces, Duqâq and his allies fled the battlefield. The crusaders swooped down on the remainder of the Muslim army, and Kurbuqa was obliged to flee in the midst of the ensuing debacle.

For the crusaders, this victory against a powerful ally was a miracle. Some of the Latin chroniclers attributed it to the discovery of the Holy Lance, in Antioch, a few days before the battle—the lance with which the Roman soldier Longinus had pierced Jesus' side after he died on the cross. The chroniclers speak of a celestial army that intervened in the battle, led by Saint George, in which (according to Petrus Tudebodus) the "pilgrims" who had already suffered martyrdom returned to wreak vengeance on the "pagans."[12]

Since the chroniclers know next to nothing about Kurbuqa, they make him into a stereotypical adversary, a pagan king, powerful and arrogant, like those that one finds in the chansons de geste. In three Latin chronicles and in the *Chanson d'Antioche*, there is a dialogue between Corbaran and his mother, who tries to prevent her son from fighting against the Christians. The relations between these texts are complex and have provoked disagreements among their modern editors.[13] Here I wish simply to present the portrayal of Corbaran in the *Chanson d'Antioche*, since this is the version of the story that the *Chrétienté Corbaran* will continue.

The *Chanson d'Antioche* presents itself as the work of a crusader, Richard le Pèlerin, who according to Suzanne Duparc-Quioc, composed it around 1100. While the Latin chroniclers (such as the anonymous author of the *Gesta Francorum,* Raymond of Aguilers, or Raoul de Caen) sought to glorify the exploits of one or another of the principal barons (Bohemond of Antioch, Raymond of St. Gilles, and Tancred, respectively), Richard seems to favor the crusaders from Lorraine and Flanders.[14] This primitive version was then reworked between 1180 and 1190 by Graindor de Douai, who put it together with his versions of two other epics, *Les Chétifs* and *La Conquête de Jérusalem.* But the oldest manuscripts, dating from the middle of the thirteenth century, contain other adventures of the fictive ancestors of Godfrey of Bouillon; it seems that this cycle was composed in order to lionize certain noble families associated with the Crusades, particularly those of the kings of Jerusalem.[15] To this collection of heterogeneous (though thematically coherent) texts is added (in the Arsenal manuscript and in two other manuscripts) the *Chrétienté Corbaran.*[16]

In the *Chanson d'Antioche*, the crusaders confront not divided Muslim armies but the forces of a powerful pagan empire. Corbaran, king of

Oliferne, is a vassal of the sultan of Persia. He participates in battles in which the historical Kurbuqa did not fight, for example at Civetot, on the shores of the Marmora, where Christian troops are martyred and perform miracles.[17] Corbaran and his men worship idols, in particular those of their principal god, Mahomet. The spiritual center of this pagan world is Mieque (Mecca), where devotees chant hymns in honor of "Mahon," a golden idol inhabited by a demon, "Sathanas." The spiritual leader of Mieque, the "Calife de Baudas" (caliph of Baghdad), promises indulgences to those who will fight the holy war against the Christians. In this way, the anonymous poet amplifies the importance of the battle for Antioch: it is part of the war to end all wars, the struggle to the end between Christ's army and the devotees of Mahon-Sathanas. One of the pagans, Sansadoines, predicts defeat: the Christians, he says, will come to Mieque to destroy the idol and eliminate paganism.[18] Later in the *Chanson d'Antioche* (and also in the *Chanson de Jérusalem*), Godfrey of Bouillon promises to destroy Mieque.[19]

"Li fel Corbarans" [Corbaran the felon] (v. 7879), "l'orgellous et le fier" [proud and haughty] (v. 6997), leads an army of hundreds of thousands of pagans, including "xxx. mile Turs del linage Judas" [thirty thousand Turks of the lineage of Judas] (v. 8803). Sure of his might, he does not take seriously Sansadoines' prophecies of defeat and dreams of ill portent.[20] Before the battle, the *Chanson d'Antioche* introduces Corbaran's mother, Calabre, an astrologer and magician who is over 140 years old.[21] She tries to stop her son from waging war. It is madness, she says, to fight against the God of the French; did He not shame the Pharaoh when He delivered the people of Israel? Moreover, ancient pagan prophecy and the stars themselves indicated that the French would win and that Corbaran, if he fought them, would die before a year was over. Haughty and disdainful, Corbaran does not heed his mother's warning; he prepares for battle.[22] When the Christian emissaries come to ask him to surrender Antioch, he offers them riches and lands if they will agree to "guerpir lor loi haïe" [betray their hated law] (v. 7375). The Christians refuse.

The poet describes the battle in detail, in the epic tradition, as a series of exploits and single combats among the chief knights. Corbaran and the other pagans constantly invoke the aid of their gods Mahomet and Tervagant, in vain. The enemies hurl insults at each other in the heat of battle, but they do not invite each other to convert, as they do in other chansons de geste.[23] Robert, count of Normandy, unhorses and injures Corbaran (8749–67), but the turning point is only reached with the arrival of the celestial troops led by St. George (9058–9106). In the debacle, Corbaran invokes Mahomet one last time, now to curse him:

Ohi! Mahomet sire! com vos soloie amer
Et de tot mon pooir servir et honorer!
Se jamais en ma terre puis un jor sejorner,
Jo vos ferai ardoir et en porre venter
U jo vos ferai tot a cevals defouler.

Oh! Lord Mahomet! How I once loved you
And with all my might served you and honored you!
If ever I shall abide one day in my land,
I will have you burned and your ashes scattered in the wind,
Or I will have you trampled by horses. (vv. 9112–16)

In accordance with the epic topos, the pagan king acknowledges the powerlessness of his idols and destroys them. Here the destruction is merely threatened, while in the *Chanson de Roland* (vv. 2580–91) the defeated Saracens attack their own idols, and in the *Conquête de Jérusalem,* the caliph himself decapitates the statue of Mahon.[24] While Corbaran, in the *Chanson d'Antioche*, curses Mahomet, he does not convert to Christianity. Death awaits this humiliated enemy, leaving the field clear for the victorious Christians.

Corbaran here incarnates the decadence of paganism: pagans and Christians are implacable enemies, but the final victory of Christianity is near. This reflects the optimism with which Christian Europeans received the news of the victories of the First Crusade, an optimism that was still alive when Graindor de Douai reworked the epic cycle around 1180. Victory, not conversion, is the subject of the *Chanson d'Antioche;* even if certain pagans (Sansadoines or Calabre) predict their inevitable defeat, they do not convert to Christianity. Reconquest and vengeance are the order of the day for the Christian knights of the *Chanson d'Antioche*. At the outset of the poem, Graindor depicts the Crucifixion: Christ, on the cross, promises the good thief that in a thousand years a valorous race, the Franks, will arise in the West in order to avenge the death of "their father" and reconquer "his land."[25]

There are few conversions in the *Chanson d'Antioche,* and none correspond to the Constantinian model. The only one described in detail is that of Datien, who delivers the city of Antioch to the crusaders after Christ himself orders him, in a series of dreams, to do so. Here we have a historical person, but he was not one of the enemy leaders. At the end of the *Chanson d'Antioche*, after Corbaran's defeat, the guards of the fortress surrender and are given the choice: to leave unharmed or, if they wish to stay in Antioch, to accept baptism; a number of them choose to convert. These conversions also are confirmed by other chroniclers; we are far from the traditional chansons de geste, where the choice would be between conversion and death. The admiral of the fortress then tells them what convinced him to convert: he describes the celestial army that he saw descend from heaven to massacre Corbaran's army.[26]

This admiral's testimony, like the predictions of Sansadoines and Calabre, confirms that God is on the side of the "pilgrims." The admiral, contrary to the Constantinian model, converts after a military defeat. If one hopes to convert the infidel, it is only after crushing him militarily. As in the *Chanson de Roland,* Christianization is imposed by armed force. Even though Charlemagne and his warriors invited their enemies to embrace Christianity, they did not convert, even when (as in the case of Marsile) they had promised to do so. Benjamin Kedar has shown that no contemporary text attributes to the First Crusade the role of converting the Muslims.[27] The goal is neither alliance nor rapprochement with the enemy; it is total and final victory. When divine grace causes the conversion of the infidel, it does so at the point of a Christian lance. The reader does not expect or hope for the spontaneous conversion of a powerful pagan king, particularly not the "felon Corbaran."

Corbaran's image is softened in *Les Chétifs;* here he becomes the friend and admirer of his Christian prisoners. Graindor includes this epic in his "primitive cycle," between his versions of *Antioche* and *Jérusalem.*[28] *Les Chétifs* continues the adventures of Corbaran and serves as a sort of sequel to the *Chanson d'Antioche,* but it is very different in tone and character: we are far from the apocalyptic triumphalism of *Antioche,* closer to the fabulous exploits of knightly romance.

At the outset of *Les Chétifs,* Corbaran, fleeing after his defeat at Antioch, arrives in the court of the sultan of Persia, who asks him if he has captured the Christian leaders, as he had sworn he would. Corbaran tells him of the rout at Antioch and of the death in battle of the sultan's son. The sultan threatens to have Corbaran burned alive, but the king of Nubia says in his defense that the Franks are so valorous that one of them could vanquish thirty Turks. In *Les Chétifs,* we are far from the aura of the miraculous that surrounded God's army in the *Chanson d'Antioche*. The king of Nubia makes no allusion to the intervention of St. George and his celestial knights (which is the turning point of the battle, according to the *Chanson d'Antioche*), speaking only of the military prowess of the Franks.

In order to convince the sultan, Corbaran proposes a judicial duel between a Frankish knight and two Turks. He returns to Oliferne, where he has two Frankish prisoners, taken in the battle of Civetot. One of them, Richard de Caumont, offers to fight if Corbaran will free him and his fellow prisoners. The pagans of Oliferne shower presents on the freed captives. Among other treasures, Corbaran's mother, Calabre, gives Richard the sword with which Herod had massacred the Innocents (vv. 651–54). This sword shows us the fictive continuity of the "pagan" world; Calabre and Corbaran are the heirs of the persecutors of antiquity. The sword (like the Holy Lance of Longinus in the *Chanson d'Antioche*) is both a relic and a weapon. This reintroduces us into the world of the *chanson de geste,* in which swords contain relics and each has a name (Durendal, Joyeuse) and a history.

The abbot of Fécamp, as he celebrates a mass to bless Richard's arms, narrates the miraculous conversion of Longinus, the blind Roman soldier who pierced Christ's side with his lance, whose eyes, splashed with the divine blood, could see anew. Next the poet recounts the fight: Richard, strengthened by the Holy Spirit, kills the two Turks. The second enemy, in his death throes, acknowledges that his God, Mahomet, "is nothing but a rotten Dog" and that Richard's God beat him. He asked to be baptized, invoking Longinus once again. Richard himself fills the Saracen's helmet with water and empties it on his head to baptize him; he then gives him three blades of grass as communion. Once again, God's will is done through the arms of a valorous Christian knight. A blade of steel provides the definitive "argument" that leads to the infidel's conversion. No need, apparently, for priests: the knight himself baptizes his enemy in a strange rite.

This conversion seems in some ways a precursor of that of Corbaran himself in the *Chrétienté Corbaran*, yet the poet of *Les Chétifs* seems in no hurry to get there. He subsequently recounts the fabulous adventures of the liberated captives: they wage battle against Sathanas (a dragon possessed by a demon), against lions, wolves, strange monkeys, and bandits. We seem to have left behind the miracles of epic for the *merveilleux* of romance. When the occasional saint intervenes, it is for rather banal miracles: St. Jerome chases off some lions, and three saints in the guise of white stags help Corbaran find the knight Harpin, besieged by bandits.

As for Corbaran, he has become a supporting player. He indeed tags along on several adventures, but his role is chiefly to witness and admire the captives' exploits—and then to richly reward them. The sultan plays roughly the same role. With the exception of the defeat and conversion of the Turkish combatant, there is no sign here of the religious hostility found in the *Chanson d'Antioche* or more generally in the chansons de geste. Corbaran had sworn in the *Chanson d'Antioche* that he would destroy the idol of Mahomet; here he shows no intention of doing so.

The mood changes again in the *Chrétienté Corbaran*, which follows the *Conquête de Jérusalem* in three manuscripts of the cycle. At the beginning of the *Chrétienté Corbaran*, an envoy arrives in Oliferne to announce the sultan's defeat at the battle of Rames (narrated at the end of the *Conquête de Jérusalem*). This defeat convinces Corbaran of the superiority of Christianity: "Vous veez," he says to his mother, "de Mahom qu'il ne vant pas .i. gant . . . Li diex as crestïens est assés plus poissant." [You see that Mahom is not worth one glove; the God of the Christians is much more powerful] (vv. 80–82). He proposes to go to Jerusalem to be baptized and to become the vassal of King Godfrey. Calabre refuses to convert (here, contrary to the *Chanson d'Antioche*, it is Corbaran, not his mother, who sees the futility of the fight against Christianity). Corbaran has her locked up in a tower, from which she escapes. Accompanied by four kings, Corbaran goes to Jerusalem, where he is greeted with joy and pomp. Two bishops, along with the abbot of Fécamp, baptize him. King Godfrey and Raymond of St. Gilles raise him out of the baptismal fonts.[29]

Conversion and baptism create feudal ties. Now vassal of King Godfrey, Corbaran will take with him the two bishops who baptized him; he later names them bishops of Tyre and Oliferne. Compared with the *Chanson d'Antioche*, we are here much more in the traditional world of the chansons de geste: a clear hierarchy with the king on top, his loyal and valiant vassals around him, and the obedient clergy under him.[30] In contrast with the church-centered representations of the baptism of Constantine and Clovis, here it is not a holy bishop who raises the new Christian from the font, but his suzerain king and a principal vassal. The bishops, instead of thundering, "Put away your necklaces, Sicamber," are happy to accept ecclesiastical benefices from the new Christian king. The illumination of the Arsenal manuscript seems to reestablish some sort of balance: King Godfrey and a bishop raise Corbaran from the baptismal font. This is no surprise, coming from an artist of one of the principal workshops of liturgical manuscripts.[31]

Corbaran's conversion is related briefly at the outset of the *Chrétienté Corbaran* in order to leave space for what really interested the epic poet: the description of bloody battles. The sultan of Persia here—like Corbaran in the *Chanson d'Antioche*—plays the role of the humiliated pagan king. Before the battle, he exhorts Corbaran to worship the idols of Mahomet and Tervagant; Corbaran retorts by asking the sultan to accept baptism. In the following battle (described in great detail, once again), Corbaran and his allies crush the enemy forces, but the sultan escapes and vows revenge, as the epic then closes with a description of the victory celebrations in Oliferne. Corbaran's sister is baptized and marries King Godfrey; Calabre, who had encouraged the sultan to fight her son, is brought to Acre; a herald announces that she will be baptized and will become a nun, thanks to the victory of the Christians.[32]

The *Chrétienté Corbaran* embodies the spirit of the traditional chansons de geste; in this way it is very different from the *Chanson d'Antioche*. Perhaps this retreat into the fictive and idealized world of epic is a response to the troubling situation of the crusader realms in the thirteenth century. The optimistic triumphalism of the *Chanson d'Antioche* is now impossible: there are no prophecies of the imminent and final Christian victory. Corbaran converts and beats the sultan, but the sultan is still a powerful enemy, licking his wounds and plotting his revenge. Thus we find both pessimism and a vague hope that a few Saracen kings could convert to Christianity and come to the aid of the crusaders. The same hope is seen in the fictive conversions of other Saracens in contemporary chansons de geste.[33]

The scribe of the Arsenal manuscript brings the epic to a close with these conversions. However, in the two other manuscripts that contain the *Chrétienté Corbaran*, the second branch of the Continuations goes on, describing events in the Kingdom of Jerusalem in what Karl-Heinz Bender calls a "return to history" and which is perhaps better described as a return to the celebration of the half-legendary, half-historical exploits of the kings of Jerusalem. These episodes evoke the conflicts among Christian barons, presaging disaster, although they also present pagan kings who follow Corbaran's example and accept baptism.[34] While the poet predicts, in an echo of the *Chanson d'Antioche* and the *Conquête de Jérusalem*, that King Godfrey will capture Mecca,[35] the good king is prevented from doing so by the patriarch Eracle, who poisons him. King follows king amid succession disputes, and the poet notes the prowess of a young Turk named Saladin.

Saladin embodies, once again, the valiant pagan king who could have converted to Christianity—but does not. Before his first battle against the Christians, Saladin swears, in the typical manner of a pagan tyrant, "ferai crestïens ocire et lapider, s'il ne croient Mahom ou fuient outremer" [I will have the Christians killed and stoned, if they do not believe in Mahom or flee across the sea] (vv. 6212–13). But after two defeats at the hands of the Christians, he asks them for a truce. He is invited to the crowning of the heir Baudouin (who corresponds probably to the historical king Baldwin IV). Impressed by the king and his barons, and by their riches, Saladin proclaims, "Hounerablement est li diex des Frans servis" [Honorably is the God of the Franks served] (v. 6315). Saladin acts here like Corbaran in *Les Chétifs* (or like Balan in the *Chanson d'Aspremont*). The next step, logically, would be his conversion, a step never taken, because "li princes du Crac qui tant a felounie" [the prince of Kerak who is so felonious] (v. 6379), Reynald of Châtillon, attacks a Muslim caravan, breaking the truce. In the battle that follows, Baudouin enjoins Saladin to "relenquir Mahoumet Goumelis / Et servir Jesu Cris qui pardon fist Longis" [abandon Mahoumet Goumelis / and serve Jesus Christ who pardoned Longinus] (vv. 6477–78). The rift between the Christian king and the pagan Other has reopened; once again, the poet calls the enemy "roi Salehadin qui onques Diu n'ama" [king Saladin who never loved God] (v. 6694). After a bloody battle, Baudouin and Saladin decide to proclaim a new truce. Saladin promises not to attack the Christians as long as Baudouin lives. Four years later, Baudouin dies, and his subjects declare that there has not been since Alexander a king so good, so just, so valorous. The cycle ends here: each of the barons goes home to mend his fortifications and wait for Saladin's imminent invasion. The poet does not narrate the crushing defeat at Hattin or the loss of Jerusalem. This epic cycle, which lionized the lineage of Boulogne/Bouillon, closes with the death of Baldwin IV and makes no allusion to the following king, Guy, first of the Lusignan kings.[36] The loss of Jerusalem, suggests the poet, could have been avoided, if we had only had a king as valorous as Baldwin, and if the barons of Jerusalem had been united. The poet seems briefly to dream of another facile conversion of an enemy prince, a dream which the events—in particular, the treason of the "prince of Kerak"—finally dissipated.

The failed conversion of Saladin fascinates other thirteenth-century authors. Gilles de Corbeil, in his Latin poem *Ierapigra ad purgandos prelatos*, tells how Saladin listened eagerly to the doctrines of Christianity and wanted to convert, but he wished first to see what life the Christians led. He found them wallowing in lust, filth, fraud, jealousy, and hatred, so he abandoned the idea of converting. Gilles berates his Christian readers: on account of our sins, we have lost a valorous prince—and his extensive kingdom.[37]

Another thirteenth-century author has him convert. The *Récits d'un ménestrel de Reims* are an anthology of *exempla* for princes, recounting the adventures and the virtues of valorous kings and knights, particularly King Philip II Augustus of France, Emperor Frederick Barbarossa, and Saladin. In one of these stories, Saladin's uncle enumerates, to King John of Acre, the qualities of his nephew, presenting Saladin as a model of generosity, justice, and wisdom. Saladin did only one thing that displeased his uncle. On his death bed, he asked that a bowl of water be brought—and he baptized himself with it.[38] Here is an unusual baptism, without baptismal fonts, without priests. We have gone from the baptism of Constantine or Clovis, in which the king humbly accepted the sacrament (and the verbal reprimands) of the bishop, to the baptism of Corbaran, where the important relations were those uniting lord and vassal while the clerics were subservient (as they exercised their specific ecclesiastical functions), and finally to Saladin's baptism, where the priest has become superfluous.

At the end of the thirteenth century, despite the repeated failures of the crusade, some writers still dreamed of the conversion of powerful "pagan" enemies. History repeats itself; hence the need to present these formidable enemies not as Muslim monotheists but as pagans who are apt to convert and—like so many new Constantines—to fly to the aid of Christendom.[39]

⁖ 6 ⁖

Mirror of Chivalry

Saladin in the Medieval European Imagination

Saladin, according to Voltaire, "never persecuted anyone for his religion: he was at the same time conqueror, humane, and a philosopher."[1] Treating captives mercifully, distributing alms to the poor (be they Christian, Jewish, or Muslim), allowing all to worship in their holy places, signing and faithfully keeping peace treaties that his Christian adversaries were to break, he is, for Voltaire, a model of an enlightened monarch. "Few of our princes," he says, "displayed such magnificence, and few of the chroniclers with which Europe is overloaded knew how to do him justice."[2]

Yet in fact many medieval writers painted a similar picture of the sultan Salâh al-Dîn, or "Saladin," as they more frequently called him.[3] While we might expect the victor of Hattin and captor of Jerusalem to be demonized by Latin Christian writers, he is more frequently lionized: Salâh al-Dîn, sultan of Egypt and Syria, becomes, in the medieval European imagination, Saladin, epitome of chivalry, generosity, and tolerance. Little better symbolizes his special place in the medieval European imagination than his position in Dante's "City of Light."

In the first circle of Dante's hell is a "noble castle," emanating the light of human reason. In it, Dante places the great poets, philosophers, and heroes of antiquity. Far from the torments of hell's other inhabitants, these virtuous non-Christians repose in verdant prairies, amicably discussing the nature of the Good and the True. Prevented by Christian dogma from admitting these non-Christians into heaven, Dante has fixed up a pleasant corner of hell for his beloved Virgil, for other Latin and Greek poets, and for philosophers from Socrates to Ibn Rûshd (Averroes). An avid reader of history, Dante has also made room here for the great heroes of Troy and Rome, among whom he sees "by himself, apart, Saladin."[4] Indeed, Saladin stands alone in many respects. He is one of three Muslims (along with Ibn Sîna [Avicenna] and Ibn Rûshd) admitted into this most exclusive corner of hell, reserved in general for "virtuous pagans." He, crusher of crusader armies, is the only Muslim to figure among the castle's great heroes and statesmen: towering over his contemporaries, Richard the Lionheart of England and Philip II Augustus of France (who receive not so much as a mention in the *Commedia)* and even over Alexander the Great, with whom many medieval authors compare him, but whom Dante relegates to the tyrants in the Phlegethon, a river of boiling blood.[5]

If Dante, characteristically, evokes Saladin's special place in one brief line of his *Commedia,* dozens of medieval authors developed the story of his life and adventures in lavish (and mostly imaginary) detail.[6] While these stories vary widely, the picture of Saladin for the most part remains the same: bold and brave warrior, humane and gentle captor, generous bestower of lavish gifts, pious and tolerant in religious matters—in short, a model of chivalry.

Yet "chivalry," for these writers, was a Christian ideal: an elaborate code of behavior, with its rituals (dubbing, blessing of weapons by priests, jousting, etc.), ideals, and history. Could a non-Christian be a model of chivalry? Could this knightly code of honor exist outside of the Church? This question fascinated those who wrote about Saladin. For some of them, chivalry was a universal moral code that needed no ecclesiastical props: Saladin (along with the heroes of pagan antiquity) offered proof of this. Other authors tried to annex him into the Christian (and French) model of chivalry: in the later Middle Ages, authors would claim that Saladin was the descendant of a French noblewoman, that he had one of his Christian captives dub him, that he traveled to Europe incognito and jousted, that he was secretly attracted to Christianity—even that he converted!

If these legends take us further and further from the historical Salâh al-Dîn, their roots are in the writings of those who saw and knew the sultan. Often, of course, it is impossible to draw a clear line between the "real," historical Salâh al-Dîn and the Saladin of legend. A clear and intriguing example is furnished by the Saladins of Anglure. The story tells that a knight from Anglure, in Champagne, goes off to fight in the Third Crusade and is taken captive by Salâh al-Dîn. He asks his captor to let him go home and raise his own ransom money, and the sultan asks him what he will leave as a guarantee. "Something more precious than gold," the captive replies. "My word as a knight." Saladin lets him go, and the knight returns to Champagne to find his lands racked by war and famine. Unable to raise the ransom money, he returns to captivity. Saladin, touched by his honesty, sets the knight free, showering him with gifts, but having him promise to place crescents and bells on his family coat of arms and to have one son in each generation of the knight's descendants named "Saladin."

This, it seems, is the stuff of which chivalrous legends are made: the unlikely scene of a knight crossing the sea to return to captivity, knightly virtue rewarded (in gold, thank you) by the chivalrous sultan—in short, the story of a pair of valorous knights whose respect for the code of chivalry and mutual admiration are unimpeded by barriers of military and political allegiance, language, or religion. It would seem easy to write this legend off as a flight of literary fancy, were it not for the fact that the lords of Anglure did indeed have coats of arms with bells and crescents and that they continued to name their sons "Saladin" until 1732; indeed, the name "Saladin d'Anglure" has survived into the late twentieth century. A fifteenth-century French *Armorial* contains what purport to be coats of arms for Alexander the Great, Saladin, and other knights of old: Saladin's coat of arms corresponds with that of the Anglures.[7] Yet the sources closest to the Third Crusade say nothing about a lord of Anglure taking part. The first member of the family on record with the name "Saladin" was born at the end of the thirteenth century; the legend is not found in written form previous to the sixteenth century. What we have is a romantic, no doubt embellished, sixteenth-century legend meant to link the Anglure nobility with that great chivalrous adventure of the twelfth century. The legend may already exist by the time the first Saladin of Anglure is christened in the late thirteenth century. How much—if at all—the legend corresponds with historical fact, of course, is impossible to say.

In the dozens of European texts about Salâh al-Dîn, fact and fancy, legend and history are so tightly woven together that they become impossible to unravel. What I propose instead is to look at the gradual creation of the hero Saladin in the European imagination, his transformation over several centuries from the scourge of the Lord into the epitome of chivalry. My study falls into three parts: First, we will see how many Europeans reacted to Salâh al-Dîn's victory at Hattin and his capture of Jerusalem by painting him as a scourge of the Lord, an instrument of Divine punishment for

Christian sins. Second, we will see how narrative and artistic portrayals of the Third Crusade portray the sultan as a valorous adversary, a shrewd and humane ruler, and in every way a match for his Christian foes. Finally, we will examine a series of legends, from the thirteenth century to the fifteenth, in which European authors increasingly portray Saladin as the epitome of knighthood.

Salâh al-Dîn, Scourge of the Lord

"O that my head were waters, and mine eyes a fountain of tears, that I might weep day and night for the slain of my people." So Peter of Blois bemoans the loss of Jerusalem to Salâh al-Dîn, echoing the lament of the prophet Jeremiah, and calls for a new crusade.[8] A century earlier, Christian writers had composed glowing accounts of the victories of the First Crusade, which culminated in the capture of Jerusalem in 1099. Clearly, it seemed, God was on the side of the "pilgrims" (as they called themselves); He showed his favor by helping His small army rout a multitude of enemies.[9] How then, were Europeans to interpret Jerusalem's fall to the armies of Salâh al-Dîn? To Christians (as to Muslims or Jews) such an event was ordained by the will of God, Whose judgment was invariably just. Pope Gregory VIII, on October 29, 1187, issued his bull *Audita tremendi*, in which he expressed the horror and confusion that he and his fellow Christians felt upon "having heard of the tremendous severity of the judgment which the Divine Hand imposed on the land of Jerusalem."[10] The devil, the pope says, caused dissension among the Christian ranks, and God allowed Salâh al-Dîn to defeat the Christian host. "We must not think," he says, "that these things happened because of the injustice of the Judge; rather, they are the result of the iniquity of a derelict people." Sins, dissension, and scandal caused God to turn away from the Christians; here Gregory can find plenty of precedents in the prophetic books of the Old Testament. He finds apt words of the prophet Hosea (4:1–2): "There is no truth, nor mercy, nor knowledge of God in the land. By swearing, and lying, and killing, and stealing, and committing adultery, they break out, and blood toucheth blood."

Yet if the Old Testament provides precedents for such manifestations of divine wrath, it also provides hope. "For we read," Gregory says, "that when the people converted to God, one man defeated a thousand and two routed ten thousand—even (with the people doing nothing) that the army of Sennacherib was destroyed by the hand of an angel." Gregory calls for penance, moral reform—and for preparations for a new crusade.

Salâh al-Dîn plays a curiously secondary role in Gregory's scheme. He is a divine scourge, whom God sent to punish sinful Christians. If Christians turn toward God, He will allow them to defeat the sultan. Gregory makes no effort to demonize Salâh al-Dîn. He has, in fact, little to say about him, considering him a minor player in this drama of sin and repentance.[11] Peter of Blois refers to Salâh al-Dîn as "that son of perdition, with whose name I do not wish to pollute this letter."[12]

The Latin Christians in Palestine also portrayed Salâh al-Dîn as a divine scourge: they, however, showed much more interest in describing him and his achievements. An anonymous poet who composed his *Carmen de Saladino* in the late twelfth or early thirteenth century tried to blacken Salâh al-Dîn's name by casting aspersions on his birth and his rise to power.[13] For this poet, the Christian Franks are facing a scourge such as those announced by the Hebrew prophets.[14] He vilifies Salâh al-Dîn by maliciously deforming the events in the sultan's rise to power, accusing him of committing adultery with the wife of Nûr al-Dîn.[15] He also claims that he killed both Nûr al-Dîn and the Judex of Babylon (by whom he seems to mean al-ʿÂdid, Fatimid caliph of Cairo).[16] In order to be immortalized by the writings of Christians, the poet continues, Saladin begins to attack the Franks.[17] The poem narrates the defeat of the Christian army at Hattin: the deaths, the prisoners led away in chains. The cause of this catastrophe, the poet makes clear, is the sins of the Christians.[18]

Other chroniclers repeated parts of this malicious tale—in particular, the purported murder of the Egyptian caliph. According to the thirteenth-century *Jerusalem Continuations* to the epic *Cycle de la Croisade*, Saladin is son of the Egyptian king Eufranius. At Eufranius's death, his brother Alfadins claims the throne and exiles Saladin. Saladin returns, kills him, and reclaims his rightful throne. The king of Cairo, Amulaine, wishes all to worship him as a god. This character seems a mix of distorted reports of the Fatimid caliph and biblical images of the pharaoh. Amulaine orders Saladin to come to him. Saladin complies, picture of feigned humility, dressed in a simple cloak- -under which he hides the sword with which he slays the evil king (v. 5749). The pejorative stories of his treachery have been transformed to make Saladin into a clever hero who uses ruse to claim his rightful throne and thwart the megalomaniac Amulaine. Saladin has become not quite a protagonist (he is still "Roi Salehadin qui onques Diu n'ama," "the King Saladin who never loved God," v. 6694), yet he is a heroic, clever, and chivalrous adversary.[19] One letter from a Latin crusader to the pope claimed that Saladin had thrown the True Cross into a fire and the Cross had leaped out of the flames. Such a story was intended no doubt to show both Saladin's implacable hostility toward Christianity and God's ability to work miracles against him.[20] The anonymous *Book on Saladin's Capture of the Holy Land* sees Saladin's offensive as an effort to blaspheme and pollute the holy places of Christendom.[21] Yet if a few authors tried to tarnish Salâh al-Dîn's name through hostile tales of treachery, most of his adversaries (Arab and Latin) beheld his exploits with grudging admiration. For William of Tyre, whose *Chronicle* narrates the story of the Kingdom of Jerusalem from the First Crusade to 1184, "Salahadinus" is "a man of genius, wise in counsel, a vigorous fighter, unusually generous."[22] William describes in detail his rise to power in Egypt and Syria and his military expeditions against both Christians and Muslims, watching anxiously as the power of this redoubtable enemy grows: "We watched each of his successes and everything that happened to him, and it seemed that we were losing everything."[23] William died in 1186, a year before Hattin, but he could read the writing on the wall.

William's clearheaded assessment of Salâh al-Dîn's skills and strengths in no way lessens the image of the divine scourge. It is often asked, says William, why our fathers, few in number, succeed in defeating large armies and conquering, while in our day we are often defeated by small armies. William gives three reasons, the first of which is that to our fathers, "religious men who feared God, were born sons of perdition," whose sins have provoked the righteous ire of God. The second cause, opines William, is that the early crusaders were skilled and practiced soldiers, while their adversaries were not. The third cause is that each Muslim city had a different ruler and that these rulers were often fighting each other. Now Salâh al-Dîn—like his predecessors Zanqi and Nûr al-Dîn—had succeeded in unifying them into a formidable force. For William, these dark political and military changes in the region are merely manifestations of the main cause, the working out of God's righteous anger against the sins and dissentions of the Christians.

Those chroniclers who followed William generally made the same assessment in explaining the losses of Hattin and Jerusalem: Christian sins—particularly Christian in-fighting—led to defeat.[24] Many authors blame the loss on Raymond, count of Tripoli, who had previously made an alliance with Salâh al-Dîn,[25] and on Reynald of Châtillon (known as Arnât of Kerak by the Muslim Chroniclers), who attacked a Muslim caravan in defiance of a treaty with Salâh al-Dîn and who was almost universally vilified by Christian and Muslim authors alike.[26] Yet as bitterly as many of these authors bemoan Christian losses, they generally express a grudging admiration—even awe—for Salâh al-Dîn, echoing the judgment of William of Tyre.[27] Several authors tell of his generous freeing of Christian prisoners after the capture of Jerusalem.[28] We have two images of the sultan, often existing together in the same author: the divine scourge and the noble, valiant adversary. The latter image will come to the fore in chronicles of the Third Crusade.

"Never Did Better Saracen Set Foot in Stirrup": The Valiant Adversary of the Third Crusade

The Third Crusade, a huge expedition led by three crowned kings, seemed destined for victory.[29] Yet when Holy Roman Emperor Frederick Barbarossa died while swimming across an Anatolian river, his army broke up in confusion. Philip Augustus of France and Richard the Lionhearted of England were bitter enemies who spent as much time quarrelling with each other as fighting the Muslims. The indigenous Latin Christians were divided over the disputed succession to the crown of Jerusalem. After an initial success in capturing Acre, Philip returned to France, and Richard struggled to control an unruly army. Following a series of indecisive skirmishes with Salâh al-Dîn, Richard negotiated a peace settlement and set off for home. The Third Crusade, upon which so many hopes had been heaped, had managed only to take Acre. Salâh al-Dîn remained as strong as ever, securely in control of Jerusalem.

European chroniclers almost unanimously imputed the failure of the crusade to Christian in-fighting. The English blasted Philip; the French lambasted Richard. Others blamed both of them. The anonymous author of a Latin chronicle says that after the crusaders captured Acre, they could have gone on to take Jerusalem, had the devil not stirred up discord between Richard and Philip: "Saladin would have willingly given up the Holy Land," he says, "if only our kings had simply *pretended* that they unanimously wished to invade and to make peace among themselves."[30] In this ritual distribution of blame, scapegoats were not hard to find, given the fighting between various groups of crusaders: French against English, Pisans against Genoans, Hospitalers against Templars, not to mention the split between the partisans of the two pretenders to the throne of Jerusalem, Guy of Lusignan and Conrad of Montferrat. In none of these accounts is Salâh al-Dîn the principal villain.

Before the crusade, European writers such as Pope Gregory VIII or Peter of Blois could portray the sultan as a divine scourge whose dominion over the Holy Land was oppressive, as an adversary who could—and must—be crushed by a crusading army. In the wake of the failure of the Third Crusade, Salâh al-Dîn seemed more redoubtable than ever, and Christian authors came to terms with the inevitable. They portray the sultan as a noble adversary, a wise and humane ruler who, far from being a threat to Christianity, shows respect for it. This change of heart is dramatically illustrated within the *Estoire de la guerre sainte* of Ambroise.[31]

Ambroise, a poet who accompanied Richard on the crusade, sets for himself the rather formidable task of portraying Richard's expedition as a glorious success and of deflecting blame for its failures onto Richard's Christian enemies. Ambroise pours out his bile on the various Christian rivals who get in Richard's way, especially Philip II Augustus and Conrad of Montferrat. Philip is cast as the supreme scoundrel: he stirs up the people of Messina against Richard,[32] he wrongfully tries to make Conrad king of Jerusalem in place of Guy,[33] and most woefully, he abandons the crusader army in Acre. God refused to grant Jerusalem to Richard, Ambroise implies, because of the sinfulness of the French knights, who go on all-night drinking binges, visit brothels, brawl, and swear. In the good old days, laments Ambroise nostalgically, when Charlemagne waged war against pagans, or when (during the First Crusade) the Franks took Antioch, there was no such division and strife within the ranks. The French knights should have followed this example and united behind Richard. Thus would they have taken Jerusalem.[34]

In addition to blaming the French, Ambroise glorifies the victories that Richard and his men did achieve (the siege of Acre, the capture of a Bedouin caravan, several victories in minor battles against Saladin). The third element in Ambroise's justification of Richard's failure is a glorification of the victorious enemy: Saladin and his men. He gives a series of apparently contradictory portrayals of Saladin and his soldiers: depicted as evil and incompetent when Richard first arrives at Acre, they become steadily more redoubtable and more chivalrous as Ambroise's narrative progresses. Such dichotomy is standard in war propaganda: on the one hand, the enemy must be denigrated enough to make aggression against him seem justifiable; on the other hand, a certain prowess and valor must be accorded him to make one's victory over him appear glorious—or to justify defeat at his hands.

When Richard takes Acre and subsequently kills the Muslim hostages there, Ambroise asserts that, because of this, Saladin lost "his renown which had stood so high."[35] In a pique of fury similar to that of a proud pagan from a *chanson de geste,* Saladin orders the destruction of Ascalon. According to Bahâ al-Dîn, he had in fact been opposed to its destruction.[36] Ambroise dwells lovingly on the details of Richard's victory in the battle of Arsûf,[37] saying that Saladin roundly chastised his men for their defeat. One of his knights responded that it was not their fault, that they indeed fought bravely and fiercely but that they had not been able to pierce the rock-hard Frankish armor. Moreover, one of the Franks, "Melek Richard," fought like no other man they had ever seen. It was only right that a man like him should win battles and conquer land.[38] This is a common trope in medieval chronicle and epic: the admiration of the enemy becomes the ultimate compliment. Ambroise subsequently tells us that the Turks bemoan their losses, for which they revile Saladin.[39]

In Ambroise's transition from Saladin-as-despised-leader to Saladin-as-noble-ally, he recounts a strange story of an event which, he says, took place on Easter. Every year, the Jerusalem Christian community waited eagerly for the miracle of the "holy fire" that would descend upon a lamp in the Church of the Holy Sepulcher. This annual miracle, by the way, had long been a source of discord between Orthodox and Latin Christians: first monopolized by the Orthodox clergy, then condemned as a pyrotechnic trick by the Latin clergy, and ultimately co-opted by them.[40] Ambroise tells us that Christian prisoners, in chains, were weeping in the Church when the fire miraculously descended upon the lamp. The Saracens marveled at this and muttered that it must be enchantment. Saladin, wishing to get to the heart of the matter, ordered the lamp put out. It reignited. A second time and a third time, Saladin had the lamp put out, and each time, Ambroise tells us, God relit it. "And when Saladin beheld the faith of the Christians and their confidence, then he said to his Turks that verily and without any doubt either would he himself die right soon, or at least the city would not remain his much longer. And he lived thereafter according to my knowledge and my reckoning, only until the Lent which followed."[41] Saladin is not the victorious sultan who drove Richard away, Ambroise is telling us. He is a sage who could read the prophecy of defeat in God's miracle and who submitted to a noble peace.

Indeed, as Ambroise's chronicle proceeds (and as he has fewer and fewer crusader victories to recount), the negative portrayal of Saladin gives way to mutual admiration. As Richard retreats to the coastline and fights a few last desperate battles, Saladin has become, for Ambroise, "that generous, that valiant Saracen."[42] Ambroise had earlier told how his brother al-ʿÂdil Saîf al-Dîn (known to Europe as Saphadin) had given two magnificent steeds to Richard during the heat of battle, urging him to take them as a testimony to his prowess and valor, and hinting that if Richard survived the battle he would find a way to repay Saphadin.[43] Whatever historical fact may underlie this story, its purpose in Ambroise's narrative soon becomes clear: Richard, preparing to return to Europe and failing to procure from the Templars and Hospitalers any assurance that they would be able to hold the coastal towns in his absence, "saw that all the world, which is neither loyal nor without guile, had flatly failed him." "My lords," continues Ambroise, "marvel not if he but did the best that he know according to the occasion he had; for whoso feareth shame and followeth honour, he chooseth, of the two evils, the lesser one. So would he rather seek a truce than leave the land in danger."[44] Richard sent for Saphadin, "who greatly loved the king because of his prowess," and asked him to negotiate a peace with Saladin. Saphadin "parleyed so well that a truce was determined and declared by Saladin."[45] Ambroise then gives the terms of the truce: the destruction of Ascalon, the assured safety of Frankish coastal towns, a pact of nonaggression for three years, and free passage for Christians to visit the holy places in Jerusalem. Ambroise wants to portray this truce as advantageous and honorable and hence to deflect criticism from Richard. Through this special friendship with Saladin's brother, he implies, Richard was able to procure an unusually advantageous peace. Richard also swears that he will return in three years, when the truce is up, to battle Saladin again, if he dares. If Richard failed to do so, implies Ambroise, it is only because of the evil machinations of his enemies in Europe, chiefly Philip Augustus.[46]

Saladin, Saphadin, and the other "noble Saracens" ensure the pilgrims' safety and respectfully let them visit the holy places and kiss the True Cross. Ambroise describes how Saladin received the bishop of Salisbury with honor. The bishop tells the sultan that Richard "is the best knight in the world and the best warrior, and bounteous and full of good qualities. I take no account of your sins; but if your qualities were put with his and joined to them, then we lightly say that not in all the world—within all the circuit thereof—could any two such princes be found, so valiant and so well approved."[47] Saladin then asks the bishop to request a gift, whatever he desires; after deliberation, the bishop asks for assurance that Latin clergy should serve in the Church of the Holy Sepulcher in Jerusalem, the Church of the Nativity in Bethlehem, and the Church of Nazareth. Saladin grants his request, "and well might the bishop boast that he had given back to God the song that then was silent there."[48] Here once more, it is hard to know how much of this is true: such a gift would certainly be in character for Salâh al-Dîn. What is clear, again, is the point of the story in context: to blunt accusations that Richard has abandoned the churches and clergy of Jerusalem, we have Saladin as generous foe-turned-friend, protector of the church, benefactor of bishops. This image of Saladin grows out of the needs of Ambroise's apologetics, just as the negative image did in the earlier passages of the text.

After the bishop returns from Jerusalem, Ambroise describes the departure of Richard and the pilgrims, and here the apologetic tone comes to the forefront:

> But many folk that were without understanding said many a time thereafter in their folly that these had nothing wrought in Syria, since they had not taken Jerusalem. But they had not well enquired into the matter, but blamed an emprise whereof they knew nought, in a place where they never set their feet.[49]

The memory of a heroic struggle against a valiant and chivalrous adversary will be carefully preserved and cultivated by the descendants of the crusaders—so much so that even the claim to have an ancestor taken prisoner by Saladin becomes a sign of prestige, as we saw in the case of the Saladins d'Anglure. As part of a propaganda campaign for a crusade he was preparing in 1252, English king Henry III had scenes from his uncle Richard's crusade painted on the walls of his rooms in several of his castles. In particular, he had painted a heroic, by now mythical, duel between Richard and Saladin.[50] It was a fitting subject for artistic propaganda: whereas Ambroise was required to place glowing descriptions of Richard's victorious battles amid awkward apologies for his failures, the painter could depict the king at his moment of glory, now imagined, it seems, as a hand-to-hand battle with the sultan. While the English royal artists would naturally play up the confrontation between Richard and Saladin, other artists portrayed a dozen valorous knights holding off Saladin's men in a mountain pass, in a legendary battle that became known as the Pas Saladin.[51] This scene, which glorified Richard and his knights at the expense of Philip Augustus, became well enough known to lead to French propaganda: an early fourteenth-century poem entitled the *Pas Salhadin* puts Philip at the head of the expedition; Richard and his knights indeed perform heroic feats, but under the direction of the French king.[52] In 1389, when the French queen, Isabeau of Bavaria, enters Paris in pomp, the *Pas Saladin* is performed for her on a stage erected in the street; Jean Froissart, who witnessed the spectacle, describes it in his *Chronicles:*

> On the street was a stage, and on the stage was a castle, and along the stage was arranged the Pas of king Salehadin, all made up of characters, the Christians on one side and the Saracens on the other, and there were depicted all the lords of renown who were at the Pas Salhadin at the time, and they were armed with their [coats of] arms as they were at that time. A little below them was the character of the king of France, and around him the twelve peers of France, all armed with their [coats of] arms. And when the queen of France was brought in her litter before the stage where these things were arranged, King Richard left his companions and came to the king of France and asked leave to go attack the Saracens, and the king gave him leave to do so. Having thus taken leave, King Richard returned to his twelve companions, and they assembled themselves and went immediately to attack the King Salhadin and his Saracens, and there was a great and entertaining battle, which lasted a good while. And everything was watched right willingly.[53]

Richard is subservient to Philip, and the twelve knights of Richard's entourage are curiously doubled by the "12 peers of France," annexing the Saladin legend into the *matière de France,* the epic celebration of the ancestral French kings. Once Richard's subservience to Philip had been duly shown, his exploits in battle could be enjoyed with gusto, even in a spectacle staged for a French queen.

We saw earlier how Ambroise made Saladin into a noble foe and ultimately into a protector of Christians. Philip and his allies such as Conrad of Montferrat are the real enemies. The king of France has his own apologists, notably Guillaume le Breton, who casts the king as the hero of a classicizing epic poem, the *Philippide*. Guillaume's strategy is to deny any differences between the two kings: Richard is Philip's dutiful vassal, and the two get along just fine during the crusade. Saladin trembles at Philip's name and wishes to surrender the besieged Acre to him; Philip, wishing to share the glory with his vassal Richard, awaits his arrival before accepting Acre's submission. After Philip leaves the Holy Land, Richard's crusading efforts are marked by failure, and he begins to make enemies.[54]

The anonymous *Récits d'un Ménestrel de Reims* (composed about 1260) uses a different strategy to explain the failure of the Third Crusade, vilifying Richard the Lionhearted.[55] Writing roughly seventy years after the crusade, the minstrel no longer associates Richard with the cause of King Guy and Philip with Conrad; rather, he chooses to justify King Guy (who had been, in fact, Richard's ally) and Philip, while vilifying Richard, Conrad, and the other treacherous barons. Subsequently, the minstrel narrates Philip's conquest of Normandy from King John, "the worst king that ever was."[56] In this version of the Third Crusade, Saladin is not once mentioned as foe of Philip and Richard. The minstrel deliberately omits mention of Richard's exploits against Saladin's army after the capture of Acre (and after Philip's departure); he also skips over Saladin's failure to raise the siege of Acre. The only mention of Saladin's fighting against Christians is that of the battle of Hattin, in which it is Christian treachery that gives him the victory. Saladin comes across as a powerful and chivalrous knight, one who recognizes and rewards nobility of spirit, but one who was never tested against mighty King Philip because of Richard's treachery.

The *Pas Saladin* celebrated the exploits of French and English knights against the sultan: by emphasizing the victorious battle, the failure of the Third Crusade is mitigated. If Saladin is the defeated enemy of the *Pas*, he is one whose victorious exploits were known to all—indeed, this is the source of prestige in being associated with the battle. The same sorts of glorification of the heroics of the crusaders—and of their descendants—probably inspired the creation of two epic cycles of the crusades, both of which culminate with the rise of Saladin. The first cycle, completed in the mid-thirteenth century, abruptly ends shortly before the Christian defeat at Hattin; in the second cycle, composed in the fourteenth century, Saladin's adventures are removed from the plane of history, and he becomes the ultimate chivalrous adversary in the culmination of the cycle, the *Roman de Saladin*.[57]

Saladin as Epitome of Knightly and Courtly Virtues

The portrayal of Saladin as valorous adversary, in the context of narratives and images of the Crusades, serves the purposes of glorifying the accomplishments of his Christian adversaries and excusing their failures. Beginning in the thirteenth century, stories about Saladin become common in collections of tales and *exempla* stripped of these apologetic concerns. These stories insist not so much on the sultan's military successes (all too well known to European audiences) but on his virtues. Saladin becomes an exemplar of chivalry, of justice, of honor, a model of behavior for knights and princes. His qualities serve as a challenge to the universalist claims of Christian morality: Saladin, like the ancient heroes of Greece and Rome, follows the universal code of knightly valor. He is admitted into Dante's City of Light and into the pantheon of valorous heroes in Petrarch's *Triumph of Fame*.[58]

Similarly, Saladin is one of fourteen knights (from Hector to Young King Henry) among the (mostly Roman) heroes of the *Conti di Antichi Cavalieri* (Tales of ancient knights), composed in Italian at the end of the thirteenth century. Five of the twenty-one stories involve Saladin. In the first of them, the troubadour Bertran de Born comes to Saladin to see if rumors are true that the sultan is faultless. Bertran is amazed to find that there is nothing in the sultan's words or deeds with which he can find fault. He soon discovers the cause: every evening, Saladin holds council with his wisest advisors to see if he has done or said anything that day that he should not have; in the same meeting he discusses plans for the next day. Saladin's perfection comes from his constant self-correction and his humbly seeking out the best advice he can find.[59] Self-correction is the theme of another of the tales: One day, we are told, Saladin, riding through territory that he has given to one of his knights, sees that it is the most beautiful land of his dominion, and he plots to take it for himself and give another piece of land to his knight. Then he immediately repents of his evil thoughts and begins to fast—so much so that he almost starves to death.[60] He is chivalrous even to the point of aiding his enemies. When he sees Richard the Lionhearted fighting on foot, he sends Richard a horse as a gift, proclaiming that it is not proper for a king to fight on foot.[61]

Indeed, if Saladin is a model of chivalrous virtues, he becomes a model of morality as well. In an era when Christian theologians speculated on the connections between natural, universal moral codes and Christian morality, Saladin became, by the thirteenth century, a symbol of the former: like great pagan heroes of antiquity, he obeys God's natural moral laws without recourse to His church or His scriptures.

The *Récits d'un ménestrel de Reims* tell how one day King John of Acre spoke with Saladin's uncle, a tall, noble, proud, white-bearded man who was John's prisoner. The king (through an interpreter) asks him to tell of his nephew's deeds, which he gladly does, in a series of short tales all dealing with Saladin's morality and sagacity. The uncle describes how one day Saladin heard of the great charity shown by the Hospitalers in the Hospital of St. John of Acre; one said that they would accept the poorest of the sick and give them whatever they wished to eat, refusing no request. Saladin, having decided to put them to the test, disguised himself as a poor Christian pilgrim and went to the hospital, where he was welcomed, put into bed, and asked what he wished to eat. He responded that he was dying of starvation and that there was only one thing he could eat to cure him, but he dared not ask for it. When the master of the sick insisted that he tell him what it was, Saladin replied that he would only eat the foreleg of the finest steed of the Grand Master of the Hospital, and only if he saw it cut off before his very eyes. The Grand Master, judging that it was better for a horse to die than a man, ordered that the horse's foot be cut off in the sick man's presence. Just as a man raised an axe to cut off the foot, Saladin called on him to stop, that he did not want such a noble animal to be killed, and that he would prefer to eat mutton. When Saladin returned home, he issued a charter to the Hospital of St. John, promising to send them a thousand gold bezants each year, so that they might continue to serve the poor. He promised that these donations would continue "despite any war which may arise between us and the Christians." The Master and the brothers were overjoyed, "for they knew concerning Saladin that never for any cause would he lie."[62]

Here Salâh al-Dîn and the Hospitalers, bitter enemies, are posthumously inducted into a mutual admiration society. The story serves to glorify both the sultan and the Hospitalers, as well as to indulge in a sort of moral fantasy: Saladin, tolerant protector of the Church at the end of Ambroise's *Estoire*, here becomes the model of non-Christian morality giving his approval to an institution epitomizing Christian charity. Saladin is a cunning master of disguise and intrigue, but here all is done in the name of moral justice. We see again his mythic liberality as he showers gold on all who deserve it.

If this idealized Saladin rewards Christians who show proper charity and generosity, he also punishes Christians who indulge in avarice. Immediately after recounting Saladin's grant to the Hospitalers, the uncle tells us that the Christian Marquis of Caesarea was so avaricious that instead of paying his soldiers to defend his city, he dismissed them and kept their pay in his own coffers. Having thus weakened his defenses, he was no match for Saladin, who took the city easily. He then had the marquis brought before him and told him that since he never seemed to be able to sate his appetite for gold, Saladin would do so for him: he had the nobleman's gold melted and poured down his throat.[63]

A dozen or so medieval texts recount the story of how the dying Saladin gave his subjects a lesson in the vanity of earthly power.[64] In the *Récits d'un ménestrel de Reims*, it is the uncle who tells:

> I saw my nephew Saladin, who was king of Babylon and had thirty kings to govern under him, how he caused one of his retainers, a wise man and prudent, to mount and to ride abroad through all his good cities. And he bore three ells of cloth fastened to a lance, and he cried at every crossing of the streets: "Nothing more shall Saladin carry away with him, of all his kingdom and of all his treasure, than these three ells of cloth for his winding sheet."[65]

Saladin has become a non-Christian model of virtue: a just ruler, generous patron, brave knight, humble in the face of death.

Yet there is a tension in many of these texts between the desire to paint the ideal ruler in non-Christian, non-European colors and the need to squeeze him into more familiar canons of behavior: to domesticate Saladin. Thus we will see the legendary Saladin falling in love with Christian women, traveling to Europe, speaking French and Italian, jousting, and having himself dubbed. In the *Conti di Antichi Cavalieri*, as we have seen, the troubadour Bertran de Born comes to Saladin to see if he is indeed faultless. Having spent months in Saladin's court, he finds the sultan's single fault: although he has several wives, he does not know what love is. Bertran gives the sultan a lesson in love and describes the virtues of "the finest of all women," a Christian who lived in a city that Saladin was then besieging. The sultan falls in love and subsequently abandons his siege when the lady he loves asks him to—proper form for a true courtly lover, if out of character for the real Salâh al-Dîn.[66]

The author of the *Conti* is not alone in his desire to make a courtly lover out of the sultan. One commentator to Dante makes Saladin the lover of Queen Isabel of Cyprus.[67] Yet if this most noble of Saracens is to have a lover worthy of him, who better than the French queen? Moreover, what better candidate than Eleanor of Aquitaine, that most famous (or infamous) of French queens who was later to be sent packing by Louis VII to become wife—and mother—of France's most bitter rivals? And what better opportunity than the Second Crusade (1147–48), during which Eleanor accompanied Louis and the two bickered famously? Granted that Salâh al-Dîn would have been a ten-year-old boy at the time, the anonymous minstrel of Reims, with fearless disregard for such problems of chronology, makes Eleanor and Saladin lovers—almost. Eleanor, we are told, accompanies Louis to Tyre and is disgusted to see him refuse to combat the gallant Saladin, with whom she grows more and more enamored. Finally she sends a message to him, telling him to come in a ship to take her away. The ship arrives at midnight, but one of Eleanor's maids wakes Louis, who catches her with one foot on the ship and brings her back. When they return to France, Louis sends her packing, and she immediately sends for a consort who will match her in evil: "King Henry of England—him who caused Saint Thomas of Canterbury to be put to death."[68]

The fifteenth-century prose version of the *Roman de Saladin,* perhaps wishing to correct the minstrel's anachronism, makes Saladin's lover the unnamed queen of Philip Augustus. In a similar though more elaborate scene, she attempts (and fails) to escape from a boring husband into the arms of the valorous Saladin. Indeed, according to the *Roman,* the entire crusade was not Philip's idea at all, but part of the queen's elaborate scheme to run off with Saladin. For Saladin, we are told, had been to France earlier, on which occasion he became the queen's lover.

The *Roman de Saladin* is not the first medieval text to claim that Saladin visited Europe. According to several Italian tales of the fourteenth century, Saladin came to Europe in disguise to see the preparations being made for the crusade against him.[69] According to his biographer Bahâ-al-Dîn, Salâh al-Dîn once looked out to sea and mused that after he had driven off the Franks, he would like to pursue them across the sea and conquer their lands.[70] The *Roman de Saladin* has him do just that. He sets off with a large army to conquer England, and in a heroic battle for a mountain pass (the *Pas Saladin* is strangely transposed here) the English and French knights drive him back.

Saladin's European adventures allow the *Roman de Saladin* to have its hero do two of the things European knights enjoy most: make love and joust.[71] Far from being a foreign prince with foreign customs, Saladin becomes like the European nobles, even more so; in the *Roman de Saladin,* as in the Italian stories of his spying, he travels incognito with ease. No one notices that he is a foreigner. He stands out only through his exceptional virtue and prowess.

In these stories Saladin is at the same time celebrated and domesticated.

This most prestigious of foreign heroes, we are told, wished to become a knight, and he asked to be dubbed. The thirteenth-century *Ordene de chevalerie* (Order of chivalry) enjoyed great popularity throughout the Middle Ages.[72] The poem tells how Hugh, Count of Tiberias, is taken prisoner by Saladin, who tells him he will set him free on one condition: that he dub his captor according to the Frankish ritual. Hugh, after some hesitation, agrees: at each step of the elaborate ritual, he explains to Saladin the importance and symbolism of the ritual acts. Saladin, in gratitude, allows Hugh to go free without ransom.

The *Ordene de chevalerie* was meant to glorify the order of knighthood and to offer a clear explanation of its increasingly elaborate rituals. Why would the author of such a text choose Saladin for his novice, of all people? There are two reasons. First, Saladin's supposed desire for dubbing testifies to the value and importance of the ritual. If this great and powerful ruler and warrior longs to become a knight, surely knighthood must be a great thing. The poet is attempting to give universal, timeless value to a ritual that is in fact culturally specific. Second, Saladin is not a Christian. The dubbing ritual, stripped of all liturgical underpinnings, becomes completely secular.[73] No priest is present, no admonitions to defend the church and its clergy are made, no warnings of hell are given to the church's enemies. Medieval authors assimilated Saladin into the order of knighthood in the same way they assimilated the great warriors of antiquity: the Roman warriors who accompany the sultan in the *Conti di Antichi Cavalieri* and in Dante's city of light; Theseus in Chaucer's *Knight's Tale;* or the greatest of the kings of antiquity, Alexander the Great, whom Saladin claims as an ancestor in the *Roman de Saladin.*[74] The knight could hold his head high, knowing that his code of behavior was older and more broadly recognized than that of the church.

If his dubbing is an attempt to domesticate the great sultan, to pull him into the orbit of the Frankish nobility, why not make the process complete and give Saladin a noble French ancestor? This is precisely what several romances of the later Middle Ages do. Weaving complex adventures of pilgrimage, shipwreck, and capture, they tell of a French noblewoman who ends up wife of a Muslim ruler and eventually mother (or great-grandmother in another version) of Saladin.[75] Somehow, such fantastic legends may have lessened the trauma of losses to Saladin at Hattin, Jerusalem, and the Third Crusade. No longer an epic battle between foreign civilizations, Saladin's exploits were due in part to his noble French ancestry: a noble-blooded knight, duly dubbed, speaking French and Italian; in sum, one of us.

One element was still missing in this domestication of the sultan: his religion. Here there are two distinct tendencies in the later legends of Saladin. On the one hand, we read of the sultan's supposed penchant for Christianity; on the other hand, we hear of him being repulsed by the venality of Christian churchmen and resting firmly in his ancestral faith. The *Jerusalem continuations* to the French crusade cycle imagined that Saladin, during the coronation ceremony of Baldwin IV, was impressed by how well the Franks served their God.[76]

Two texts go so far as to have him baptize himself on his deathbed. In the *Récits d'un ménestrel de Reims*, Saladin's uncle remarks:

> One thing he did which sorely vexed us. For when he was so forspent that he perceived clearly that he must die, he called for a basin filled with water. And immediately a servant ran and fetched a silver basin and set it at his right hand. And Saladin caused himself to be raised up until he was sitting, and with his right hand he made the sign of the cross over the water, touching the basin in four places and saying: "So far is it from this place unto this as from this unto this." This he said so that it might not be perceived what he was doing. And then he poured the water upon his head and upon his body, uttering therewithal three words in French, which we understood not; but verily it seemed, inasmuch as I could see, that he baptized himself.[77]

The uncle then relates that Saladin was buried in the Christian cemetery of St. Nicholas of Acre and that the Hospitalers keep an oil lamp burning in the magnificent tower that marks his tomb. Saladin, scourge of crusaders, has been brought into the Christian fold. The *Roman de Saladin* describes Saladin's deathbed baptism in similar terms.[78] Saladin, for the *Roman*, is no longer the Saracen model of virtue, showing that moral virtue can exist independently of Christianity: rather, he is the French nobleman who through a series of accidents is a Saracen king of Babylon, but whose virtue brings him instinctively back to the Christian faith of his noble ancestors.

This baptism, however—in both of the versions cited here—is far from a standard one. Most notable, of course, is the absence of a priest: there is no Remigius on hand to tell this new Clovis to abandon his talismans.[79] Saladin baptizes himself. This baptism indeed reaffirms the universal claims of Christianity, since the virtuous non-Christian wishes to die Christian and attain paradise. Yet he hopes to do so without having once benefited from the services of a cleric—except for the attention that (according to the minstrel) the Hospitalers are to give his tomb. If this model of moral and knightly virtue is drawn to Christianity, he is able to get along just fine without priests. The *Roman de Saladin* has the sultan berate his Christian friends for their slavish obeisance to the pope. For Christian knights and rulers who often resented clerical meddling with their affairs, getting to heaven without ever having to submit to the wrangling of a priest must have seemed ideal.

Most stories about Saladin have him remain in his ancestral faith. He indeed becomes something of an anticlerical weapon for many authors: a non-Christian prince who through liberality, modesty, and charity outshines the petty, venal Christian priests and princes. Latin poet Gilles de Corbeil in the early thirteenth century recounts how Saladin listened with interest to the exposition of the Christian faith and desired to convert. First, however, he wished to inquire into the morals of the Christians, clerics, and laymen. Having found them indulging in lust, filth, fraud, envy, and hatred, the sultan chose to remain true to his faith. Gilles laments that through sin the Christians have lost the conversion of such a man—and of so much territory—to Christianity.[80]

Saladin and other pious Muslims become foils with which to criticize the lack of piety among Christians. Peter the Chanter, writing his *Brief Discourse,* a manual for preachers and teachers composed in the late twelfth century, bemoans the fact that Christians no longer know how to fast. The saints of old, he says, such as Paul the Hermit or Mary the Egyptian, could live for months or years on a few loaves of bread and some roots; because we are corrupted, we can no longer do so. Indeed, he laments that "the sobriety of the Mahometans today surpasses the sobriety of the Christians." Hence Saladin decides that "such men are not worthy of the Land."[81] Far from being a mere scourge of God, Saladin and his Muslim associates are more pious and worthy of the Holy Land than the unabstemious Christians; it is for this reason that they take it. Indeed, Saladin obeys rules of piety and justice that transcend the differences between Christianity and Islam.

The *Conti di Antichi Cavalieri* also emphasize Saladin's tolerance of Christians. Two friars, out of concern for Saladin's soul, come to him to preach the Gospel and to try to convert him. Saladin's advisors tell him that according to their law, these men must be put to death. "This is true," Saladin replies, "that our law is so. But I must follow a greater law. These men have come here out of a concern for my soul. It will not please God if I repay them for this concern by sending them to their deaths." He honors the two friars greatly and lets them go in peace.[82] Saladin does not convert, and he treats the friars the same way he treats his own holy men—politely and respectfully, but keeping them subservient.[83] The sultan claims to be following "the law which most pleases God," which presumably is above and beyond the petty disputes of Christian and Muslim clergymen.

There are several stories of debates, in Saladin's presence, about the respective virtues of Judaism, Christianity, and Islam. Some of these stories by Christian authors, unsurprisingly, show a clear Christian bias. According to one, Saladin, before dying, has Christian, Jew, and Muslim debate religion; after some hesitation, he divides his possessions between devotees of the three faiths.[84] Voltaire retells the same story; for him it reflects not Saladin's uncertainty but his conviction that Muslims, Jews, and Christians are brothers.[85]

The most famous and popular of these stories was the "fable of the three rings," in which Saladin asks a Jew which of the three monotheistic religions is the greatest. The Jew responds with a parable: "There was a father who wore a beautiful ring of gold and jewels. He had three sons, each of whom asked him for the right to have the ring when he died. The father went in secret to a master goldsmith and had him make two rings identical to his own; only the father could tell the difference between the three. Thus he gave a ring to each of his three sons, and they argued vainly about which was the real one. So it is with our three religions; we all claim to follow the true religion, but only God, our father, can truly tell which is the best." The sultan, impressed with the reply, lavishes gifts upon the Jew.[86] The story was retold many times throughout the Middle Ages and beyond.[87] It emboldened Menocchio, a sixteenth-century miller, to proclaim to the Inquisition that "the majesty of God has given the Holy Spirit to all, to Christians, to Heretics, to Turks, and to Jews; and he considers them all dear, and they are all saved in the same manner." The miller was subsequently burned as a heretic.[88]

While few Christians would be as rash as Menocchio and declare to an inquisitor that Islam and Christianity were both legitimate paths to God, various medieval authors hint that this is so. Jean de Joinville recounts that during his captivity in Egypt (during Louis IX's crusade), the admiral of Egypt told him that Saladin had once declared that he had never seen a bad Christian become a good Muslim, nor a bad Muslim become a good Christian; for Saladin (and, apparently, for the admiral and Joinville), Muslims and Christians should each stay loyal to their ancestral faith.[89] Far from the spirit of the early crusade chronicles, the thirteenth-century *Chronicle of Ernoul* shows Salâh al-Dîn as a wise and pious ruler who, upon recapturing Jerusalem, offers humble prayers of thanks to "Nostre Seigneur"—our Lord—the same God as the Christians.[90] Indeed, the contrast is stark between the sultan's simple and pious prayers and the desperate pleas made by the Christians of Jerusalem, whose prayers could not reach God's ears because of their sins.[91]

Ironically, it is in the midst of the bloody struggle for Jerusalem that Christian chroniclers come to see the fundamental similarities between themselves and their Muslim adversaries. In the wake of the failure of the Third Crusade, Europeans accepted that Salâh al-Dîn was ruler of Jerusalem by the judgment of God, and they increasingly idealized him. Yet the picture of Saladin that they painted reflected less their knowledge of the twelfth-century Kurdish sultan than their idealization of what a virtuous non-Christian knight and king should be: tolerant, generous, wise, just, pious, powerful, free from the constraints of money and politics, free from struggles with clergy.[92]

⁖ 7 ⁖

VENERATIO SARRACENORUM

Shared Devotion among Muslims and Christians, According to Burchard of Strasbourg, Envoy from Frederic Barbarossa to Saladin (c. 1175)

Few Latin Christian authors of the twelfth and thirteen centuries express respect or admiration for Islam. Respect for Muslims, yes: for individual Muslim men and (less often) women, for the thriving cities of the Muslim world, for the riches found there, for Muslim culture and learning; one could cite the praise of numerous Latin writers. But when it comes to Islam, to the religious rites and beliefs of Muslims, we find at best a discreet silence, more often outright hostility. There are occasional exceptions: William of Tripoli and the anonymous author of the *De statu sarracenorum* (until recently attributed to William) praise Muslims' devotion to Jesus and the Virgin Mary, but both authors qualify praise with predictions of the imminent conversion of all Muslims to Christianity. They minimize the differences between Islam and Christianity in order to affirm that Islam will soon disappear. The pilgrim Burchard of Mount Zion, in the midst of a catalogue of different denominations of Oriental Christians, devotes a short chapter to the rites and beliefs of the "Saracens," without emitting the slightest criticism: nothing in his description would lead his readers to believe that their religion is less legitimate than that of the Latin Christians.[1] Yet these authors are exceptional: the great majority of Latin authors who mention Islam express their hostility to the religion and in particular to its prophet, Muhammad.

It is thus all the more surprising to find frank praise of Muslim piety and in particular of Muslim devotion to the Virgin Mary in a text written in the entourage of Emperor Frederick Barbarossa, a travel narrative by Burchard, Vidame of Strasbourg and imperial notary.[2] Burchard was sent to negotiate with Saladin, Ayyubid sultan of Egypt. Yet he does not say if he succeeded in meeting up with Saladin, nor does he speak at all about his diplomatic mission to the sultan. What he does relate is his voyage: his departure from Genoa, the crossing to Alexandria, then up the Nile to Cairo and finally across the desert to Damascus. He describes cities and countryside, the heat of the desert, the crocodiles, the pyramids,[3] and the customs of the locals. In particular, he describes the rites and beliefs of the "Saracens" in a way that is remarkably free of invective or disapprobation. He repeatedly stresses that numerous Christians and Jews live in the Muslim territories he visits and that they are free to practice their religion. And he paints a striking portrait of two shrines devoted to the Virgin Mary, where Muslims and Christians pray together and where all benefit from her miraculous protection.

Burchard and His *Itinerarium*

The author of this singular text presents himself as "Burkardus" and affirms that in the year 1175 Frederick I Barbarossa sent him to "the king of Babylon." Some historians have identified this Burkardus with Frederick's imperial notary, a native of Cologne,[4] author of two letters addressed to Nicolas, abbey of Siegburg, a Benedictine monastery in the Rhine Valley that played an important role in the monastic reform movement of the eleventh century. In the first of these letters, dated 1161, Burchard tells of his diplomatic embassies to Aquileia, to Salzburg, and to Hungary.[5] The second letter, from 1162, recounts the siege and the destruction of Milan by imperial troops in 1162.[6] Long passages of these letters are subsequently incorporated into the *Chronica regia coloniensis*.[7] The next document that we have from Burchard is the *Itinerarium* in which he relates his 1175 voyage, if indeed this text is authentic and from the same Burchard (a problem to which we will return). Next we find a certain Burchard, notary and chaplain in the imperial court, who signs a number of charters in 1177 and 1178.[8] Finally, various documents mention a certain Burchard, Vidame of Strasbourg, between 1182 and 1194.[9] It seems probable that all these documents refer to the same Burchard, who produced the text of his journey to Egypt and Syria in 1175.

Burchard's diplomatic embassy was not an isolated event, but rather part of ongoing diplomacy between the Frederick and Saladin. The *Annales colonienses maximi* tell of the arrival, in 1173, of legates sent by the "King of Babylon" to the emperor.[10] By "King of Babylon," the annalist no doubt means Saladin, master of Egypt since the death of his uncle Shirkûh in 1169 and the abolition of the Fatimid Caliphate in 1171. Babylon was the name of the old Roman fortress at Cairo and the name many medieval authors used to refer to the Egyptian capital. What was the purpose of this embassy, at a time when Saladin was trying to affirm his power against Nûr al-Dîn, when he made frequent razzias against the Kingdom of Jerusalem, and when he tried to establish more solid commercial relations with the Italian maritime republics? Did Saladin imagine an alliance against a common enemy, perhaps Sicily, whose king, William II, was preparing a raid against Alexandria (this attack took place the following year, 1174)? The annalist tells us nothing; he simply affirms that the "king of Babylon" proposed a matrimonial alliance between his son and the daughter of the emperor and that he promised to convert to Christianity along with his son and all his people and to release all his Christian captives. The annalist also says (and this is more plausible) that the emperor retained the legates many months, having them visit different cities, and that they departed from Ratisbon on the Feast of St. John the following year (June 24, 1174).[11] Whatever the real purpose of this embassy, when the legates returned to Egypt the situation had changed: Nûr al-Dîn had died on May 15, 1174, and on July 28 the Sicilians arrived at Alexandria and besieged it; four days later, the Sicilians were routed by the Alexandrians and they quickly fled.

It is most probably in order to pursue the negotiations with the Egyptians that Frederick sent Burchard to see Saladin the following year. Burchard says that he departed from Genoa on September 9 ("VII. idus Septembris"), 1175. Frederick was in Italy in September 1175, bogged down in negotiations with Pope Alexander III and the Lombard League concerning the terms of the Peace of Montebello. Burchard landed at Alexandria and then traveled to "Babylon," Cairo. This itinerary is quite logical: Burchard took the most direct route, that frequented by Genoese merchants, to reach the capital of the Egyptian sultan. But Saladin was not in Cairo: he had left Egypt in October 1174 in order to take possession of the inheritance of Nûr al-Dîn in Syria.[12] Burchard then went to Damascus, no doubt accompanied by an Egyptian escort party; he says that this trip across the desert took twenty days and that he passed through a region "once inhabited by Christians . . . but now by Saracens." Chronicler Arnold of Lübeck identifies this region as *Busserintinum* (Busrâ), indeed a common stop on the itinerary of those travelers going from Egypt to Syria, if they sought to go around the Kingdom of Jerusalem.[13] Burchard subsequently gives a description of Damascus and of the Marian sanctuary of Saydnâyâ (to which we shall return). He then writes of the Assassins, who made quite an impression on him largely, no doubt, because of their two attempts to assassinate Saladin in January 1175 and in May or June 1176. He tells us very little about his return to Egypt, indicating only the number of days that it took him to go from Damascus to Tiberias, to Acre, Jerusalem, Ascalon, and Cairo. He gives no description of these places, except for a brief portrait of Ascalon. It is worth noting that Saladin also returned from Syria to Egypt via the Kingdom of Jerusalem in 1176.[14] The sultan and the imperial ambassador may well have traveled together. In any case, Burchard then provides his reader with a rambling discussion of the sexual mores and religious rites of the Saracens of Cairo; on this note, his text comes to an abrupt halt, without saying anything about his return to Europe.

Burchard's diplomatic mission is quite plausible: it would be a logical follow-up to the visit of the Egyptian embassy to Frederick. The itinerary is also credible, as we have seen, given what we know about Saladin's movements in this period. Did this embassy in fact take place? I have found no documents, Egyptian or imperial, that confirm it. Yet this lack of documentation is hardly surprising. It seems quite implausible that Burchard's mission is a mere invention of the author of the *Itinerarirum*. Burchard probably did go to Egypt and Syria in 1175 and 1176.

This does not necessarily mean that Burchard wrote the *Itinerarium* in its extant version, which exists in three manuscripts, one from the thirteenth century and two from the fourteenth.[15] Arnold de Lübeck became abbot of the new monastery of St. John the Evangelist in Lübeck in 1177. Continuator of Helmhold's *Chronica Slavorum*, Arnold narrates events from the years 1171–1209. He incorporates Burchard's text, with a few minor modifications, into his *Chronica Slavorum*, in the midst of the events of the year 1207, no doubt the year that he discovered Burchard's text.[16] The *Itinerarium* is subsequently used and cited by a number of medieval authors, such as the chronicler Jacques de Vitry and various pilgrims who insert Burchard's descriptions into the narratives of their own travels (real or fictive), beginning with a certain Thietmar who traveled to Jerusalem and Saydnâyâ in 1217.

But what is at first glance most puzzling about this text is that it says nothing at all about Burchard's diplomacy. It is only in the incipit that any mention at all is made of Burchard, the emperor Frederick, and the diplomatic mission to the "King of Babylon." Saladin's name appears nowhere; nor do we find the names of any of his predecessors, be they Fatimids in Egypt or Zengids in Syria. Burchard says nothing of the rapid rise to power of Nûr al-Dîn or of his successor Saladin, which had so troubled Latin writers such as William of Tyre; nothing, either, about the Kingdom of Jerusalem or the other Latin principalities in the Orient. On the contrary, Burchard portrays a rather static Orient, where harmony reigns between Saracens, Christians, and Jews. Only once, when he briefly describes lands south of Damascus devastated by "Saracens," does he hint at the existence of military conflict. Even when he describes the infamous Assassins, he presents them more as an ethnographic curiosity than as a real threat to peace; he does not seem to imagine that the machinations of the *veteres promontani* could destabilize the region.

With its descriptions of travels, of the sea and the desert, its lists of churches and especially its long passages devoted to the Marian sanctuaries of Matariyya and Saydnâyâ, this text seems closer to a pilgrimage narrative than a diplomatic dispatch. It is not the least bit surprising that this emissary should be silent about the diplomatic negotiations he participated in. As a traveler, pilgrim, and astute observer, Burchard penned a lively testimony of his voyage and of the holy sites he visited. But even if we consider the *Itinerarium* as a pilgrimage narrative, it remains unusual: Burchard describes only the churches and sacred sites that he saw in Muslim territory; he insists in particular on the two sites associated with the Virgin Mary. He says not a word about Jerusalem, principal goal of every European pilgrim, nor of any of the sites surrounding the holy city. This difference is striking if we compare Burchard's text with those of later pilgrims who used it, for whom Matariyya and Saydnâyâ become minor sanctuaries in the spiritual orbit of Jerusalem.

The Harmony between Saracens and Christians, According to the *Itinerarium*

The opening of the *Itinerarium* resembles the beginning of a pilgrimage narrative, containing a mix of ethnogeographic curiosities and an enumeration of churches, relics, and holy sites. Burchard relates that he set sail from Genoa and stopped in Corsica, Sardinia, and Sicily (he describes the flora, fauna, and the inhabitants of these islands); we learn of the fish of the Mediterranean and of the famous lighthouse of Alexandria, which he saw as he approached the African coast. He describes Alexandria as an "eminent city, adorned with edifices and with a great multitude of men, inhabited by Saracens, Jews and Christians, under the rule of the king of Babylon."[17] In his description of this flourishing city, he insists in particular on the harmony that reigns between the three religious communities. "In Alexandria, everyone freely follows his religion. In this city there are many Christian churches." He describes a number of these churches, in particular that devoted to Saint Mark the Evangelist.[18]

Elsewhere in Egypt, the situation is the same: "Everywhere in Egypt, Christians live in the cities; they pay a tribute to the king of Babylon, and almost every city has a Christian church. These men are miserable and live in great poverty."[19] This final sentence introduces a discordant note, in contradistinction to the rather idyllic *convivencia* that reigns elsewhere. Burchard affirms, for example, that in Cairo "Saracens, Jews and Christians live; each nation follows its own law and there are many Christian churches in this city."[20] He presents Damascus in the same way: "Damascus is a very noble city. The city and its surroundings are irrigated by the will of men; it is like a veritable terrestrial paradise, and there are many Christian churches. Near Damascus an excellent wine is produced. Damascus is a very healthy city and contains numerous elderly people."[21]

It is in Burchard's description of the Marian sanctuaries of Egypt and Syria that *convivencia* becomes common devotion. Let us first look at Matariyya, near Cairo. Burchard gives the following description:

> This garden has a spring which irrigates it; it cannot be irrigated from any other spring. Note that balsam grows nowhere else than in this place. The blessed Virgin and our Savior came here when they were fleeing Herod's persecution. She stayed there a certain time and washed her son's diapers (necessary on account of his human nature) in the above-mentioned spring. Because of this, this spring is up to our day the object of veneration on the part of the Saracens: they bring incense and candles and wash in the spring. During Epiphany, a great multitude of people come from the surrounding area and wash with this water.[22]

Indeed, beginning in the seventh century, Coptic texts associate Matariyya with the Holy Family, said to have stopped at the spring during the flight into Egypt. By the twelfth century, it is an important and well-established pilgrimage site. Coptic author Abû al-Makârim gives a detailed description of the site; he evokes the construction (c. 1155) of a church on the site and describes the cultivation of the balsam and the production of balm from it.[23] He affirms that "the emissaries of the Greeks, the Franks, the Ethiopians, and the Nubians have the custom, when they come to the Gate [the court of the caliph] to come to Matariyya, to set up altars for their celebrations, and to take communion after having bathed in this water."[24] For Abû al-Makârim as for Burchard, the Virgin's devotees at Matariyya are a diverse group coming from as far afield as Ethiopia and Europe. But Burchard particularly insists on the fact that Muslims join the Christians in these festivities, whereas for Abû al-Makârim, it is a purely Christian gathering. Burchard presents Matariyya as a testimony to the warm relations between Muslims and Christians in the lands of the "sultan of Babylon." This insistence on the interconfessional nature of the Virgin's cult at Matariyya is found in the accounts of other European pilgrims during the thirteenth and fourteenth centuries (some of them reiterate Burchard's description).

After his description of Matariyya, Burchard describes a palm tree that is also an object of devotion to the Virgin Mary for Christians and Muslims:

> Moreover, near Cairo is a very ancient and very tall palm tree, which bowed down before the blessed Virgin when she passed that way with our Savior: the tree let her pick its dates and then straightened itself up. The Saracens of the time saw this and, jealous of the Virgin, chopped up the tree. The following night, the tree was found erect and solid, and today one can still see its scars. The Saracens venerate this tree still; they illuminate it every night by lighting candles. There are many other places where the Virgin stayed in Egypt which are venerated by the Christians and the Saracens.[25]

The date palm that shows its reverence to the Holy Family and feeds it corresponds to a well-know topos in hagiography: nature recognizes its Creator and serves Him. For Muslims, this tree has a Qur'ânic analogue: the date palm under which Maryam (Mary) gave birth to Isa (Jesus) and which also furnished dates miraculously.[26] For Burchard, the date palm's devotion provoked the jealously and anger of the "Saracens of the time"; here (as often in the Middle Ages) the term "Saracen" can be used broadly to designate any non-Christian and non-Jewish person—even from before the rise of Islam.[27] The impiety of these early "Saracens" is in contrast with the pious devotion of the modern "Saracens" who, the author affirms, venerate the tree by lighting candles.

This story corresponds to classic hagiographical practice. The legend serves to sanctify the site and to justify the cult practiced there. The proof of the sanctity of Mary and Jesus (and in consequence of the venerated site) is double: the date palm bows down before Jesus and his mother, then is miraculously restored after its destruction at the hands of impious "Saracens," whose hostility the first miracle did not lessen. In accordance to the standard hagiographical topoi in such narrations, the second miracle should normally have resulted in either a divine punishment of the Saracens who chopped down the tree or, as here, in the confirmation of the first miracle—which normally leads the infidels to convert. Yet here, if we can speak at all of conversion, it is a partial conversion: the Saracens learn to venerate the Virgin at the site of the double miracle, but they do so while remaining "Saracens," not in converting to Christianity. By this anachronistic presentation that exploits the ambiguous nature of the term *Saracen*, Burchard makes the miracle into a founding legend of the harmony between Christians and "Saracens"; this harmony is nothing less than the product of a miracle performed by Jesus and his mother during their stay in Egypt.

We find the same image of common devotion to the Virgin in Burchard's description of the sanctuary of Saydnâyâ:

> Four miles from Damascus is a site in the mountains called Saydnâyâ, inhabited by Christians. On a rock there is a church dedicated to the Virgin, in which twelve virgin nuns and eight monks sedulously serve God and the Virgin. In this church, I saw a wooden tablet that measured a cubit in length and half a cubit in width; it was placed behind the altar in the wall of the sanctuary, in a window, enclosed by an iron grate. On this tablet was a resplendent image of the blessed Virgin, but now, miraculous to say, the image on the wood has incarnated and from it issues continuously perfumed oil, redolent of balsam. Many Christians, Saracens, and Jews suffering from diverse illnesses have been cured by this oil. This oil never diminishes, even if one takes great quantities of it. No one dares touch this tablet, but all may look at it. This oil is carefully conserved by a Christian religious and it augments. When it is taken in conjunction with masses in honor of the Holy Virgin, beyond any doubt one obtains the cure that one wishes. During the feast of the Assumption of the Virgin and during the feast of her birth, all the Saracens of this province come to this place, together with the Christians, to pray. And the Saracens offer

> their ceremonies with great devotion. This painting was first made in Constantinople and painted in honor of the Blessed Virgin and subsequently taken from there to Jerusalem by a certain patriarch. At that time a certain abbess from this place went to Jerusalem to pray and, having obtained the painting with the permission of the patriarch, full of joy she brought it back with her and gave it to the above-mentioned church. This was in the year 870 of the Lord's incarnation. But after that, the holy oil started issuing forth for a long time.[28]

At Saydnâyâ the object of veneration is an icon, a painted wooden tablet representing the Virgin; the image has become "incarnated" and produces oil that smells of balsam (here again, balsam is associated with the Virgin). Many other texts contemporary to Burchard's (in Arabic and in Latin) confirm the importance of this site and concur in general with his description; some give a more elaborate and miraculous story to explain the arrival of the icon. We also know that Knights Templar frequented this sanctuary as early as 1186 and brought back the precious oil to Europe.[29]

As with the Egyptian sites, these other texts allow us to confirm the interconfessional nature of the devotion to the Virgin at Saydnâyâ. Here again, it is Burchard who particularly emphasizes this aspect of her cult. He affirms that, thanks to this miraculous oil, numerous devotees—Christians, Muslims, and Jews—obtained cures for different diseases. Burchard's Virgin is an ecumenical saint who makes no fine theological distinctions among her devotees. The local Saracens participate in the Christian festivals of the Nativity and the Assumption of the Virgin and offer her "their ceremonies with great devotion." Throughout his narration, and in particular in his descriptions of the Marian sanctuaries, Burchard affirms that Saracens, Christians, and even Jews are united in their devotion to Mary. She grants miracles to all her faithful, apparently showing no preference for the Christians.

This is not to say that Burchard ignores or minimizes the ritual and doctrinal differences between Christianity and Islam. On the contrary, he presents them succinctly and on the whole accurately. For example, just after his description of the pious devotion of the "Saracens" to the Virgin Mary at Matariyya and just before his description of the date palm that miraculously succored her, Burchard offers the following explanation to his readers:

> The Saracens believe that the blessed Virgin conceived Jesus Christ with an angel, that she gave birth, and that she subsequently remained a Virgin. They say that this son of the Virgin was a great prophet and

> that he was miraculously borne off into the heavens, body and soul; they celebrate the day of his nativity, but they deny that he is son of God and that he was baptized, crucified, that he died and was buried. They affirm that it is they who follow the law of Christ and the apostles because they practice circumcision, whereas we do not. They say that the apostles were also prophets, and they venerate many martyrs and confessors.[30]

This passage is remarkably free of the polemical tone that most Christian authors employ when describing Muslim Christology. Burchard relates, briefly and more or less accurately, Muslim doctrine concerning Jesus and his mother: Mary's virginity, the miraculous conception and birth of Jesus, a "great prophet." Burchard knows that Muslims reject the incarnation, baptism, crucifixion, and resurrection of Jesus. He even recognizes that Muslims claim to follow the example of the apostles more closely than do the Christians, since the Muslims, unlike the European Christians, are circumcised. What is particularly surprising here is that Burchard does not propose either any refutation of these Muslim beliefs or any defense of Christian belief or practices. Would Burchard's reader come away with the impression that the religion of the "Saracens" is as legitimate as that of the Christians? Such an impression could only be reinforced by the fact that the Virgin performs miracles for her Saracen devotees.

At the close of his description of Egypt, à propos of nothing, Burchard presents his reader with a description of the paradise awaiting the Muslims:

> The Saracens believe that there is a terrestrial Paradise where they will go after this life. There, they say, there are four rivers: one of wine, a second one of milk, a third of honey, and a fourth one of water. They believe that all sorts of fruits grow there and that they will be able to eat and drink as much as they please and that each day, for the sake of their enjoyment, they will be able to lie with a new virgin. And if one of them is killed by a Christian during a battle, he thinks only of the paradise where ten virgins await him. But concerning these women, who according to them are corrupted every day, they were not able to answer my questions.[31]

Burchard does not hesitate to show his skepticism concerning these beliefs, but this is as close as he comes to criticizing Islam. This is all the more striking if we bear in mind the invectives that most Latin authors used when describing the Muslim paradise.[32] But Burchard simply changes the subject, returning to the enumeration of the plants and birds of Egypt.

At the very end of his *Itinerarium* Burchard gives a few last details concerning the habits and beliefs of the Saracens of Cairo:

> Close to Cairo, there is a public brothel of sodomites [or of prostitutes]. The Saracens' women go out only veiled and covered with cloth; they never enter into their temples. They are carefully guarded by eunuchs, because the great ladies never leave their houses without the permission of their lords. Without his permission, no one dares enter to see these women, not even their brothers or others close to them, men or women. The men go to the temple five times a day and use criers instead of bells. Every hour, the Saracen religious wash with water, from head to foot, and they go pray. They never pray without piety, from what I hear. They believe in God creator of all things, and they say that Muhammad was a prophet and the author of their law. They venerate him in their pilgrimages. They also venerate the authors of the other laws. Each Saracen may have seven legitimate wives at a time; among them, he shares his resources according to the stipulations of each marriage contract. Moreover, he may licitly sin with all his servants and slave-girls, as if it were not a sin. If one of these slaves becomes pregnant, she immediately becomes free. And he may divide his inheritance as he sees fit between the children born to his free wives or his slaves. Many Saracens don't even have one wife. They may have less than seven wives, but not more, except for the concubines, as we said.[33]

This paragraph proffers a somewhat haphazard catalogue of observations on the rituals, social practices, sexual mores, and laws concerning marriage and inheritance. A mixture of accurate and inaccurate information: four, not seven, is the number of lawful spouses for a Muslim. Here again, Burchard presents key elements of Muslim practice (veneration of Muhammad as a prophet, ablutions and prayers, pilgrimage) without the slightest criticism. He does not hesitate, on the other hand, to note his disapproval of their sexual habits: the Muslim sins with impunity when he sleeps with his slaves. But this disapproval is milder than that of anti-Muslim polemicists, and he insists that such behavior implicates only a part of the population; he underlines the chastity of Muslim men of religion, who have no wives.

Immediately after this passage, Burchard's text (as it is preserved in the three extant manuscripts) closes abruptly with this sentence: "May they live and rule with the Devil for all eternity."[34] This invective, which contradicts what had preceded, could well be the addition of a scribe; it is at any rate absent from Arnold's version, where we find, in conclusion, a long reflection on the "immense clemency of the Redeemer," Who permits the infidels to enjoy all the joys of earthly life.[35] It is impossible to know if this conclusion was penned by Burchard (who would have tried in this way to insert his observations into a more standard vision of Christian history) or by Arnold (who would thus express the reflections that Burchard's text inspired in him).

What was the purpose of this unusual text? What was its audience? Burchard tells us nothing: he offers no prologue and no conclusion to his *Itinerary*. This reinforces the impression that this text is poorly organized and incomplete. Perhaps Burchard had intended to rework it into a more structured text, a text that he perhaps never completed or that, in any case, has not survived. The *Itinerary* reflects its author's curiosity, his acute gift of observation, and his open-mindedness. We see this most clearly in his descriptions of Muslim rites and beliefs, particularly in his portrait of Muslim devotion to the Virgin Mary, devotion that brings together Muslims and Christians. If this text indeed is the product of Burchard's diplomatic mission from Frederick Barbarossa to Saladin, this positive image of Islam corresponds to diplomatic purpose of his embassy, if we presume that the goal of Burchard's embassy was to forge an alliance or at least a treaty between emperor and sultan. If the "Saracens" are so pious, so devout to the Virgin, if they allow Christians to freely practice their religion, what could be more natural than to seek a peaceful alliance with them? Just as other Latin authors denigrated Islam and its prophet to justify wars of conquest against Muslims, Burchard paints a glowing picture of Muslim-Christian harmony to justify peace with Saladin. If the Virgin herself bestows the grace of miracles on the Saracens, who are we to consider them enemies of her Son?

∴ 8 ∴

Saracen Philosophers Secretly Deride Islam

The Dominican Giordano da Pisa (1260–1311), in one of the sermons of his *Quaresimale fiorentino*, tries to convince his listeners that all wise men, in all places and times, have rejected earthly delights and sought out intellectual and spiritual pleasures. In the course of his sermon, he makes the following remarks:

> Of all of the philosophers who were great philosophers, I mean those who were right and important philosophers, none of them could love the things of the world; they damned the law of the Saracens as it was, since they [the Saracens] look to earthly delights. And if one were to ask: "Are there not philosophers among them?" I answer that there were: Avicenna was a Saracen and was a philosopher, and he mocked their law and ridiculed it. And if there is any philosopher or great wise man, they themselves make fun of their own law and mock it.[1]

For Giordano, Avicenna (Ibn Sînâ) was not a true Muslim. Because he was a philosopher, he saw through Muslim law and ridiculed it. What makes the "Saracen law" irrational, for Giordano, is its emphasis on "earthly delights": Giordano no doubt has in mind (in the tradition of medieval Christian polemics against Islam) Muslim polygamy and in particular Muslim notions of a paradise replete with eating, drinking, and lovemaking. True wise men can only despise such pleasures, Giordano asserts, and thus they deride Muslim law.

There are several interesting things about this passage. First, the Florentine Dominican makes this point not in a work of anti-Muslim polemics, or even a sermon about the errors of the religious Other, but in a sermon stressing how wise men reject the pleasures of this world (a familiar trope not only in Christianity but also of course in stoic and neoplatonic philosophy, not to mention Sufism). He is anticipating a counterargument from his listeners who may know (he seems to think) two important facts: Muslims "look to earthly delights" and many wise men (philosophers and scientists) are Muslims. Giordano seeks to affirm the first of these ideas and to vigorously deny the second. In order to do so, he maintains that Muslim philosophers are in fact not really Muslims—that they reject and deride their own law. He cites Avicenna as the best known of these philosophers.

We do not have to look far to see where Giordano got these ideas: from Riccoldo da Montecroce, a Dominican at the same convent in Florence, who had spent years in Baghdad learning Arabic, studying the Qur'ân, and vainly trying to convert Muslims. We will look at Riccoldo's arguments at the end of this chapter. What interests me now is that Giordano felt a need to include this in his sermon: clearly the existence of Muslim philosophers and scientists, and their imperviousness to the "rational" polemics of Dominican missionaries like Riccoldo, rankled. In order for the Christian to affirm that his religion is "rational," Islam (and Judaism) must be demonstrably "irrational"—and therefore he could not acknowledge the existence of philosophical minds among their adherents.

This chapter explores how several twelfth- and thirteenth-century authors dealt with what became a major intellectual problem: could one affirm (or even try to prove) the rationality of Christianity? If so, why do so many apparently rational and learned people reject its truth? These two centuries saw a tremendous flow of scientific and philosophical texts from Arab to Latin. Those who read and admired these texts knew that their authors were not Christian. They also struggled to believe that their own Christian religion was rational. Out of this struggle came the need to present the religious other, Jew and Muslim, as irrational.

This problem is, of course, not unique to Christianity, nor is it limited to the twelfth and thirteenth centuries. Jews, Christians, and Muslims have often had to contend with the conflicting claims of reason and revelation, grappling with the difficult relations between scripture and classical philosophy and science and between rival religious traditions. The Bible and Qur'ân both contain passages that describe God in anthropomorphic terms: references to God's hand and throne, to his walking, talking, or expressing human emotions or needs. God does not really have a hand, so when the

Qur'ân speaks of "God's hand," it is in fact, for theologian Fakhr al-Dîn al-Râzî (born c. 1150), referring to "God's protection," just as Qur'ânic references to God's look refer to divine providence.[2] Commentators of Bible and Qur'ân generally affirmed that such passages were to be understood allegorically, while polemicists attacked the anthropomorphic passages in rival scriptures to show how erroneous those scriptures were.[3]

While Qur'ân commentators have almost unanimously agreed that Qur'ânic passages that attribute anthropomorphic features to God should be interpreted allegorically, they were far from unanimous on how to interpret the descriptions of the physical delights that the Qur'ân promises to the faithful in the next world.[4] Both Christianity and Islam assert that we are to resurrect with our bodies at the end of time, and for both, the punishments of the damned in hell are quite physical: "Flames of fire shall be lashed at you, and molten brass. There shall be none to help you" (Qur'ân, Sûra 55). Yet the Qur'ân, unlike most Christian texts, lavishes more description on the joys of heaven than on the torments of hell, and they are joys that ascetically minded Christians would dare not hope for in the Hereafter:

> But for those that fear the majesty of their Lord there are two gardens planted with shady trees. Which of your Lord's blessings would you deny?
>
> Each is watered by a flowing spring. Which of your Lord's blessings would you deny?
>
> Each bears every kind of fruit in pairs. Which of your Lord's blessings would you deny?
>
> They shall recline on couches lined with thick brocade, and within their reach will hang the fruits of both gardens. Which of your Lord's blessings would you deny?
>
> They shall dwell with bashful virgins whom neither man nor jinnee will have touched before. Which of your Lord's blessings would you deny?
>
> Virgins as fair as corals and rubies. Which of your Lord's blessings would you deny?
>
> Shall the reward of goodness be anything but good? Which of your Lord's blessings would you deny? (Qur'ân 55)

Various hadîths elaborate on these descriptions, describing in detail the physical and spiritual delights of the next world. For most Muslim exegetes, the resurrection of the body and the bodily pleasures of heaven promised in the Qur'ân are literally true. For others, such pleasures are poetic metaphors, meant to describe the ineffable delights of heaven in earthly language.[5]

This became a particularly thorny problem for theologians enthralled by the traditions of Greek philosophy. In the Neoplatonic tradition, the soul is prisoner to the body, and the wise man spends his life working to free his soul from the foul, earthbound tendencies of the flesh. The sage thus regards separation of the soul from the body at death as a welcome liberation. What then is he to make of the resurrection of the body at the end of time, a doctrine central both to Islam and to Christianity? At best it is an embarrassing doctrinal anomaly that has to be explained away, at worst a degradation, a new captivity imposed upon the soul. Moreover, should the wise man's soul, which had struggled to liberate itself from bodily cares and pleasures during life, after life be plunged into an orgy of eating, drinking, and lovemaking as its reward?

Avicenna was not the first Muslim philosopher to grapple with this problem, but his views were best known and most influential for later Muslim thinkers and for European Christians. Avicenna is careful not to flatly deny the literal truth of the Qur'ânic descriptions of heavenly delights, yet in some of his works he suggests that they are meant to present heaven's ineffable pleasures in terms understandable to the common people; the sage must seek to comprehend the truth behind this allegory. In his *Risâlat adhawiyya fi amr al-ma'âd* (Letter concerning the return), he affirms, "Opposed to the true happiness of man is the existence of his soul in the body, and . . . corporeal pleasures are different from true pleasures, and to return to the body would be a punishment for the soul."[6] In a number of his works, Avicenna develops physical and metaphysical arguments for the inappropriateness and impossibility of bodily resurrection.[7]

But this does not, for Avicenna, compromise the message of the Qur'ân, which he praises for its efficacy rather than for its literal truth. Prophets need to promise physical pleasure in heaven in order to mobilize the masses in the cause of the Supreme Good. Avicenna criticizes Christianity for its logical inconsistency, teaching that the bodies of the faithful will resurrect but that they will only experience spiritual and not bodily pleasures. This is not only illogical but inefficacious. Since Christianity promises only spiritual awards to its faithful, is it any wonder that it has not proved as able as Islam to rally the masses?[8] Avicenna's notions are based on a distinction between an enlightened elite (*khâssah*) and the unenlightened masses (*'âmmah*). For the former, as he explains in his *Kitâb al-Najât* (Book of salvation from error, c. 1030), the supreme joy in paradise will be the union of the individual soul with the Active Intellect and the Universal Intellect through which Divine Light may be contemplated. The souls of the latter, of those who have respected God's laws but are incapable of sublime intellectual pleasures, will experience pleasures of the imagination, which the Qur'ân presents as sensual pleasures. These pleasures experienced through the imaginative powers of the soul will be so intense that those who benefit from them will indeed believe that they are actually experiencing bodily pleasures, the only type of pleasures they are capable of comprehending and experiencing. By this compromise, Avicenna has preserved the integrity of the Qur'ânic descriptions and the veracity of the Neoplatonic ascetic tradition.[9]

Such a compromise did not win the approval of Abû Hâmid b. Muhammad b. Muhammad al-Tûsî al-Ghazâlî (1058–1111), a prominent theologian and religious reformer. In his *al-Durra al-Fâkhira* (*The Precious Pearl*), al-Ghazâlî narrates the events that await each soul from the hour of its death to that of its final resurrection and reward or punishment. This narration, which is didactic and devotional rather than theological or discursive, closely follows traditional sources.[10] He similarly affirms the return of the soul to the body at resurrection in his *Iqtisâd fî al-`itiqâd,* where he asserts that the purpose of philosophical explanations of such phenomena is to "cure the doubters of their doubts and to refute the negation of the negators."[11] Al-Ghazâlî's conservative and traditional conception of the afterlife is in stark contrast to Avicenna's. In his *Maqâsid al-falâsifa* (*Intentions of the Philosophers*), al-Ghazâlî provides a summary, without criticism, of the main doctrines of the philosophers. This text served as a sort of preamble to his *Tahâfut al-falâsifa* (*Incoherence of the Philosophers*), in which he seeks to demonstrate that philosophical arguments in the realm of metaphysics lack the solidity and assurance of their arguments in the realms of logic and the physical sciences; certainty in this domain can only be had through revelation. While al-Ghazâlî's *Tahâfut* has been presented by some scholars as an attempt to refute Avicenna, Jules Janssens has shown that there is little evidence for this and that his target seems rather to be the ancient philosophers and their more uncritical Muslim followers. While al-Ghazâlî indeed criticizes some of Avicenna's ideas (notably his reservations about bodily resurrection), on the whole both thinkers present an Islamified philosophy in which reason is an essential but imperfect tool and in which prophetic revelation is the key to certainty for fundamental religious doctrines. Rather than an attack on Avicenna's thought, the *Tahâfut* could be seen as al-Ghazâlî's attempt to continue and perfect the work of his illustrious predecessor.[12] He seeks to show the lack of certainty of philosophers' speculations on metaphysics; certainty in such matters can only be attained through prophetic revelation. Moreover, philosophers have been led into three fundamental errors, as al-Ghazâlî explains in his conclusion:

> If someone says: "You have explained the doctrines of these [philosophers]; do you then say conclusively that they are infidels and that the killing of those who uphold their beliefs is obligatory?" we say:
>
> Pronouncing them infidels is necessary in three questions. One of them is the question of the world's pre-eternity and their statement that all substances are pre-eternal. The second is their statement that God's knowledge does not encompass the temporal particulars among individual [existents]. The third is their denial of the resurrection of bodies and their assembly at the Day of Judgment.
>
> These three doctrines do not agree with Islam in any respect. The one who believes them believes that prophets utter falsehoods and that they said whatever they have said by way of [promoting common] utility, to give examples and explanation to the multitudes of created mankind. This is manifest infidelity which none of the Islamic sects have believed.[13]

Al-Ghazâlî categorically rejects Avicenna's allegorical interpretation of the bodily resurrection and physical rewards and punishments promised in the Qur'ân. Whereas Qur'ânic passages that refer to God's hand or to God walking must be understood allegorically since they are literally impossible (since God is incorporeal), the same is not true of the passages involving future bodily punishments and rewards in the next life: since God is capable of resurrecting the body and since the Qur'ân affirms that he will do so, the text must be understood as literally true. Without citing Avicenna by name, al-Ghazâlî gives two arguments against his ideas:

> One is that the anthropomorphic utterances are amenable to interpretation in accordance with the customary practice of the Arabs in using metaphor. But what has come down [in the law] describing paradise and the fire and the detailing of these states has attained a degree [of explicit statement] that does not [render it] subject to metaphorical interpretation. Nothing, then, would remain but to take [such utterances] as obfuscation by making one imagine what is contrary to truth for the benefit of creatures. But this is what the position of prophethood is sanctified high above.

> The second is that rational proofs have shown the impossibility of [attributing] place, direction, visage, physical hand, physical eye, the possibility of transfer, and rest to God, praise be to Him. Metaphorical interpretation [here] is obligatory through rational proofs. What He has promised in the hereafter, however, is not impossible in terms of the power of God, exalted be He. Hence, one must follow the apparent [literal meaning of the revealed] speech—indeed, according to its signification, which is explicit.[14]

Al-Ghazâlî goes on in great detail to refute arguments that various philosophers had used to show the impossibility of bodily resurrection. His *Maqâsid al-falâsifa* was translated into Latin in Spain in the mid-twelfth century and was widely read in scholastic circles throughout Europe. His *Tahâfut al-falâsifa* was not known, however, to Latin readers, who as a result often portrayed al-Ghazâlî as an uncritical follower of Avicenna.[15] In the 1170s, Ibn Rushd (known to the West as Averroes), composed a long refutation of al-Ghazâlî's *Tahâfut al-falâsifa*, entitled the *Tahâfut al-Tahâfut* (*Incoherence of the Incoherence*). Robert of Anjou, king of Naples, commissioned a Latin translation of Averroes's text, completed in 1328. This translation was little known, and it is primarily those who could read Arabic who had access to al-Ghazâlî's *Tahâfut* and to Averroes's refutation.[16] Meanwhile, throughout the twelfth and thirteenth centuries, several of Avicenna's works, in philosophy, theology, and medicine, were translated into Latin and were widely read in scholastic circles.[17]

During Averroes's lifetime these philosophical and theological works of Muslim authors began to have a considerable impact on Latin Europe. In the midst of a broad revival of learning and scholarship commonly referred to as the "Renaissance of the Twelfth Century," scores of texts in philosophy and the sciences were translated from Arabic to Latin.[18] The impact of this transmission of texts and ideas was to be tremendous: the new Arabic texts were championed by a large segment of the emerging clerical elite, although some looked on in alarm at the growing vogue for the new Arabic texts.[19]

Peter of Cluny is ambivalent about the impact of this Arabic learning on Christian Europeans. We have seen in chapter 4 how, during a trip to Castile in 1142–43, Peter assembled a team of translators whom he commissioned to produce a full, annotated Latin version of the Koran, along with translations of other Arab texts on Islam, and how he composed two anti-Islamic tracts: the *Summa totius haeresis Saracenorum* and the *Contra sectam siue haeresim Saracenorum*. He addressed the *Contra sectam* (1156) to a fictitious Muslim audience, although in his preface he affirms that even if his treatise is never translated into Arabic, it will be useful to "cure the hidden cogitations of some of our people, thoughts by which they could be led into evil if they think that there is some piety in those impious people and think that some truth is to be found with the ministers of lies."[20] In other words, if some Latin Christians admire Muslims and think their religion may be legitimate, this tract is meant to show how wrong they are. Peter does not say which Christians he has in mind, but it is most probably those in Spain with regular contact with Muslims, particularly those who read and admire the philosophical and scientific works of Muslim thinkers. In the same way, he had sought in an earlier work of polemics against Petrobrusian heretics to combat "secret thoughts of certain Catholics" who might be convinced by some of the heretics' arguments.[21]

Peter of Cluny knew little if anything about the debates between Avicenna and al-Ghazâlî about bodily resurrection. He was, however, aware that the Arabs were widely renowned for their learning. He had also read the Qur'ân in Robert of Ketton's Latin translation and presented the Qur'ân's passages about Moses and Jesus, about the torments of hell and the carnal pleasures of paradise. Peter holds Muhammad's life—in particular his polygamy—up to opprobrium. Mixing good and evil, sublime and ridiculous, Muhammad created a monstrous cult, similar to the monster described by Horace as having a human head, a horse's neck, and feathers.[22] Yet if Muslim law is as irrational and ridiculous as Peter presents it, how does one account for the fact, as Peter himself admits, that the Arabs are "not only rational by nature, but logical in temperament and training," that they are "learned in worldly knowledge"? Peter thinks he has found the answer:

> Hear, I say, how amazing it is, if indeed it is true, what I have heard: that no one wishing to act against your ancestral laws, no one wishing to argue against the rites transmitted to you by the same man I mentioned earlier (your prophet) will dare do so. And not only have I heard that no one dares listen to this, but that as soon as one begins to say [such things] you oppose him with stones or swords or some other kind of death. This precept of your law has become known from your East to our West.[23]

These Arab philosophers use their reason to comprehend nature. Do they not know that this nature, the highest object of the search for truth, asks Peter, the uncreated creator, the ultimate substance or essence, is God?[24] Should they not use their reason to investigate the truth concerning God?

The law prohibiting religious dispute is an "infernal counsel," a law fit for irrational sheep, not rational men. Instead of reaching for your swords or stones when a Christian comes to preach the Gospels, Peter says, follow rather the example of Christians who dispute with Jews, listening patiently to their arguments and responding wisely.

If he can only convince the philosophically minded Saracens to hear him out, Peter seems to think, he can rationally prove to them the superiority of Christianity. What is irrational about Muslim law? Much of it is that it contradicts itself and contradicts the Bible. Much of it, too, is sexual. Muslim polygamy, divorce law, sex in heaven—all of this is "irrational" for Peter for the same reasons it is irrational 150 years later for Giordano da Pisa. The "rational" argumentation that Peter of Cluny presents to his putative Muslim audience in favor of Christianity is based not on philosophy or science but on scripture. He uses selected passages from the Qur'ân that praise the Gospels and Torah to affirm that Muslims should accept the authority of the Bible and reject that of the Qur'ân. He imagines that the Saracen sages who have heard him out will be ready to accept his biblical proofs of the superiority of Christianity.

Ramon Martí

Dominican friar Ramon Martí (d. 1285) was much more knowledgeable about Islam than Peter of Cluny. Martí was part of the team of Dominican missionaries under the guidance of former Dominican master general Ramon de Penyafort. In 1250, the Dominican provincial chapter of Toledo established a school of Arabic for eight of its friars, including Ramon Martí. Martí was not only educated in Arabic and Hebrew language but he also studied the Talmud and works of Arabic philosophy: al-Ghazâlî, Avicenna, al-Râzî, others. Unlike most of his Latin contemporaries, he is aware of al-Ghazâlî's attack on the philosophers and of Averroes's refutation of al-Ghazâlî.[25] Martí became the most prolific writer of this team of missionaries; his efforts were directed primarily against Jews, and he shows the same strategy in his works of polemic against both religions: he attempts to attack the religion at its base by showing how its own scriptures invalidate its precepts. In his massive encyclopedia of anti-Jewish polemic, the *Pugio fidei* (Dagger of the faith), Martí cites both Avicenna and al-Ghazâlî; he is aware in particular of the latter's three reasons for classifying the philosophers among the infidels. Martí produced a diptych of texts for the evangelization of Muslims: *De seta Machometi* (composed before 1257) and the *Explanatio symboli apostolorum* (written in 1257). The differences between the two texts reflect the two phases of mission, according to the Dominican strategy: the *De seta Machometi* furnishes missionaries with arguments with which to attack Islam and the *Explanatio symboli apostolorum* offers the truth of Christianity. First destroy error, then expound truth.

The *Explanatio* is thus an apologetical (pro-Christian) text rather than a polemical (anti-Muslim) one. Martí uses his studies in Greek and Arabic philosophy to portray Muslim doctrine as irrational where it differs from Christian doctrine. In a long passage on marriage, he affirms that reason and natural law permit marriage only between one man and one woman; he concludes that the Saracens' marriage law permitting polygamy "is a law not of rational and honest humans but rather of pimps and whores."[26] Saracen law is opposed to natural law, opposed to reason. He develops this idea in greater length in his discussion of the carnal pleasures that the Qur'ân promises in Heaven. He presents the standard Catholic doctrine that the body will be resurrected at the end of time, to share the soul's punishment in hell or glory in heaven. There will, however, be no eating or drinking in heaven, contrary to what "Muhammad's fables" promise.

> For he led the Saracen wise men into error, so that they do not believe in the resurrection of bodies as it is portrayed in the Qur'ân. For there it says that after resurrection they will have bodily delights, such as delight in food, drink, and sex. These things, if they indeed existed in the next life, would prevent the intellect from contemplating and delighting in the Supreme Good. Therefore, since they could see that this is improper (as in fact it is), they denied the resurrection of bodies, placing man's beatitude in the soul, not understanding that the human body could live without food.[27]

He goes on to cite Avicenna, who showed that divine and spiritual pleasures were superior to those of the body.[28] He cites al-Fârâbî and al-Ghazâlî to make the same point: the highest pleasures are those of the intellect, incomparably sweeter than those of the bodily senses.[29] As a result of their (correct) perception that spiritual pleasures are superior to physical pleasures and their (correct) rejection of the carnal delights promised in the Qur'ân, these philosophers justly reject the Qur'ân's message but incorrectly assume the impossibility of bodily resurrection. The point is clear: the learned among the Saracens reject Muhammad's irrational "fables" of banquets, wine, and sex in heaven. Christian ideas of beatitude, in contrast, are in accordance with philosophical truth.

Peter of Cluny lambasted Jews for their stubborn refusal to recognize Jesus as the Messiah, which showed, he affirmed, that they were irrational, subhuman beasts. At the same time, he praised the Saracens for their rationality and learning; clearly, they must be ripe to convert, once Christian doctrine is rationally explained to them. Yet Muslims were no more apt than Jews to be converted by Christians' supposedly rational arguments. Hence Martí classifies the Muslims as irrational: it is far easier to lambast one's opponents as unthinking, subhuman beasts than to call into question the rational basis of one's own system of beliefs. The Latin Christian worldview, carefully constructed over the centuries and increasingly buttressed by philosophy, could not allow itself to be undermined by infidel objections. If many of the most acute philosophical minds of the Middle Ages belonged to Saracens, they must be somehow crypto-Christians, or they must at least secretly reject the law of Muhammad. Martí plays up intellectual division within Islam to make Avicenna and al-Fârâbî into free-thinking rationalists who rejected the Qur'ân.

Roger Bacon

This same portrayal of Arab sages who reject Islam is found in a contemporary of Martí, English Franciscan Roger Bacon, who expounds his ideas in his *Opus maius,* which he composed for Pope Clement IV between 1266 and 1268.[30] Inspired by his readings in Arab science and philosophy and by the *Itinerary* in which fellow Franciscan William Rubruck described his travels to the Mongol court at Karakorum, Bacon is optimistic that carefully trained cadres of missionary friars can use preaching and logical argumentation to prove the truth of Christianity to Mongols, Jews, and Muslims. He seeks to "prove" that only Christianity is in fact consistent with logic and philosophical truth. Bacon portrays Islam as irrational, focusing on Muslim notions of pleasures of the afterlife. The key to his argument is Avicenna and his rejection of bodily resurrection. Bacon twists Avicenna's reservations on this issue into a refutation of Muslim doctrine, affirming: "Avicenna says in the *Elements of Morals* that Muhammad offered only a glorification of our bodies, not of our souls, except in so far as the soul shares in the enjoyment of the body."[31] This is a relatively accurate assessment of Avicenna's rejection of bodily pleasures in heaven, although Bacon fails to note that Avicenna equally rejects the bodily punishment of the damned and the very idea of resurrection: in so doing, Bacon suggests that the philosopher's arguments can be used to bolster Christian notions of afterlife, when in fact they are a rejection of them. Elsewhere in his *Opus maius*, Bacon writes: "Avicenna in the ninth book of his Metaphysics proves Muhammad in error because he has set forth only physical delights and not spiritual ones."[32] Here Bacon reiterates the same idea but affirms that Avicenna showed that Muhammad was in error, making the Muslim philosopher into a sort of an anti-Muslim polemicist, implying that his writings disprove the Qur'ân (whose author, for Bacon as for most medieval Christian writers, was Muhammad himself).

Having set up an opposition between Muhammad and Avicenna, Bacon tries to go further and imagine the Muslims split into two camps: the erroneous priests and people, blindly following Muhammad's law, and the sages who reject it: "Avicenna and other philosophers contradict the rank and file and the priests [of the Muslims]. For they show that not only does glory belong to our bodies, but also, and in greater measure, to our souls; and they decide that that sect will soon be destroyed."[33] Avicenna's rejection of bodily resurrection has been transformed into a generalized rejection, by Avicenna and "other philosophers," of the doctrine of Muslim "priests." Bacon here refers obliquely to these philosophers' predictions of the imminent destruction of the "sect" of Muhammad. He explains this elsewhere by referring to the Muslim astrologer Abû Maʿshar, who, he claims, had predicted the demise of Islam within 693 years after the Hijra.[34] Hand in hand with the notion of the "irrationality" is the naive optimism (with Bacon as with Peter the Venerable) that the Muslims can be brought to see the light of Christian truth.

Bacon's Avicenna is emphatically *not* part of the Muslim team, but is rather a sort of intellectual free agent ready to sign on to Christianity. He makes this clear in another passage of the *Opus maius:*

> Avicenna, moreover, says in the *Morals* that Muhammad spoke of the glory of the body; but we know, as he says, that the glory of our souls is greater, since we are not asses, reckoning only the delights of the body; and therefore he finds fault with his own lawgiver and wishes another to investigate who promises not only the glory of our bodies, but that of our souls.[35]

Here Bacon's Avicenna not only rejects "his own lawgiver," Muhammad; he "wishes another to investigate"; in other words, that he is seeking another lawgiver, who of course for Bacon is Christ. The idea that Avicenna would find Christian notions of the afterlife more palatable than Muslim ones is patently false. Avicenna after all rejects not simply physical pleasures in the afterlife, but the very notion of bodily resurrection, a central doctrine of both Christianity and Islam. And Avicenna criticizes Christianity for illogically affirming bodily resurrection, physical punishment in hell, but only spiritual rewards in heaven. Christians, for Avicenna, naively think that they can mobilize the masses through promises of spiritual delights. Whether Bacon is aware that he is misrepresenting Avicenna is a moot point; he certainly wants to present Avicenna as part of a fifth column of Arab sages ready to recognize the truth and superiority of Christianity.

Bacon affirms that the Saracens can be brought to Christian truth through preaching, and he provides supposedly fool-proof philosophical arguments for missionaries. Exposing these arguments is beyond the scope of this article.[36] There is some irony in the fact that Bacon presents Avicenna as an intellectual maverick at odds with Muslim orthodoxy, and he uses this image as proof of the irrationality of Islam. During Bacon's lifetime, the impact of Greek and Arabic philosophy stirred tremendous controversy in Paris and in Europe's other intellectual centers, resulting in various prohibitions of the teaching of certain texts, including some of Aristotle's.[37] In the thirteenth century, Latin Christians, as much as Muslims, feel that philosophy and science may prove dangerous to orthodoxy. The notion that Christian truth was rationally provable was rejected by prominent scholastics such as Thomas Aquinas. Bacon himself may have spent a brief stint in a Franciscan prison, perhaps because he publicly criticized Bishop Etienne Tempier's condemnation of Aristotelian doctrines in 1277.[38] Islam is not the only medieval monotheistic faith that has problems with philosophy and science. It is tempting to think that, as he sat in his Franciscan prison cell, Bacon felt a certain solidarity with Avicenna (as he imagined him): both rejecting the certainties of their contemporaries in search of higher truths, both misunderstood and persecuted by an ignorant cadre of clerical purists.

Ramon Llull

Ramon Llull knows much more about Islam than either Peter the Venerable or Roger Bacon. Born on the island of Mallorca, a commercial and intellectual crossroads of the Mediterranean with significant Muslim and Jewish communities, Llull learned Arabic in order to study not only the scientists and philosophers (like Bacon) but also Qur'ân, Hadîth, and Muslim theology.[39] Llull criticized the Dominican missionary strategy of Ramon Martí, whose mission to the king of Tunis Llull presents as a failure, without ever mentioning Martí by name.[40] As Llull tells the story, Martí went to Tunis and logically proved to the king that the religion of Muhammad was false, so that he was ready to abandon it. If the good friar would prove to him the truth of Christianity, the king and all his people would convert. The friar responded that "the faith of the Christians is so transcendent that it cannot be proven by necessary reasons; it is only to be believed, nothing else. Here is the *Symbol* written in Arabic [probably an Arabic translation of Martí's *Explanatio simboli Apostolorum*]. Believe it and you will be saved."[41] The king rebuked the friar for having used reason to destroy his faith without being able to prove Christianity; he banished him from his kingdom. Llull laments that if only the friar had been properly educated in logic and philosophy he could have proven the truth of Christianity to the king. Llull's own strategy differs from that of the Dominicans. His goal, as he explained in several of his works, is to argue with infidels "not against the faith, but through the faith."[42] He sought, in other words, to bring Muslims (and Jews) to the Christian faith by positive argument, based on what they *already* believe, rather than by attacking that belief.

In his *Book of the Gentile and the Three Wise Men* (c. 1275), Llull stages a civilized debate between a Jew, a Christian, and a Muslim, in the presence of a philosophically educated Gentile.[43] Each of the three disputants tries to explain why his religion is the true one. Toward the end of the work, the Gentile raises various objections to the Muslim conception of a heaven replete with carnal delights. In the course of his "defense" of these ideas, the Saracen makes the following confession:

> It is true that among us there are differing beliefs with respect to the glory of Paradise, for some believe it will be as I said, and this they take from a literal interpretation of the Qur'ân, which is our law, of the Proverbs of Muhammad [the Hadîth], and of commentators' glosses on the Qur'ân and the Proverbs. But there are others among us who take this glory morally and interpret it spiritually, saying that Muhammad was speaking metaphorically to people who were backward and without understanding; and in order to inspire them with a love of God he recounted the above-mentioned glory. And therefore those

> who believe this say that in Paradise there will be no glory of eating or of lying with women, nor of the other things mentioned above. And these men are natural philosophers and great scholars, yet they are men who in some ways do not follow too well the dictates of our religion, and this is why we consider them as heretics, who have arrived at their heresy by studying logic and natural science. And therefore it has been established among us that no man dare teach logic or natural science publicly.[44]

The polemical intent of this passage is clear. Llull here places into the mouth of his supposedly Muslim character a harsh condemnation of Islam. The whole project of the *Book of the Gentile* is to reach spiritual truth through the logical use of "necessary reasons"; the underlying idea is that all truths concord and that no knowledge contradicts the Ultimate Truth. Yet here Llull's Saracen frankly admits that logic and natural philosophy contradict Islam and that Muslims subsequently ban them. Despite all the polite language of respect, Llull presents Islam as fundamentally irrational.[45] Llull knows about Muslim difference of opinion regarding the resurrection of the body; he has read works of both Avicenna and al-Ghazâlî. For Llull, the message is clear: "Natural philosophers and great scholars" are not good Muslims; Islam prohibits the study of logic and natural philosophy. This means, for Llull, that even ostensibly Muslim philosophers don't really believe in the Qur'ân, and that only repressive, anti-intellectual legislation ensures the survival of Islam. Llull's Arab sages, like those of Bacon, are Islam's interior enemies, testimonies to its weakness.

This Llull makes clear in many places in his works, but perhaps nowhere more clearly than in his *Doctrina pueril* (1282–83), a didactic tract in which a father instructs his son in the articles of the Catholic faith, in piety, and in morals. Llull includes a chapter on the "law of Muhammad." After narrating Muhammad's life in a derogatory caricature that is standard fare in Christian polemics against Islam, Llull's narrator affirms:

> So vile and filthy are the deeds that Muhammad performed, and so much are his words and his deeds inconsistent with the life of a prophet, that the majority of those Saracens who know much and have subtle minds and elevated understanding do not believe that Muhammad is a prophet. And for this reason the Saracens have decreed that no man should teach natural logic among them, so that their understanding remain rude, and in this way they may believe that Muhammad is

> a prophet. Dear son, those Saracens who have subtle understanding and who do not believe that Muhammad is a prophet should be easy to convert to the Catholic faith, if you should demonstrate and preach the faith to them.[46]

Here the links in Llull's notion of Christian superiority to Islam are clear: the "vile and filthy deeds" of Muhammad show that he is not a prophet. Wise men cannot fail to see this, so Saracen wise men do not believe that Muhammad was a prophet. Muslim authorities prohibit the teaching of logic so as to maintain people in their error. The Saracen wise men, for Llull as for Bacon, are close to the truth and should be easy to convert.

Llull was over seventy years old when he composed, in Montpellier in 1305, his *Liber de fine,* a plea for sweeping action: crusade to recapture Granada, North Africa and the Holy Land, and the training and sending out of an elite cadre of missionaries who could deploy Llull's system of logical argumentation to bring infidels (primarily Muslims, but also Mongols, Jews, and schismatic or heretical eastern Christians) to the Truth. For this to work, Llull needs to imagine (as did Martí and Bacon) that the Saracen sages did not really accept the veracity of Muhammad's law.

> Among those Saracens who are most learned, few believe in Muhammad (since they well know that this man was a sinner and that in their law he placed many ridiculous things). And thus some learned Arabs are Christians—among which I could number myself. Once the better Saracens are converted the lesser ones can be converted by the better ones.[47]

For Llull, the learned among the Saracens do not accept that Muhammad is a prophet and do not follow his law. This is why some Arabs are Christians. Llull seems to suggest that Arab Christians are those who have seen the light and renounced Islam for Christianity, rather than descendants of Christians present before the Muslim conquest, even though he certainly knows that this is not the case. He further confuses the issue by presenting himself, a Catalan who learned Arabic from a Mallorcan Muslim tutor, as one of these "Arab Christians." The suggestion is that learned Arabs reject the precepts of the Qur'ân, that some of them are already Christians and that others can be convinced by disputation. These learned converts will in turn convert the Saracen masses. He reiterates this idea in other works, for example, in his *De acquisitione Terre Sancte* (1309), a tract calling for a crusade and proposing a strategy for reconquest of the Holy Land; here he affirms, "Well-educated Saracens do not really believe that Muhammad is a prophet. For in the Qur'ân, which contains their law, they find many things inconsistent with sanctity and true prophecy."[48]

In none of these passages does Llull name Avicenna (as had Martí and Bacon) or al-Ghazâlî, although he may well have had them both in mind. Llull is familiar with Martí and his arguments, and he himself adapted al-Ghazâlî's *Mi'yâr al-'ilm* and his *Miakk al-Nazr* into Latin as the *Compendium logicae Algazelis* and was familiar with some of his other works.[49] Llull presents Saracen philosophers as at odds with the doctrines and the rites of Islam; he affirms that Averroes had been stoned by his fellow Muslims, an incident which for Llull shows that Muslims are hostile to philosophy and philosophers.[50] The wise among the Arabs are ready to recognize Christian truth; only the violent fanaticism of the Saracen authorities prevents them from doing so.

Riccoldo da Montecroce

This brings us back to Riccoldo da Montecroce, contemporary of Llull and resident of the same Dominican convent in Florence as Giordano da Pisa.[51] Riccoldo set out for the East in 1288 to attempt to convert Muslims and heretical Christians, continuing the missionary traditions of Dominicans such as Ramon de Penyafort and Ramon Martí. Riccoldo eventually arrived in Baghdad, where he learned Arabic, read the Qur'ân, and studied Muslim theology and philosophy. Shortly after his return to Italy (in about 1300), he composed his *Liber Peregrinationis*, in which he combines a narration of his pilgrimage to the holy sites with an ethnographical sketch of the different peoples he encountered on his travels (paying particular attention to their religious beliefs and practices). He describes in great detail his impressions of Baghdad, profusely praising the learning and piety of the city's Muslims. Yet he, like the other authors we've looked at, is unable to accept the idea that a philosophically trained person could believe in what he found written in the Qur'ân. In what seems a contradiction of his earlier praise of Muslim intellectual activity in Baghdad, Riccoldo writes:

> Their wise men began to execrate the perversity of their law. Since this law could be eliminated either through the books of the prophets, by the law of Moses, or even by the veracious books of the philoso-

> phers, therefore the caliph of Baghdad ordered that nothing should be studied in Baghdad except the Qur'ân. For this reason, we find that they know very little about the truth of theology or the subtlety of philosophy. Nevertheless, their wise men put no faith in the sayings of the Qur'ân, but deride it in secret. In public, though, they honor it, on account of their fear of others.[52]

This passage has all the explicative power and sophistication of a good conspiracy theory. If these intelligent men in Baghdad seem to be pious Muslims, they are only dissimulating on account of fear. The caliphs (whom Riccoldo does not name, implying that this is a generalized caliphal strategy), aware of the dangers that the study of either the Bible or philosophy poses to Muslim doctrine, bans their study, allowing only the study of the Qur'ân. As for Martí, Bacon, and Llull, these Muslim intellectuals who reject the Qur'ân are a potential fifth column within the Muslim world that Christians can exploit to their advantage.

Yet in his *Peregrinatio,* this idea seems to contrast sharply with his glowing image of Muslim sages in Baghdad and with his admiration for the city's madrasas. Aware, perhaps, of the contradictions in this portrayal, Riccoldo subsequently refines it in his *Libellus contra legem Saracenorum,* a polemical tract which he composed within a few years after the *Peregrinatio.*

> There arose against both groups [Sunnis and Shiites] certain Saracens expert in philosophy. They started to read the books of Aristotle and Plato and started to despise all the sects of the Saracens and the Qur'ân itself.
>
> When someone warned the caliph of Baghdad, named [name left blank in manuscript] about this, he built in Baghdad two very prestigious schools, Nizâmiyya and Mustansiriyya. He reformed the study of the Qur'ân and ordered that whoever came from the provinces to study the Qur'ân in Baghdad, these students would have rooms and stipends for their needs. He also ordered that the Saracens and those studying the Qur'ân should in no way study philosophy. And they do not consider those who study philosophy to be good Saracens, because they all despise the Qur'ân.[53]

Here Riccoldo has combined (and elaborated upon) two ideas from his *Peregrinatio,* resolving the first text's apparent contradiction by bringing two elements together, making the founding of madrasas into a clever *anti-intel-*

lectual ploy: the point of having government-funded educational institutes, he tries to make his reader believe, is precisely to squelch philosophical reading and speculation by ensuring that only the Qur'ân is read and taught, not any philosophical texts that will contradict it. Not that he is completely wrong: the Nizamiyya madrasa, founded by Sultan Nizam al-Mulk in 1067, indeed became a bastion for orthodoxy against philosophical speculation; its most illustrious teacher was none other than al-Ghazâlî. Yet these facts are twisted to fit Riccoldo's polemical needs; it is in fact in Paris, not Baghdad, that thirteenth-century clerics forbid the study of Aristotle. Yet for Riccoldo it is Islam that is illogical, and those who stubbornly adhere to it merely display their irrationality.

Riccoldo's contact with Muslim learning was through the Qur'ân and through direct interaction with Muslim scholars in Baghdad, not principally through the reading of philosophical texts in Arabic, as had been the case with Martí and Bacon (and to a certain extent Llull). Riccoldo does not name any of the Muslim sages who reject the Qur'ân, yet he certainly has Avicenna, and perhaps Averroes, in mind. It is thus easy to imagine Riccoldo communicating his ideas to his fellow Florentine Dominican Giordano da Pisa. As we have seen, Giordano puts Riccoldo's idea to good use, employing it to affirm that true philosophers despise the pleasures of this world and that such Arab sages as Avicenna mock and reject the debauched and corrupt "law of the Saracens."

The success of this separation is clear in the work of another Florentine, contemporary of Riccoldo da Monte Croce and Giordano da Pisa: Dante Alighieri. In the fourth canto of his *Inferno*, Dante describes the first circle of hell, inhabited by virtuous pagans. Here he places the "noble castle" in which the great heroes and writers of antiquity dwell. Aristotle presides over a group of scholars that includes most of the philosophers of Greek and Latin antiquity: in their midst, he places Avicenna and Averroes.[54] Removed for all eternity from contact with Muslims, the two Arab sages can eternally commune with their Greek and Latin soul mates. Far away, in the eighth circle of hell, Muhammad and 'Alî are punished as schismatics, sliced open by a demon in what for Dante is a symbolic reenactment of their own renting asunder of Christian unity. Dante separates Arab sages from Saracen schismatics for all eternity.

The various authors examined in this chapter all denounced Islam as irrational, while affirming that Christianity was rational. In order to maintain this, they created a stereotypical image of fanatical, anti-intellectual Muslim leaders who prohibited the study of philosophy and science. The corollary to this was that those Muslim intellectuals whose writings were widely admired and read in Latin Europe must not have been true Muslims; they must have rejected the Qur'ân. In order to cling to the belief in the rationality of their own religion, Christian intellectuals had to relegate the religious other to the realm of the irrational. Hermetically isolated from the "Saracen error," the Arab philosophers, like their pagan Greek counterparts, could be studied and admired without upsetting the supposed rational basis of Christianity.[55]

9

Walls of Hatred and Contempt

The Anti-Muslim Polemics of Pedro Pascual

Over the last thirty years, a number of scholars have written about the place of Muslims in Christian Spain. Some have studied the polemical and apologetical works of medieval Christian writers for whom Islam was a sordid heresy founded by Muhammad, a sly pseudo-prophet whom the devil inspired to spread his heresy by the sword. Others have elucidated the roles assigned to Muslim minorities in the societies of Christian Iberia by analyzing legal and archival sources, while the picture that these documents provide is varied and complex—in general, Muslims under Christian rule have roughly the same status as *dhimmis* in Muslim societies. Few historians have tried to elucidate connections between the theological anti-Muslim polemics of clerical writers and the legal and social role of Muslims in Christian societies. Are the legal and social restrictions imposed on Muslims based (explicitly or implicitly) on a polemical perception of Islam? Or do political, social, and military interest call for and inspire a theologically based ideology that justifies Christian hegemony and Muslim social inferiority?

If historians have little to say about the possible links between anti-Muslim polemics and the place of Muslims in Christian Iberian societies, the main reason is perhaps because the sources make no such explicit links. Dozens of *fueros* enumerate the rights and obligations of Muslims without giving any theological justification. In the rich archives of the Kingdom of Valencia, when royal documents justify the rights of Mudejars (subjected Muslims) or limitations imposed upon them, they do so by invoking the surrender treaties in which conquered Muslims had accepted their new subject status, not by referring to theological arguments about the supposed inferiority of Islam.

Yet if we examine the numerous texts that describe (and denigrate) Islam and its prophet, we can discern the social functions of this negative image of Islam. A few of these texts are meant for evangelization: their intended audience is either Muslim readers or Christian missionaries; their authors seek to demonstrate the superiority of Christianity. Such is the case, for example, of the *Contra sectam sive haeresim Sarracenorum* by Peter of Cluny, of the *De seta machometi* by Ramon Martí, and the Arabic texts of Ramon Llull.

This negative image of Islam is not limited to polemical and apologetic texts. In other texts, the denigration of the "law of Muhammad" justifies Christian kings' military conquest of the peninsula or the obligation of Muslim rulers to pay *parias* (tribute) to them. Such is the case, for example, of the chronicles of Lucas de Tuy and Rodrigo Jiménez de Rada and of the *Estoria de España* attributed to Alfonso X el Sabio, king of Castile and León (1252–84). Although theoretically limited to the history of the Iberian peninsula), these chronicles recount the life of Muhammad, whom they present as a heresiarch and a false prophet in order to affirm the illegitimacy of Muslim dominion in the peninsula. Thus the three chronicles present the Muslim invasion of 711 as an event of near-apocalyptic significance.[1] The denigration of Muhammad and of Islam justifies the *reconquista*. Here religious polemics serve political ideology. Juan Manuel uses the biography of Muhammad in the same way in his *Libro de los estados*.[2]

The social barriers between the Christian majority and the Muslim (or Jewish) minority, in theory clearly delineated by law, were far from watertight. Christians, Muslims, and Jews traversed them daily, rubbing elbows with neighbors of different religions, working with them, buying and selling with them, exchanging advice or jokes, forming friendships, and indulging in forbidden interreligious sexual relations. All of this, some members of the three communities feared, could blur the distinctions between them. The law was insufficient to maintain the desired separation without some sort of mutual repugnance. David Nirenberg has shown how the ritualized violence against the *calls* (Jewish quarters) of Catalan towns reinforced this separation. Louise Mirrer has described the warrior ideology of the Castilian *romances,* which affirmed the right of valorous Castilian men to dominate the "weak," be they women, Muslims, or Jews.[3]

It is in this context that I examine *Sobre la seta Mahometana* by Pedro

Pascual, a text that manipulates traditional anti-Muslim polemics, seeking to inspire in its readers hatred and disdain for Islam, in order to prevent them from crossing over to the rival faith. Little is known of the life of Pedro Pascual, the details of which are shrouded in hagiographic haze. Since the various works ascribed to him do not exist in any manuscript earlier than the fifteenth century, the authenticity of his works has sparked some debate, although Walter Mettmann argues convincingly that he did write *Sobre la seta Mahometana*.[4] Pedro was named bishop of Jaén by Pope Boniface VIII in 1296. In 1297 or 1298, as he was visiting his diocese, Pedro was captured by the Nasrid emir of Granada, Muhammad II, and imprisoned in Granada. Pedro watched in consternation as some of his fellow prisoners converted to Islam; he was also troubled by the divinatory practices of certain Christians, practices which he attributed to a malevolent Muslim influence. Worse yet, some Christians were ready to share their beds with the infidel. In his *Sobre la seta Mahometana*, Pedro tries to offer, in Castilian, a sort of handbook which furnishes the Christian reader with defensive arguments that he can deploy in his debates with Muslims. He also tries to cultivate, in his Christian reader, a sense of radical difference with the Muslim Other. He gives a hostile biography of Muhammad in order to inspire scorn for Islam. He affirms that the Moors (Pedro, like most medieval Castilian authors, uses the term *moros* to designate the Muslims) are naturally libidinous, violent, and stupid: this is why they follow Muhammad's irrational law, a law which gives free rein to their lust and makes them the implacable enemies of Christians. Pedro frequently employs animal metaphors to relegate his adversaries beyond the threshold of humanity: they are beasts, asses.[5] For Pedro Pascual, legal and theological distinctions are not sufficient to isolate the Christian from the malevolent influence of Islam: he needs to build walls of hatred and contempt.

In his *Disputa contra los Jueus*, Pedro describes how many of his flock, fellow prisoners, converted to Islam:

> When I, a religious, and by the grace of God bishop of the City of Jaen of the Kingdom of Castile (although not yet named to that position),[6] was captured and placed in the hands of the king of Granada, I saw each day many Christian captives, illiterate and ignorant of the faith of the Christians, turn to the evil sect of the Moors.[7]

He affirms that Jews came every day to speak to the Christians and attempt to convert them to "the false sect of the Moors." He names in particular two

Jews, "moved by great felony and maliciousness," who asked Pedro a series of questions to which he responds in his *Disputa contra los Jueus,* which he composed in Catalan. When Christian prisoners apostatize thus, it is not merely the fault of the malevolent Jews and Muslims, for Pedro; it is also because of their ignorance. He says that he sought out books on sacred history and Christian doctrine so that he could teach his fellow prisoners.

The result was the *Sobre la seta Mahometana*, which Pedro penned in his Granadan prison in early 1300.[8] In the prologue of this text, he explains his method:

> I do not wish that the sinner die in his evil sins, but that he convert and live. I saw many, in this captivity on account of their great sins, who despaired of God's mercy, as had Cain who killed his brother Abel, and despaired and was doomed, and as Judas who betrayed his Lord, and despaired and hanged himself. And on account of their lack of comprehension, for they know neither the law of the Christians nor that of the Moors—the Moors whom Muhammad led astray and who take pleasure in lying to the Christians and turning them away from their law.
>
> I, seeing this, was pained for the souls of our Christians, whom I saw lost because they did not know the truth. For this reason I translated from Latin into Romance completely, and not in rhyme, nor with concordances (because poets tend to add to or subtract from the truth) the history of Muhammad as I found it written in our books from the time in which Muhammad lived. In addition to what is written in this history, I also wrote some things which some Moors told me, trying to praise their law, and which I found written in the Moors' books. And then I wrote a few things that I found written in the Gospels, and in the Epistles, and in authentic books which are read in the Holy Church.[9]

Pedro here affirms that he is writing to save the souls of Christians in captivity who risk wallowing in sin and (like Cain and Judas) in despair. Added to this despair is another problem: their ignorance. They know neither the law of the Christians nor that of the Moors. The Moors, deceived by Muhammad, now delight in turning Christians away from the true faith. Christians and Muslims argue about their respective faiths, it seems, and few Christians are capable of defending their faith. As a remedy to despair and ignorance, Pedro must offer hope and instruction. He proposed to expound

Christian and Moorish law to his ignorant readers. He explains the plan of his treatise: first he presents the life of Muhammad *twice:* first according to Muslim authors, then according to Christian authors who, he claims, were Muhammad's contemporaries; this corresponds to the first chapter (*título*) of his tract, where he explains (and denigrates) Islam. Next he presents biblical passages: *títulos* 2–16 expound, didactically, the story of Jesus and the essential Christian doctrines. The point of these chapters is to allow the Christian reader to comprehend his faith and to defend it in arguments with Muslim adversaries. "You will find in it [the book] what you need to defend yourselves against the enemies of our law"[10]

The purpose of the *Sobre la seta Mahometana,* written for "those of us who lie in this place," in other words in prison, is to prevent apostasy: "Friends, strengthen yourselves, and take consolation in our Lord Jesus Christ, for whom you suffer chains, and jails, hunger, thirst, and many other tribulations, pains, and hardships."[11] Pedro must convince his readers that it is worth the trouble to remain steadfast in their faith, to endure the hardships of captivity, in order to receive a reward in the next life. In order to do this, he must inspire in his readers a strong revulsion for Islam, so that apostasy will seem worse to them than imprisonment.

Pedro writes for an uneducated audience. They do read Castilian, but principally "fables, love stories, and other frivolities" and the verses of the poets (*rimadores*) who deform the truth.[12] Pedro needs to present Christian doctrine so that his readers can understand it. When he cites the Bible, he first gives the Latin text and then the Castilian translation. When he cites Augustine, he explains to his readers who he was: "a holy bishop, who was one of the most erudite that the world had seen to our day, who was bishop in Africa before the sect of Muhammad began, whose name was Saint Augustine, and who wrote many books."[13]

A Defensive Tool

The purpose of this tract, as we have seen, was to give the Christian reader basic instruction in Christian doctrine and to furnish him with the essential elements of a defensive argument. Let us examine first this defensive aspect, before presenting the denigration of the Muslim other. In *títulos* 2–16, Pedro explains the central doctrines of Christianity and provides advice to his readers for their arguments with Muslims. A few examples will suffice.

On a number of occasions, Pedro presents standard Muslim arguments against specific Christian doctrines, providing his readers each time with counterarguments. Having explained the doctrine of the Incarnation, Pedro presents Muslims' objections:

> The Moors say that they do not see or understand why God could not have saved us in another manner, rather than dying on the cross for us. For [they say] he could have sent another man who would have saved us by dying or not by dying. To this argument the first response is this.[14]

Pedro then gives a series of responses that seek to prove that only the sacrifice of a man-God could save humanity. Pedro's ideas are traditional (they resemble those of Anselm of Canterbury's *Cur Deus homo*), but here they are explicitly deployed in a defensive argument against Muslims.

In a similar vein, Pedro declares, "The Moors and the Jews say that since Jesus Christ, whom we claim as our Savior, was circumcised, we, since we are not circumcised, cannot be saved."[15] This is indeed a frequent argument in anti-Christian polemic by Muslim and Jewish authors; twelfth-century Almoravid writer Ibn `Abdun, for example, fulminates against the hypocrisy of Christians who commemorate the circumcision of Jesus but who fail to circumcise themselves.[16] Here again, Pedro's response is standard: Christ replaced bodily circumcision with the sacrament of baptism, a sort of "spiritual circumcision." The very fact that Muslims and Jews do not understand this shows that they are "carnal"; we will return to this charge shortly.

Another Christian practice severely criticized by Muslim and Jewish polemicists is the use of crucifixes and images of Jesus and the saints. Moors and Jews, says Pedro, accuse us of worshiping images, but we do not—we merely show reverence to God through the images that we kiss. These practices, for Pedro, help the Christian recall and sympathize with the sufferings endured by the martyrs and especially by Jesus: hard of heart he who does not weep when he contemplates the wounds of the crucified Christ. Hence the usefulness of images:

> If they did not see the cross and the images, they would not remember so many times, nor would their hearts be so moved to compassion; and for these reasons, crosses and images are placed in the churches, and not because we think that in the stones or in the wood there is any deity or divinity, nor that they can aid or harm us.[17]

He explains elsewhere that the crucifix teaches the illiterate ("a los non letrados") Christ's passion, just as paintings teach them about the passion of the martyrs.[18] Pedro reiterates the classic distinction between the adoration of God and the devotion shown to the crucifix and to painted images. Yet in Pedro we see above all his pastoral preoccupations: the didactic and edifying function of the images which (just like Pedro's text) teach the simple and inspire devotion in them. Indeed, says Pedro, we use crucifixes to tame demons, but that should come as no surprise: if we can strike fear into the hearts of evildoers by showing them images of terrestrial kings, we can certainly terrify demons by showing them the insignia of the Celestial King.

It is reverence for Christ, Pedro asserts, that inspires Christians to kiss the crucifix and to kiss the feet of the images of Christ and his saints. These practices call for no reprimand, since vassals kiss the feet and hands of their lords, Joseph kissed the scepter of Pharaoh, Moors kiss the earth when they pray, and among the Moors inferiors kiss the heads and hands of their superiors.[19] These are the arguments Pedro proposes to his readers, in order to make them understand the principles justifying the veneration of images and to provide them with arguments to use against Jewish and Muslim adversaries. The analogies seek to show that such devotion is neither reprehensible nor exceptional, since people habitually kiss the hands and feet (or clothes or scepter) of human lords. These examples, moreover, are borrowed from Christian feudal society, from the Old Testament, and from Hispano-Muslim social practice. This shows how Pedro sought to furnish his reader with arguments that could be comprehensible and persuasive to Jewish and Muslim interlocutors.

We could multiply the examples that show how Pedro, for each key Christian doctrine, presents Muslim (and at times Jewish) objections and then provides his readers with arguments meant to refute these objections.[20] He never proposes responses that could be seen as aggressive or offensive to the Muslim interlocutor.

Pedro says that he himself had participated in disputations with Muslims. He asks wise old men (*sabios viejos*) to explain certain Muslim practices or traditions.[21] Having exposed certain "contradictions" in the Qur'ân, he affirms: "I presented this argument to some Moors who claim to be wise, and I never found anyone who could refute it."[22] He elsewhere says that a young Moor had narrated to him the capture of Jerusalem by `Umar.[23]

Pedro says that he has read "books of the Moors" and mentions the *Miʿrâj*, the Qur'ân, and the Hadith. Some of this knowledge could well be secondhand, through some of the Christian texts he cites, such as the anonymous *Risâlat al-Kindî* (*Sobre la seta*, 34, 41, 46) and Petrus Alfonsi's *Diálogi contra Iudeos (Sobre la seta,* 88–89). He uses these texts above all to denigrate Islam (as we shall see shortly) but also, at times, to prove the truth of Christian doctrine. He uses the Qur'ân as a testimony to the birth of Jesus to a virgin, to Jesus' holy life and miracles, and to the doctrine of bodily resurrection. These passages of the Qur'ân, Pedro affirms, "greatly pain" the Moors.[24]

A Perpetual Hostility, Rooted in History

Yet, for Pedro's purpose, it is not sufficient to provide his Christian reader with defensive arguments against Islam. If he is to make them prefer prison (or even martyrdom) to apostasy, Pedro needs to instill in his readers hatred and disdain for Islam and for Muslims. He needs also to explain to his readers the place that God has allotted to Islam in Christian theology and history. To these ends, Pedro presents Islam as a heresy concocted by a false prophet and spread by the sword.

Pedro says that he found in the *Istoria escolásitca* a prophecy by the martyr Methodius (the text is in fact the *Apocalypse of pseudo-Methodius,* composed in Syriac c. 692 and translated in the seventh century into Greek and Latin).[25] According to this prophecy, the reign of the Moors would last "eight weeks of years," which is to say (affirms Pedro after a long mathematical excursus) 560 years. We are presently in the year 1338 of the Spanish Era (or AD 1300), says Pedro, and this period is almost over. The hopeful message to the Christian reader is clear: destiny is on our side.[26] The Syriac original of the *Apocalypse of pseudo-Methodius* had in fact predicted that the reign of the Ishmaelites would last *ten* weeks of years, or 70 years: composed c. 692, this text proffered the hope that Muslim domination would soon come to an end.[27] Paul Alvarus, in the 850s, writing to defend the voluntary martyrs of Cordoba, finds another prophecy (Daniel 7:23–27) which, with a few mathematical contortions, shows that the reign of the "Chaldeans" in Spain should last 245 years, of which, he affirms, only 16 remain![28] In all three cases, the method is the same: find an obscure prophecy, play with the numbers until they come out right, then present it as evidence that Islam is on its last legs and that the Christians need only be patient for a few more years. Pedro adds that some of the Moors admit that Muhammad himself had predicted that Muslim dominion would last only 700 years. This period, Pedro affirms, comes to a close this year (1300); indeed, 700 AH began on 15 September 1300.

While Muslims claim that their victories show that God is on their side, Pedro insists, on the contrary, that in the battles fought by El Cid and by Alfonso VI of Castile, one thousand Christians vanquished two thousand Muslims (26–27). Spain's Christian kings will soon regain control of the whole peninsula, marking a return to the good old days of Visigothic king Witiza, who ruled all of Spain and who received *parias* from all of Africa (62).

But Pedro knows that these Christian victories may arrive too late to help his comrades in prison in Granada. These prisoners must be ready, if necessary, to endure martyrdom. Their imprisonment is a trial and an opportunity for penance. They must follow the example of the martyrs of antiquity:

> Give praises to God, and admit that you are sinners, and that you have merited and do merit what you are suffering, and even more. And in everything, bless God's name, for thus Job, and the Apostles, and the Holy Fathers, and the Confessors did, and they were imprisoned in more somber prisons and in worse jails than we are, as we clearly see in the history books.[29]

The stories of Christ's martyrs serve as *exempla* for the Christian prisoner, just as the contemplation of the crucifix should inspire the Christian to be ready to suffer martyrdom (241). In his seventh chapter (supposedly a defense of the Christian notion of martyrdom), Pedro, like a war propagandist, attempts to instill hatred in his Christian readers by describing what the Muslim "Other" does to "us." By anchoring this violent hostility in the past, he presents it as eternal and inevitable: the wall of violence cannot be traversed. Martyrdom is the great divider: Pedro writes of Christians killed by Muslims, in particular Pelayo (Pelagius), martyred in Cordoba in the tenth century (202).[30] He narrates the story of Friar Daniel and his fellow Franciscans who went to preach to the Moors of Ceuta, only to be decapitated at the order of the Moorish king. The Infante Don Pedro of Portugal was in Ceuta, Pedro says, witnessed the martyrdom and subsequent miracles of the saints, and brought their heads to the monastery of Sancta Cruz de Coimbra.[31] Pedro says that he himself saw these heads, which miraculously seemed still to be fresh and bloody (201–2). The message is clear: the violent hostility of the Muslims is permanent and implacable.

Violence, for Pedro, characterizes Muhammad and his followers: "With the sword they began, with the sword they maintain their accursed sect, and for this reason by the sword they shall end their lives."[32] Pedro tries to deny any exception to this rule, blackening the images of two sultans often presented as enlightened monarchs by medieval European writers: the caliph `Umar I and the Ayubid sultan of Egypt, al-Kâmil. In recounting the capture of Jerusalem by `Umar, Muslim and Christian chroniclers describe the caliph's humility, his simple clothing, and the respect that he showed toward the city's Christians. Pedro says that a "moruelo" (young Moor) told him that the capture of the holy city by `Umar had been predicted by the prophet Zechariah (9:9), who spoke of a king of Jerusalem who would arrive "lowly, and riding upon an ass." This prophecy, Pedro affirms, applies only to Christ. Al-Kâmil, the Egyptian sultan to whom Francis of Assisi preached during the Fifth Crusade, is presented by thirteenth-century Latin (and French) authors as an example of the good infidel: he listens politely to the saint, recognizes his holiness, offers him gifts (which the saint refuses), and lets him depart in peace. For Pedro, al-Kâmil lets Francis go not in kindness but through calculated animosity: "The sultan told [Francis], 'Be gone with you, for I do not wish to make you a martyr so that Christians will venerate you.'"[33]

A Hostility Based on Ethnic Differences

This obdurate antipathy, for Pedro, is the continuation of the hatred between the sons of Ishmael and Isaac. Ishmael, illegitimate son of Abraham, malevolent toward his brother, made clay idols and tried to force Isaac to worship them. This is why, Pedro says, Abraham expelled Ishmael from his house, increasing the hostility between the two brothers.[34] Pedro traces the history of the Arabs, the descendants of Ishmael, and concludes:

> These peoples have always persecuted and made war against the legitimate sons, descendants of Abraham, who are called the people of Israel, *and to this day they have not ceased.* And in this way the prophecy that was made to their ancestor Ishmael is fulfilled: that he would be cruel, and a thief, and that his hands would be against all

> men, and the hands of all against him, and they will pitch tents against their brothers; and the Hebrew text says that he would be *velut onager*, which means a wild ass.[35]

The prophecy that Pedro cites from Genesis (16:12) is commonplace and used to castigate Arab conquerors even before the rise of Islam and in response to the Muslim conquests of the seventh century.[36] Arabs are by nature violent, especially toward Christians, the true spiritual descendants of Isaac. The animosity between the sons of Ishmael and Isaac is thus permanent and inevitable. Pedro compares it to the enmity of the demons against the sons of Adam and Eve.[37] If Ishmael is a wild ass, his descendants are beasts of the field (*bestiae agri*) who, in a prophecy of Ezekiel (39:17), drink blood and eat human flesh (*Sobre la seta*, 70–71). Throughout his text, Pedro calls Arabs and Moors beasts and asses. The animal imagery dehumanizes the adversary.

Biblical prophecies explain the hostility and ferocity of the Ishmaelites, but Pedro does not stop there. He offers several etymologies of the word *moro*. First, the Moors are originally from *Maurica major*, a Roman province of Africa. Second, the Moors have the habit, when they are afraid of being robbed, of swallowing their gold, "and afterwards they sometimes regurgitate it through their mouths and sometimes they pass it through their bottoms, and for this reason we from Spain call them *moros*, as a sort of insult, because they pass their gold through the worst place. Hence *moro* means 'shitting gold.'"[38]

In the iconography of the thirteenth century, one finds images of demons (or the avaricious in hell) defecating gold and silver. This filthy and shameful act, for Pedro, defines the Moor. Moreover, Moors have no table manners: they use neither spoon nor knife, taking their food in their hands and ripping off pieces of meat with their teeth. And among them, he who eats the sloppiest is considered the most virile.

This hostile ethnology of the Moors is meant to underline and accentuate the differences between the Christian Spaniards and their adversaries. These differences are also meant to explain why these people embrace Islam, or rather the caricature of Islam that Pedro presents, a ridiculous and depraved law for irrational beasts. "And I say that much more of a beast than a beast is he who reads the books of your sect, O Muhammad, and your sayings, and your deeds, and believes you." This "bestiality," for Pedro, is apparent in Muhammad's lust (and that of his followers), in their "sacraments" (which Pedro qualifies as carnal and filthy), and in their lack of reason. This makes Islam an "accursed and filthy sect."[39]

A Carnal Law for Flesh-Bound Men

Accusing one's adversaries of sexual debauchery is a long and venerable ecclesiastical tradition. Jerome makes such accusations against Priscillian, Simon Magus, and other heresiarchs.[40] Twelfth- and thirteenth-century European authors made the same charges against contemporary heretics. Muslim polygamy and the promise of dark-eyed *houris* awaiting the elect in a sensual paradise could only confirm the prejudices of the hostile Christian reader. In lambasting the supposedly libidinous nature of Islam, Pedro reiterates a key element in the traditional Christian polemics against Islam.

Thus, for Pedro, before the time of Muhammad, the Arabs adored Venus, the goddess of lust, making her day, Friday, their holy day. For this reason, Muhammad decreed that Friday would be maintained as the day of prayer in honor of lust, this same day that for Christians is a day of fasting in remembrance of Christ's passion (*Sobre la seta*, 87). Their holy city is called "Meca," the Latin word for adultery (*moecha*) (4). He lambasts Muhammad's polygamy and that of his followers; he affirms that Muhammad authorized homosexuality (30–37, 81–82). His followers lust after Christian women, he says, many of whom (but alas not all) suffer martyrdom to escape the beds of their oppressors (202–3).

But it is not only their sexual proclivities that make these men carnal creatures. Their very sacraments (like those of the Jews) are carnal, in stark contrast with the spiritual and timeless sacraments of the Christians. Here Pedro reiterates a traditional saw of Christian anti-Jewish polemic, according to which the "spiritual" sacraments of the age of grace (baptism, Eucharist) are supposed to have replaced the "carnal" sacraments of the age of law (circumcision, paschal sacrifice). Circumcision and animal sacrifice are "filthy and bloody," in contrast with the "honest, pious, and clean" sacraments of the Christians (*Sobre la seta*, 192). Thus the flesh-bound Muslims believe that by washing their bodies before praying, they can purify themselves; they should rather, says Pedro, perform an "interior cleansing in their hearts" followed by baptism.[41]

Their inability to comprehend spiritual things prevents them from understanding Christian sacraments; this blindness, Pedro asserts, is predicted by Paul: they cling blindly to the letter that kills, while the Christians are inspired by the spirit that brings life.[42] When he presents the doctrine of the transubstantiation, Pedro uses Old Testament prophecies in an attempt to show that they predict not only the Christian sacrament of the Eucharist but also the blind refusal of the Jews and Muslims to recognize the sacrament.[43]

The Irrationality of the Moors and of Their Law

A carnal law for flesh-bound men, Islam is by the same token irrational, affirms Pedro, indulging in numerous animal metaphors. Peter of Cluny, in his twelfth-century tract *Against the Inveterate Stubbornness of the Jews,* an exceptionally virulent polemical text, maintains that the "irrational fables" of the Talmud show that the Jews are not rational beings but mere beasts; he calls them bovines, pigs, and dogs.[44] Pedro shows the same attitude toward the Qur'ân and toward Muslims. In a clever juxtaposition of information from Muslim sources and defamatory legend, Pedro presents the life of Muhammad in a way meant to ridicule and discredit his followers.[45] Muhammad, "he who was born on an evil day,"[46] was a sly scoundrel who trained a dove to eat seeds out of his ear and then claimed that it was the angel Gabriel who came to speak to him. Possessed by demons, he is struck with epilepsy but claims it is the consequence of his divine revelations. He composes a carnal law on a scroll that he attaches to the horns of a bull; when the credulous masses see the bull arrive with the scroll, they think that the law is sent by God. Throughout, Pedro lambasts the stupidity of the people who fall for the false prophet's ruses. The Qur'ân, for Pedro, consists of "fables, lies, vanities, contradictions, jokes, heresy, stupidity, insults to God, and shenanigans."[47]

If this law is so irrational and its devotees are so stupid, how can one explain the erudition of many Muslims in philosophy and science? Pedro asserts that Saracen philosophers reject the idea of a carnal paradise promised in the Qur'ân:

> Finally, seldom or never will you find a Moor learned in philosophy who is not a heretic in his law, since he can see clearly that Muhammad was an idiot and that he did not know what he was talking about concerning this subject and many others, as he was an illiterate man who did not know what he was saying. Hence the wise men of his own law mock Muhammad.[48]

The great Muslim thinkers, for Pedro, are in fact not Muslim: they reject the Qur'ân and mock Muhammad.

Pedro Pascual wrote in order to convince his correligionaries to resist the allure of Islam: not to apostatize, of course, but also to avoid any sexual relations with Muslims and any participation in the "diabolical arts" that he accuses the Moors of practicing. He is not the only author of this period who uses polemics against Muhammad to inspire aversion toward the Muslim Other. The *Castigos e documentos para bien vivir ordenados por le rey don Sancho IV* attempt to convince the future king Fernando IV of Castile that to make love to a Moorish woman is like sleeping with a bitch, because she follows the irrational law of Muhammad.[49] To inspire in one's readers hate and disgust for Islam, one must present the Moors as irrational beasts, lustful and ferocious, whose intense and implacable hostility is announced in the Bible. Girded with this hatred and contempt, and armed with the defensive arguments of Pedro, the Christian reader can resist the temptation of apostasy; the barriers between the Christian and the Other are strengthened, even in a Granadan prison, where the laws of Castile do not apply.

∴ 10 ∴

A Dreadful Racket

The Clanging of Bells and the Yowling of Muezzins in Iberian Interconfessional Polemics

In 997, the Andalusian Hâjib Al-Mansûr plundered Santiago de Compostela, removed the bells from the city's cathedral, and brought them, on the backs of Christian captives, to his capital, Cordoba. He had the clappers removed and the bells transformed into lamps for the great mosque of Cordoba. In this way he silenced the infidels' bells, which henceforth produced light for the true religion. In 1236, Castilian king Fernando III captured Cordoba and placed his royal insignia on the minaret, there (according to chronicler Rodrigo Jiménez de Rada) "where once the name of that perfidious man [Muhammad] was invoked." The king silenced the muezzin and sent the bells back to Compostela.

The ringing of bells represents, for some medieval Muslim authors, an audible symbol of Christianity, a noisome racket that one should silence. In the same way, various Christian authors express their disdain for the *adhân*, the call to prayer of the muezzin (*mu'adhdhin*). Once he has conquered an "infidel" city, the prince often transforms its principal religious center: the cathedral becomes the *jâmi'* (main mosque) or vice versa. Some of the texts that describe these transformations insist on the conversion of the belfry or minaret, visual and sonorous symbol of the rival religion.

In this chapter, I will trace the history of this opposition through the texts of the first centuries of Islam and then concentrate on Cordoba at three precise moments: the crisis of the ninth-century martyr movement; the arrival of the bells from Santiago in 997; and the Castilian conquest of the city in 1236, which leads to the conversion of the minaret and the restitution of the bells to Santiago.

Bells, Audible Symbols of Christianity, in Muslim Texts

Let us first look at the earliest Muslim texts concerning church bells. According to one Hadith, one day in Medina, a Muslim suggested that the Muslims use a bell (*nâqûs*) to call the faithful to prayer; another suggested that they use a trumpet, like the Jews; ʿUmar ibn al-Khattab recommended a vocal call to prayer. Muhammad turned to his servant Bilâl and said: "Bilâl, call the Muslims to prayer." Bilâl climbed onto the roof of the Mosque at Medina and became the first to call out the *adhân*.[1] From the very beginning of Islam, according to this Hadith, the muezzin's call is both compared to and distinguished from church bells: the Hadith identifies the *nâqûs* (a word which designates at times a bell, at times a simander, σήμαντρον, a wooden percussion instrument used in certain Eastern churches)[2] as the audible symbol of Christianity and proposes the *adhân* as a similar symbol for Islam. Another Hadith, transmitted by the traditionalist Muslim, relates that Muhammad disliked the sound of bells and that he even said that angels avoided coming to places where bells could be heard.[3]

This same process of imitation and distinction that we see between bells and the *adhân* is found, a generation later, in sacred architecture, with the construction of the first minarets. The first Muslims had no minarets: their muezzins, such as Bilâl, simply called out the *adhân* from the roofs of the mosques. For this reason, some Muslim communities (in particular Wahhabites) still refuse to use minarets. The first minarets were probably constructed during the reign of Mu'âwiya (661–80), the first Umayyad caliph. These minarets are the monumental expressions of an Islam that seeks to affirm itself over and against Christianity, still the majority religion in much of the caliphate. The first minarets should be seen as part of a monumental building program (including the Dome of the Rock and al-Aqsa mosque in Jerusalem and the Umayyad mosques in Damascus and Medina) that affirms the legitimacy of the new Umayyad dynasty, which had emerged victorious from the *fitna*.[4] The minaret rises up across from the church bell tower, against which it competes for the conquest of the urban skyline, soon rising well above the height from which the *adhân* can best be heard.

During this same period, in the first decades of the Umayyad dynasty, this opposition between bells and muezzins appears in legal texts, particularly in prohibitions or restrictions on bell ringing. Such restrictions may have been placed on Christians who submitted to Muslim rule during the conquest. Abû Yûsuf Ya'qûb (d. 798) affirms that during the conquest of Syria, General Abû 'Ubayda negotiated a peace treaty that stipulated, among other things, that Christians "will not ring the *nâqûs*, either before our call to prayer or during theirs"; the Christians of 'Anât receive guarantees that they may ring their *nâqûs* at any hour, day or night.[5] The same author says that the treaty of Hîra guarantees that Christians may ring the *nâqûs* as they please during their feast days.[6] Occasionally religious rivalry is seen in sonorous battles between bell ringers and *muezzins;* some Muslims complain that Christians deliberately ring their bells at the hours of the *adhân.*[7]

More sweeping prohibitions are found in the Convention of 'Umar, which, according to Muslim tradition, the second caliph, 'Umar ibn al-Khattab (634–44), imposed on the Christians of Syria. Antoine Fattal has shown that these restrictions were in fact imposed little by little upon the *dhimmis* over the course of the first Muslim century and confirmed by 'Umar II (717–20).[8] The first author to give us the full text of this convention is al-Turtûshî (d. 1126), in his *Sirâj al-mulûk.* In this text, the conquered Christians of Syria address a letter to the Caliph 'Umar, reminding him of the promises they made when they surrendered to him. They present a long list of prohibitions which they promise to respect: against the construction of new churches and monasteries, against teaching the Qur'ân to their children, against wearing "Muslim" clothes or turbans, bearing arms, etc. Some of these measures seek to limit or prohibit the public expression of Christianity. Hence the Christians promise not to place crosses on the exterior of their churches, show their sacred texts in public, make public religious processions, or pray noisily or ostentatiously. It is in this context that they promise: "We will sound the *nâqûs* very softly in our churches."[9] Other authors transmit variant versions of the convention. According to Ibn 'Asâkir (d. 1176), 'Umar decreed that the Christians "will not sound the *nâqûs* before the Muslims' call to prayer."[10] The treaty of Damascus, which, according to Ghâzî b. al-Wâsiî (d. after 1292), was negotiated between 'Umar and the Syrian Christians, stipulates that the Christians "will not ring the *nâqûs* outside of their churches."[11]

Such restrictions are frequent, but they are neither ubiquitous nor uniform.[12] In spite of local or temporary prohibitions, church bells continued to ring in the different regions of the dâr al-Islâm. Ibn Qutayba (d. 889) relates that the Caliph Mu'âwiya, suffering from insomnia, was bothered by the *nâqûs* from the Melkite churches. He finally became so upset that he sent an ambassador to Constantinople to complain to the emperor![13]

These conflicts occasionally result in the destruction of bells or churches. Mas'ûdi tells that the Caliph al-Walîd b. 'Abd al-Malik was preaching one day in a mosque when he heard the bells of a neighboring church. He ordered that the church be destroyed, which prompted the emperor of Constantinople to send a letter of protest.[14] Similarly, a Seljukid governor had a monastery in Mayyâfâriqîn destroyed because of the noise of its bells.[15] According to Abû Makârim, a twelfth-century Coptic author, when the guardian of the Egyptian church of Matariyya rang the bells in the presence of Muslims, this became a pretext for the Muslim authorities to confiscate the church and transform it into a mosque.[16] We could cite other examples of bell ringing that provoke either the destruction of churches or new restrictions, but this would only serve to underline that these prohibitions are far from universal.[17]

Sometimes the chronicles of conquest insist on the fact that the victorious Muslims silence the infidel bells. According to Maqqarî, when Mûsa ibn Nusayr invaded Spain in 712, he destroyed all its churches and broke all the *nâqûs* that he found.[18] 'Imâd al-Din describes how Saladin, after conquering Jerusalem, purified and restored the al-Aqsa mosque, silencing the bells and replacing them with the *adhân*.[19] In this context, the bells taken from the churches of the dâr al-Harb represented a prestigious booty: a later example is that of the Marinids who hung bells taken during raids on Christian Spain in the Qarawiyyîn mosque in Fez.[20]

Muslim jurists, including the founders of the *madhhab*, continue to tackle this problem. Al-Shâfi'î (m. 819), founder of the Shafite *madhhab*, proposes, in his *Kitâb al-'umm*, a model *dhimma* (pact of protection) to impose on infidels. He affirms: "You should not show the cross, manifest your polytheism, build churches or meeting-places for your prayers, ring the *nâqûs*, proclaim your polytheist beliefs concerning Jesus son of Mary before a Muslim."[21] Mâlik rules that one should simply forbid *dhimmîs* to ring the *nâqûs*.[22] Some Muslim rulers of the Maghreb and al-Andalus, faithful to their Malikite principles, enforce these prohibitions. Yet bells continue to ring in many regions of the dâr al-Islâm, and many texts, such as the *Sîrat 'Antar* (a twelfth-century romance) associate bells with Christians.[23] Some geographers imagine that in Rome, emblematic capital of Christendom, 120,000 church bells ring.[24] Bells do not always inspire hostility in Muslim authors; Abû 'Amir ibn Shuhayd (992–1035) tells how he passed a night in a church in Cordoba, listening with delight to the sound of the bells.[25]

Ninth-Century Cordoba

Eulogius of Cordoba and Paul Alvarus, apologists for the Cordoban martyrs of the 850s, testify to the animosity and derision that this rivalry between *nâqûs* and *adhân* could inspire: Muslims' mockery of the Christians' bells, the hatred and revulsion that the call of the muezzin arouses in some hostile Christians, the demolition of bell towers, and the dreams of converting minarets into bell towers.[26]

Eulogius and Alvarus exhibit an extreme and unbridled hostility toward Islam; they reproach their coreligionaries for not being hostile enough toward the religion and the rule of their "Chaldean" masters. The martyrs of Cordoba publicly denounced Islam and its prophet and in so doing merited the death sentence according to the *sharî'a*. The martyr movement provoked the Umayyad emirs 'Abd al-Rahmân II (822–52) and Muhammad I (852–86) to impose punitive restrictions on the entire Christian community of Cordoba, even though it seems that they were generally hostile toward the martyrs. In order to prove that the martyrs were right to denounce Islam, even if in so doing they were condemned to death, Eulogius and Alvarus attempt to show that the "Chaldeans" persecute their Christian subjects. Among other crimes, says Eulogius, they mock the rites and solemnities of the Christians. It is in this context that he presents Muslim reactions to the ringing of church bells:

> The masses, seduced by vulgar superstition, as soon as their ears catch the sound of clanging metal [bells], do not hesitate to proffer all sorts of maledictions nor to pronounce all sorts of vulgarities. Hence it is not wrong to curse them, they who inspire in their followers such hatred toward God's prophecy.[27]

Alvarus attempts to show that Muhammad is a precursor of the Antichrist; for this he gives, in his *Indiculus luminosus,* a detailed exegesis of Job and the prophets, who, he says, had predicted the coming of Muhammad and his deadly heresy. Alvarus affirms that the Muslims, when they see Christian processions pass by, throw stones and sing obscene songs. The sound of ringing bells also provokes their derision:

> But when they hear the sound of the basilica, that is the ringing in the air (which sounds at the canonical hours to call the faithful together), they stand there, rolling their heads in derision and contempt; they moan and proffer profanities. Not only do they insult the whole of the flock of our Lord Christ, both sexes and all orders together, but moreover they attack them and mock them with a thousand sordid infamies.[28]

We must not forget the nature of these sources, whose authors are particularly hostile to any entente with their "Chaldean" masters. We cannot accept these caricatures as accurate portrayals of Cordoba Muslim attitudes toward Christians. But these passages show us, first of all, that the Christians of Cordoba still rang their bells in the middle of the ninth century; they demonstrate, moreover, that the bells could provoke reactions of hostility or derision on the part of some Muslims.

For some hostile Christians, the call of the muezzin could provoke the same aversion, although here it is the hostility of a repressed minority, not that of a disdainful majority. For Eulogius, the *adhân* is both the emblematic expression of the heresy of Muhammad's acolytes and the means of its diffusion. He claims that the devil incited Muhammad to repudiate the prophets and the Gospels and to affirm that Christ was a mere man: a holy man, indeed, through whom God performed miracles, but still a man like Adam, inferior to God the Father. The minaret and the *adhân,* for Eulogius, are the most nefarious visible and audible manifestations of this heresy:

> But even as he preached other unheard of crimes, products of the imagination of this demon that dominated him and who transfigured himself into an angel of light, he [Muhammad] had temples built for the celebration of his accursed dogma, establishing as the ultimate seat of his idolatry a very high tower that dominated the other buildings, from which he could issue the decrees of his insane sacrilege to those infected by the poison of his iniquity. And today, the priests of his impiety, educated by him, observe this rule: like donkeys, their jaws gaping, their filthy lips open, they bray their horrible edicts, but first block both ears with their fingers, as if they themselves could not bear to hear the wicked edict that they proclaim to others. Each time my grandfather of pious memory, Eulogius, heard this impious braying, he immediately protected himself by marking his forehead with

> the sign of the cross and moaned this Psalm: "Keep not thy silence, O God: hold not thy peace, and be not still, O God. For, lo, thine enemies make a tumult: and they that hate thee have lifted up their heads" (Ps. 83:1–2). We also, as soon as we hear the voice of the herald of lies, we immediately pray: "Confounded be all they that serve graven images, that boast themselves of idols" (Ps. 97:7).[29]

For Eulogius, it was Muhammad himself who had the first minaret constructed: a tower that rose above the surrounding buildings and became the supreme symbol of the Chaldeans' idolatry, the place from which their "heresy" was diffused. In the absence of evidence from archaeology or from Arab texts, these passages show us that there were indeed minarets in Cordoba at this time and that they had become symbols of Islam for at least some Christians.[30] Eulogius and Alvarus repeatedly use comparisons with animals to denigrate their adversaries.[31] Here the muezzin's call is presented as the braying of a donkey, "horrible" both in form and in content. The fact that the muezzin covers his ears when he proclaims his "criminal edict" suggests that he is ashamed of it. Eulogius's reaction, like that of his grandfather, is not to openly mock the *adhân* but rather to protect himself with the sign of the cross and to mumble an appropriate Psalm, emphasizing in this way the continuity between the new "Chaldeans" and the biblical "Chaldeans" who once persecuted God's people. Little did it bother Eulogius that these verses condemning idolatry could scarcely be applied to Muslims.

Eulogius makes little comment about the contents of the *adhân*. Alvarus addresses this question when he invokes the muezzin in the same chapter of his *Indiculus luminosus* in which he describes the Muslim reaction to church bells.

> And lo! Every day, by day and by night, they curse God in their towers and in their obscure mountains, praising at the same time, in their testimonies, God and their shameless, perjuring, rabid and evil prophet.[32]

The muezzin's praise of God becomes for Alvarus a curse, because the muezzin invokes in the same breath God and Muhammad as his prophet.

Alvarus attempts to situate Islam in Christian eschatology by making Muhammad a precursor of the Antichrist. He affirms that the prophecies of Daniel 11, normally interpreted as referring to the persecutions inflicted by Antiochus IV, may also be understood as predictions of the nefarious heresy of Muhammad. The Muslims' prophet is the king who, according to Daniel, "shall honor the God of forces [Deum Moazim]: and a god whom his fathers knew not shall he honor with gold, and silver, and with precious stones, and pleasant things. Thus shall he do in the most strongholds with a strange god, whom he shall acknowledge and increase with glory: and he shall cause them to rule over many, and shall divide the land for them" (Dn. 11:38–39).

Who is this god Moazim? Alvarus explains that the Hebrew word means "fortis uel fortissimus."[33] Muhammad simulated veneration of the one strong God in order to impose his rule over the nations.

> And hence they vociferate every day in their smoky towers, in a loud and monstrous battle-cry, their snouts gaping like savage beasts, their lips hanging down, their throats belching, they vociferously proclaim that they must protect Maozim along with a foreign god that he knew. That is to say that they must protect Maozim, whom they call Cobar (which means "great") along with a foreign god, that is that demon who appeared to him in the form of Gabriel, that they be protected by one name, so that this error be hidden in the hearts of the believers, while by the name of the Great God he exalt the rite of vociferation and infect noble souls by his superstitious efforts and his impious spirit. But in order to avoid appearing to be speaking in enigmas, or to prefer the products of human ingenuity to those inspired by divine spirit, I must present clear proofs of what I mean. These people preserve some terms similar to those in the Hebrew language. Those days in which these devotees consecrate their insanity in the house of their idol they call *Almozem*, for in ancient times it was in this period that this gentile nation flocked from all around to worship this idol. At the same period this accursed mob meets every year and continues to perpetually serve the self-same demon who, in the greatness of their faith, they believe to have been born in this same place. To this very day, then, they venerate Maozim in his stronghold, in accordance with the prophet inspired by God, and in these days they call him by his traditional name, during the month that they call *Almoarram,* just as once the idolaters honored him, they today, with a heightened perfection, as they believe, lift him up toward heaven.[34]

Alvarus then tries to link four names. First there is Moazim, the strong God or God of forces of the prophet Daniel; the Arabic translation of this word is *akbar* (great), a word which the muezzins bellow from their "smoky towers," and which Alvarus deforms into "Cobar." This god Moazim/Cobar, affirms Alvarus, is the demon who, in the form of the archangel Gabriel, revealed the Qur'ân to Muhammad.[35] The second word is *Almozem* (probably Alvarus's deformation of *al-mawsim al-hajj*), referring to the pilgrimage rites in Mecca.[36] Third, *Almoarram* is the name of the Muslim month of Muharram. And finally, *muezzin* (*mu'adhdhin*) is a term which Alvarus does not explicitly mention but which seems to be the inspiration of these passages concerning Moazim.[37]

Alvarus, in this complex exegetical exercise, deforms the *adhân* into a call to idolatry or heresy. This god Moazim, about whom the prophet Daniel warned us, is worshipped by the Chaldeans in their obscure rites and their distant pilgrimages. To better hide this infamy, Muhammad and his adepts do not use the name Moazim, but discreetly call him simply akbar, great. A naive Christian could think that to call God "great" is pious. But Alvarus's tortuous exegesis permits him to denigrate the content of the call to prayer and not only the form, which he compares to the belching of savage beasts.

In response to the martyr movement, the emir Muhammad I proclaimed punitive restrictions against the entire Christian community: he banned Christians from his court and ordered the destruction of a few recently constructed churches. Moreover, says Eulogius, "He toppled the towers of the basilicas, demolished the summits of the temples, and prostrated the peaks of the pinnacles."[38] The destruction of bell towers struck at the most visible and audible symbols of Christianity and affirmed the superiority of Islam against its Christian detractors. A century later, when Caliph 'Abd al-Rahman III renovated and expanded the principal mosque of Cordoba, he erected a high minaret which dominated, triumphant, the caliphal capital.[39] Alvarus, for his part, dreamed of the conversion of the earlier minaret, pernicious symbol of infidelity:

> Alas and alack! Our days are ignorant of Christ's wisdom and are filled with diabolical zeal. No one can be found who, in obedience to God's edicts, makes the air ring on the mountains of Babylon and who bears the standard of the cross of the faith onto the dark towers of insolence, offering the evening sacrifice to God.[40]

Al-Mansûr and the Bells of Santiago

Many authors, Arab and Latin, describe the fifty-six devastating raids that Al-Mansûr inflicted on the Christian principalities of northern Spain. In what is probably the most infamous of these raids, the *hâjib* and his army sacked Santiago de Compostela in 997.[41] Ibn Darrâj, poet at Al-Mansûr's court, who accompanied the expedition, subsequently wrote three poems (preserved in his *Dîwân*) celebrating the exploit. He also composed the official communiqué of the expedition; this text is now lost but may be partially preserved in such texts as the *Muqtabis* of Ibn Hayyân or the *Jadhwat al-Muqtabis* of al-Humaydî (both texts date from the eleventh century); it is subsequently used by Ibn 'Idhârî, a Maghribi chronicler of the fourteenth century.[42] According to Ibn 'Idhârî, when Al-Mansûr arrived in Compostela, the city had been abandoned by its inhabitants, who had taken flight. The *hâjib* systematically razed the city, including the basilica, "which is for them the equivalent of the Ka'ba for us." But he spared the tomb of St. James, expressly ordering that it be left intact.[43] Al-Mansûr's destructive jihad targeted the Christian cities that had rebelled against the authority of Muslim Cordoba, razing their churches, but stopped short of profaning the tomb of the apostle James, a Qur'ânic saint worthy of veneration.

We can glean information here and there from other Maghribi chroniclers who no doubt had access to early texts that have since been lost. Ibn Khaldûn's description of the expedition is similar to Ibn 'Idhârî's, although he adds that Al-Mansûr brought the doors of the church of St. James back to Cordoba and had them incorporated into the roof of the great mosque.[44] In the seventeenth century, Al-Maqqarî reiterates Ibn Hayyân's narration; he affirms that the *hâjib* brought the church bells to Cordoba on the backs of Christian captives and hung them in the mosque of Cordoba. He also made chained Christian captives work on the renovation and expansion of the mosque.[45]

Numerous Latin chroniclers also describe the expedition. Sampiro, notary at the Leonese royal court from 990 and subsequently bishop of Astorga from 1034 to 1040, composed a chronicle of the reigns of the Asturian and Leonese kings from Alfonso III (866–910) to Alfonso V (999–1028). He describes how, during the reign of Vermudo II (982–999), "their king who falsely usurped the name of Almanzor" devastated, during twelve consecutive summers, the kingdoms of the Franks, of Pamplona, and of León. This false king fought his way to Compostela, sowing desolation in his wake and arrived, full of rage, at Saint James's tomb. But the saint repelled him and in terror he took flight. Sampiro says nothing of the church bells.[46] The *Historia Silense,* composed at the beginning of the twelfth century, makes a brief allusion to the sack of Compostela in the midst of a catalogue of depredations made by this "barbarian," but makes no mention of the bells.[47] We find more or less the same presentation of the raid in the twelfth-century *Chronica Najerensis.*[48] The anonymous author of the *Historia Compostellana* minimizes the shame this raid represented for the apostle by letting him have his revenge: James terrifies Al-Mansûr and makes him flee, then strikes the Muslim army with diarrhea and dysentery and thus kills the "king Almanzor," who gives his soul up to Muhammad.[49]

It is with the chroniclers of the thirteenth century that the confrontation between minaret and bell tower takes on its full polemical value. Lucas de Tuy, in his *Miracula Sancti Isidori,* tells how the miracles that St. Isidore performed in Seville caused the Muslims to admire him and even led some of them to convert. The "Miramolin" (the Almohad caliph), in order to put a stop to this, had the church of St. Isidore destroyed and built in its stead a mosque with a minaret. But the good St. Isidore took vengeance by making three muezzins successively fall to their deaths when they tried to make the call to prayer.[50] This same Lucas de Tuy, in his *Chronicon mundi,* gives a version of Almanzor's expedition based on those of Sampiro and the *Historia Silense.* He describes how Almanzor destroyed the whole city and the church and then "came to the tomb of the blessed Apostle James to destroy it, but, terrified by some sort of lightning, he left." Lucas adds that the saint wrought vengeance, striking the *hâjib*'s army with diarrhea and dysentery. He adds, "The barbarian Al-Mansûr took the small bells from the church of Saint James and had them brought back to Cordoba as an emblem [*ob insigne*] and had them hung as lamps in his oratory."[51] Lucas closes his *Chronicon* with the capture of Cordoba by Fernando III and the conversion of the great mosque into the cathedral. Once "all the filth of Muhammad was eliminated," the ex-mosque was reconsecrated.

> They found the bells which, long ago, the king of Cordoba, Almanzor, had symbolically removed from the Church of the Apostle Saint James. Fernando, Catholic king, had them brought back to the church of St. James on the shoulders of Saracens. The city of Cordoba was taken in the year 1274 of the Hispanic era [1236 AD] and the illustrious king Ferdinand returned to Toledo victorious and full of glory. What

> a blessed king, who erased the insult to the Spaniards, toppling the throne of the barbarians and restoring to the church of the Apostle Saint James, with great honor, the bells which had long been in Cordoba, a mark of infamy and obloquy to Christ's name.[52]

Lucas emphasizes that the removal of the bells is a symbolic act; he twice uses the words *ob insigne*. The taking of the bells is an insult to Christ's name; their restitution removes the shame and transforms it into glory; the Catholic king now covers the "barbarians" with shame: their throne (*solium*) is toppled; their religion (or rather "the filth of Muhammad") is banished from their former capital.

For Rodrigo Jiménez de Rada, the transformation of the mosque and its minaret is a restoration. In his *Historia Arabum,* Rodrigo affirms that Muhammad decreed that the precepts of his law should be proclaimed "from the towers where once bells rang."[53] For Rodrigo, the minarets are bell towers that have been usurped, perverted from their proper purpose: Christian princes have the duty to return them to their original function. Little does it matter that the minarets of Cordoba had never been bell towers. The symbolic importance of the conversion of Cordoba's minaret was clear to both Christians and Muslims long before the conquest of the city in 1236. In the first half of the twelfth century, Ibn Bassâm affirms that Alfonso VI "had prepared for the great mosque of Cordoba—may God protect its precinct from such a horrific calamity—a bell, which he had taken great pains to have cast."[54] Valencian poet Ibn 'Amira (thirteenth century) laments that James I of Aragon, after his conquest of Valencia, replaced the muezzin's call with the clang of bells.[55] An associate of Rodrigo, Mark of Toledo, writing c. 1210 (well before the capture of Cordoba), denounces the scandal represented by the perversion of churches into mosques and justifies their reconquest: "In those places where once priests offered the holy sacrifice to Jesus Christ, now the name of the false prophet is exalted, and in the church towers where the bells once rang out, now profane proclamations deafen the ears of the faithful."[56]

When, in his *De rebus Hispaniae,* Rodrigo Jiménez de Rada describes the transformation of Toledo's mosque into a church, he says that the archbishop Bernard "entered into the principal mosque during the night, accompanied by Christian knights, and, having eliminated the filth of Muhammad, erected altars and hung in the great tower bells for calling the faithful."[57] He offers a narration of the capture of Cordoba, emphasizing the parallels between minaret and bell tower, *adhân* and ringing. He presents the raid of 997 in essentially the same terms as Lucas de Tuy, telling how Al-Mansûr "as a sign of victory brought back the small bells and placed them in the mosque of Cordoba as lamps. They stayed there a long time."[58] His description of the capture and "purification" of the mosque of Cordoba deserves to be examined in detail. Rodrigo relates that after the surrender of the city:

> The Arabs of the city left safe and sound and on the feast day of the Apostles Peter and Paul [June 29th] the patrician city was purged of the filth of Muhammad. The king, in the main minaret, where the name of the perfidious one [Muhammad] used to be invoked, now undertook to lift up the wood of the vivifying Cross, and all began to acclaim with him, with joy and tears, "God help us!" Then the royal insignia was placed next to the Lord's cross, and a voice of joy and delight was heard coming from the tabernacle of the just, as the priests and monks intoned the *Te Deum:* "God we praise you, Lord in you we trust."
>
> Then John, venerable bishop of Osma, chancellor of the royal court, with the bishops Gonzalo de Cuenca and Domingo de Baeza, Adam de Plasencia and Sancho de Coria, entered into the mosque of Cordoba, which surpassed all the mosques of the Arabs in its size and decoration. And since the venerable John exercised the primacy for Rodrigo, archbishop of Toledo, who was at this time in Rome, once the filth of Muhammad had been eliminated and holy water had been sprinkled, John transformed it into a church, erected an altar in the honor of the Blessed Virgin, and solemnly celebrated mass. . . .
>
> And since, to the shame of the Christian people, the bells of the church of St. James at Compostela had been placed in the mosque of Cordoba, where they had served as lamps, ever since they had been taken by Al-Mansûr (as I related earlier), King Ferdinand had them brought back to the church of blessed James, to which they were properly restored.[59]

Rodrigo describes how Fernando climbed the minaret, visual and audible symbol of conquered Islam, to place there the insignia of both Christianity and of royal power. This "great tower" from which the muezzins had called out the *adhân,* invoking Muhammad as a prophet, the king himself

Christianizes. The bells can obviously not yet ring, but the *Te Deum* already replaces the *adhân*. Fernando is the counterpart of al-Mansûr: the infidel prince destroyed churches and absconded with the bells of Santiago; the Christian king transforms mosques into churches and restores the bells to their rightful place and function.

The examples we have examined represent only a small part of the conversions of minarets into bell towers during the *reconquista*. In general, the laconic documentation makes only brief mention of the transformation of mosques into churches and seldom mentions the installation of bells in the former minaret, even though we may suppose that this was one of the fundamental acts of this transformation. There are a few other documented instances, for example, the mosque of Murcia. James I of Aragon relates, in his *Llibre dels feyts,* that he had a mosque near his palace transformed into a church because it was inadmissible that he hear the "sabaçala" (call to prayer) proclaimed when he was trying to sleep.[60] While James here affirms that the Murcian muezzin's call disturbed him, elsewhere he guaranteed to Muslims the right to call to prayer. Throughout the Iberian peninsula, everywhere that Muslim communities survived, the call of the muezzin continued to ring out. It was only in 1311 that the Council of Vienna prohibited the *adhân* in an attempt to silence the muezzins of reconquered Christian Spain.[61]

Notes

Introduction

1. Jacques de Vitry, *Lettres,* 1:34–46.

2. See Thomas of Cantimpré, *Vita Sanctae Lutgardis virginis cistercensae; Supplementum ad vitam Sanctae Mariae Oigniacensis.*

3. "Tuo namque ipsius gladio occidere te multum cupio." Petrus Alfonsi, *Diálogi contra Iudeos,* 10; *Dialogue against the Jews,* 44.

4. "Insistendum est ad confutationem tam perfide legis, et ostendendum quod non sit lex Dei, et quod Saraceni tenentur recipere auctoritatem Euangelii et ueteris Testamenti. Hoc autem ostendere possumus per ipsum Alchoranum, ut Golias proprio gladio iuguletur." Riccoldo da Montecroce, *Libellus contra legem Saracenorum,* ch. 2, p. 68.

5. Peter Abelard, *Historia calamitatum,* trans. B. Radice, in *The Letters of Abelard and Heloise,* 61; Bernard of Clairvaux, *Letters,* 239 (to Pope Innocent II).

6. Mentioned by Ghâzi Ibn al-Wâsitî, *Radd ʿalâ ahl al-dhimma wa man tabiʿahum;* cited by Anne-Marie Eddé and Françoise Micheau, *L'Orient au temps des Croisades,* 359.

Chapter 1. Antihagiography

1. Moore, *The Origins of European Dissent;* Moore, *The Formation of a Persecuting Society;* Frassetto, ed., *Heresy and the Persecuting Society in the Middle Ages: Essays on the Work of R. I. Moore.*

2. See Tolan, *Saracens,* ch. 5.

3. See Tolan, ed., *Medieval Christian Perceptions of Islam;* Southern, *Western Views of Islam;* Daniel, *Islam and the West;* Kedar, *Crusade and Mission,* 3–41.

4. See Moore, *The Origins of European Dissent,* esp. 1–114.

5. See ibid., 82–101; Landbert, *Medieval Heresy,* 44–48.

6. Embrico of Mainz, *La vie de Mahomet.* Cambier discusses Embrico's possible sources in his introduction (5–37). See Tolan, *Saracens,* ch. 6.

7. Ward, *Miracles and the Medieval Mind*, 17.

8. This parallels some of the contemporary beliefs about Antichrist: while some commentators believed that Antichrist would work real miracles with the aid of the devil, others maintained that he would only feign the outward attributes of sanctity and perform false miracles through magic. See Emmerson, *Antichrist in the Middle Ages*, 92–93. Embrico's Magus and Mammutius fit the latter model.

9. See G. Cambier's introduction to Embrico's *La vie de Mahomet* for examples.

10. See Madeleine Tyssens, "L'epopée latine," in Regis Boyer, *L'epopée*, 39–52. At 40n, Tyssens gives a long list of medieval epic and hagiographical poems in hexameters. She summarizes, "L'hexamètre (souvent l'hexamètre léonin) se prête au développement de tous les thèmes sérieux" (39).

11. George, *Venantius Fortunatus*, 126.

12. See de Ghellinck, *L'essor de la littérature latine*, 403–6. Hexameters are occasionally used for the life of a recent saint: e.g., the two lives of St. Hugh of Cluny (cf. Ghellinck, 405) and the anonymous *Gesta Alberonis Metrica* (Ghellinck, 418).

13. This structure is expounded by Altman, "Types of Opposition and the Structure of Latin Saints' Lives"; see also Olsen, "De Historiis Sanctorum."

14. Ferreiro, "Jerome's Polemic," 315–17.

15. These two authors' works are in PL 171. On them, see W. Jackson, "Hildebert of Lavardin" and "Marbod of Rennes." On Hildebert's use of classical poets, see W. von den Steinen, "Les sujets d'inspiration chez les poètes latins du XIIe siècle." On Marbod's hagiographical opus, see degl'Innocenti, *L'opera agiografica di Marbodo di Rennes*.

16. Hildebert's poem is based on the ninth-century Latin prose translation of Paul the Deacon, which survives in over 120 manuscripts, making it the most popular of the Latin versions. Kunze, *Studien zur Legende der heiligen Maria Aegyptiaca*, 26–28, 173–78. Hildebert's text was the most popular of the Latin verse versions; it survives in 40 manuscripts. (Kunze, 59n6, adds 15 manuscripts to the 25 listed by Manitius, *Geschichte der lateinischen Literatur des Mittelalters*, 3:644 and 861.) On the relationships of the various versions (Greek, Latin, and vernacular—primarily German), see Kunze, *Studien*, 166–67. On the medieval French versions of the text, see Peter Dembowski's introduction to his edition of *La vie de Sainte Marie l'Égyptienne*, 13–32. Dembowski says (9) that version T of the French text was translated into Spanish around 1215: *La vida de Santa María Egipciaca*. On the German and Dutch versions (and their relations to the various Latin versions), see Kunze, ed., *Die Legende der heiligen Maria Aegyptiaca*.

17. "Annos undenos quadrupliciterque novenos," PL 171:1333C.

18. See Cambier, "Embricon de Mayence," esp. 468. The manuscript is Paris, Bibliothèque Nationale MS Latin 5129; two later MSS (Douai 825 and 882) also attribute the text to Hildebert, but according to Cambier, they derive this attribution from the Paris MS.

19. On this, see Cambier, "Embricon de Mayence," 47

20. Cambier gives the full text of the poem, along with a French translation. "Embricon of Mayence," 469.

21. Max Manitius attributed it to another Embrico who was dean of Mainz, became bishop of Augsburg in 1064, and died in 1077. Manitius, *Geschichte der lateinischen Literatur des Mittelalters*, 2:582–87. Two German scholars argued against this thesis, object-

ing that the *Vita auctoris* does not mention that the the author of the *Vita Mahumeti* was ever bishop of Augsburg and that the text's style places later than 10779–in particular, that his mastery of the Leonine hexameter show the influence of poets such as Hildebert. Wolfram von den Steinen, "Literarische Anfänge in Basel," esp. 282–85. Von den Steinen argues that 1090 is the earliest possible date, saying that c. 1120 is more likely. G. Cambier attempts to answer these objections in his "Embricon" and to argue for the attribution to the bishop of Augsburg. He declares that the poem is a parody of events in a succession crisis in Constantinople in the 1030s; therefore, he dates the text between 1034 and 1041. I must agree with Richard Southern, however, in finding Cambier's arguments unconvincing (*Western Views of Islam,* 30n). Both the content and the style (not least Embrico's apparent familiarity with the work of Hildebert and his school) argue for an early twelfth-century date.

22. He later asserts: "Nam gens exosa Christo, gens perniciosa, Gens Mahumet parens et ratione carens " (ll. 191–92).

23. Thomas Burman has suggested to me a possible origin of this association with Libya. Yathrib, the Arabic name for Medina, was at times transliterated as Trib, Tribus, or Tripus, and was hence at times confused with Tripoli (in Libya).

24. Tunc rex inuictus Theodosius et benedictus,
Hostis perfidie, filius Ecclesie
Summus erat regum sub quo sacra sanctio legum
Predicante pio floruit Ambrosio. (ll. 121–25)

25. See Cambier's introduction to his edition of Embrico's *La vie de Mahomet,* 12–14.

26. See Yvan Lepage's introduction to his edition of Alexandre du Pont's *Roman de Mahomet*, 18–32; A. Abel, "Bahira," EI[2] 1:922–23.

27. Ferreiro, "Jerome's Polemic," 314.

28. See Flint, *Rise of Magic,* 331–54.

29. Marbod's poem is in PL 171:1593–1604.

30. Ferreiro, "Jerome's Polemic."

31. Marbod of Rennes, *Epistolae* VI, in PL 171, 1483–85; translated by Robert I. Moore in *The Origins of European Dissent*, 84–85.

32. "Pater urbis," 109 and 150; "pontificem," 151; Embrico also says that the Magus was "potificari | Adspirans auide," 111–12.

33. The same is true of the related terms "pontificare," "pontificium," and "pontificalis": see, e.g., Niermeyer, *Mediae Latinitatis lexicon minus*, 812–13.

34. Emmerson, *Antichrist in the Middle Ages*, 91.

35. The story of Simon Magus and his confrontation with the apostle Peter is attested in many medieval sources. One of the oldest and most widely known versions was that of the apocryphal *Actus Petri cum Simone*; English translation with introduction and bibliography by Elliot, *The Apocryphal New Testament*, 390–443.

36. See Daniel, *Islam and the West,* 85–86, 89–90.

37. On this episode and similar episodes in other lives of Muhammad, see Cambier, "L'épisode des taureaux."

38. This *topos* is found in hagiography from the very beginning. Rufinus Aquileus,

in the *Historia monachorum in Aegypto,* says that Abbas Bes drove away hippopotami and crocodiles through the invocation of Jesus and that he and his companions similarly warded off an attack by crocodiles. *Historia monachorum in Aegypto* (iv.3 and Epilogue 11–13); English translation by Norman Russell, *Lives of the Desert Fathers.*

39. He also has wild asses and other beasts do his bidding (*Historia monachorum in Aegypto,* xii.5–9). A mother Hyena asked another hermit to cure her blind pups; when he did so, she showed her thanks by giving him a ram skin (ibid., xxi.15–16).

40. See Flint, *Rise of Magic,* 197–99, 259–60.

41. The speaking dog is in *Actus Petri cum Simone* 9 (Lipsius and Bonnet, eds., 56–57; Elliot, trans., 406–7). The ravenous dogs are not in the *Actus*; the only source I have been able to identify is from the thirteenth century: Jacobus de Voragine, *Legenda Aurea*, cap. 89, p. 373.

42. See, for example, *Historia monachorum in Aegypto* i.1–3, 10–11, 28; vi.1; viii.48; x.12; xii.10–11; xxii.6–9.

43. PL 171:1327.

44. PL 171:1336.

45. PL 171:1335–36.

46. PL 171:1337.

47. See Daniel, *Islam and the West.*

48. In the *Gesta Pontificum Cenomannensium,* quoted by Moore in *The Origins of European Dissent,* 86–87.

49. See Flint, *Rise of Magic*, esp. 333–38, where she discusses the legends surrounding Noah's son Ham.

50. On Christian accounts of Muhammad's supposed epilepsy, see Daniel, *Islam and the West*, 28–29, 90, 104–5.

51. "Vis coelica," PL 171:1331.

52. This episode was often counted among the miracles of the Virgin. See Ward, *Miracles and the Medieval Mind*, 15, 123, 144.

53. See Daniel, *Islam and the West,* 209–11.

54. On the various versions of this legend, see below, chapter 2.

55. Gregory the Great (*Dialogues* I.4.6) tells of a magician monk Basilius, who, out of dislike for his abbot, suspended the abbot's house in midair by invoking demons. Flint, *Rise of Magic,* 121.

56. See, e.g., Daniel, *Islam and the West*, 83–86, 209, 342. Daniel refers to the author of the *Vita Mahumeti* as Hildebert of Lavardin (on the attribution to Hildebert, see discussion above).

57. My thanks to Deirdre Stone for her comments and corrections to an earlier version of this article.

Chapter 2. A Mangled Corpse

1. Gibbon, *The Decline and Fall of the Roman Empire,* 3:113n.

2. On these polemics, see Tolan, *Saracens,* chs. 3 and 4, where fuller bibliography is given.

3. Guibert de Nogent, *Dei Gesta per Francos.*

4. Matthew Paris, *Chronica maior,* 3:360. Matthew's work is a compilation, and he includes several different (and conflicting) lives of Muhammad, culled from different sources: see 1:269–72 and 3:344–61. On Matthew Paris's *Chronica maior*, see Gransden, *Historical Writing in England*, 356–79; Vaughan, *Matthew Paris*; S. Lewis, *The Art of Matthew Paris*. The fifteenth-century French epic *Ogier le Danois* also has Muhammad killed by pigs on a dung heap.

5. The first description of his death is found in the anonymous *Iniquus Mahometus,* ed. A. Mancini, in "Per lo studio della leggenda di Maomette in Occidente," 345–49. The other is the *Liber Nycholay,* 14.

6. Daniel, *Islam and the West*, 104–5.

7. The author was probably from the area near Seville in the eighth or early ninth century, according to Wolf, "Christian Views of Islam," 93ff. See also Wolf, "The Earliest Latin Lives of Muhammad," 90–91.

8. *Historia de Mahometh pseudopropheta*, in Eulogius of Cordoba, *Liber apologeticus martyrum*, in CSM, 483–86. Also edited by Diaz y Diaz and Ceinos, "Los textos antimahometanos." Cited here from the edition and translation by Wolf in "The Earliest Latin Lives of Muhammad," 97–99.

9. Pedro Pascual, *Sobre la seta Mahometana,* in *Obras* 4:1–357; the description of Muhammad's death is at 138–42.

10. Mancini, "Per lo studio," 348.

11. Pedro Pascual was familiar with the *Miraj,* as shown by Cerulli, *Il libro della scala,* 264–328.

12. See Tolan, *Saracens,* ch. 5.

13. See Emmerson, *Antichrist in the Middle Ages.*

14. *Toledoth Yeshu,* 53; see Tolan, *Saracens,* 17. Thanks to Nina Melechen for bringing this text to my attention.

15. Hildebert of Lavardin, *Vita beatae Mariae aegyptiacae,* PL 171:1321–40.

16. Petrus Alfonsi, *Diálogi contra Iudeos,* 102–3; *Dialogue against the Jews,* 162–63. Similar stories are told by the above-mentioned ninth-century Latin life from Spain, *Chronica maior* by Matthew Paris, and by Fidentius of Padua, *Liber recuperationis terrae sanctae,* 16–21. On Petrus Alfonsi, see my *Petrus Alfonsi.*

17. Eckhardt, "Le Cercueil flottant," concludes that Embrico invented the legend of the floating coffin.

18. Embrico of Mainz, *La vie de Mahomet,* vv. 1140–45, p. 92.

19. Ibid., v. 1118, p. 91.

20. See Hildebert of Lavardin, *Vita beatae Mariae aegyptiacae,* PL 171:1327d, where the praying Mary levitates.

21. Gauthier de Compiègne, *Otia de Machomete,* in Alexandre du Pont, *Roman de Mahomet,* ed. R. B. C. Huygens, vv. 1077–86, p. 206.

22. In some crusader chronicles Cairo is referred to as Babylon, after the nearby town of Fustat, known to the ancients as Babylon of Egypt. It is unclear to which of the two the poet is referring, or if he is even aware of the distinction. In either case, "Babylon" still carried its negative biblical connotations. The very fact that the Christian chroniclers

refer to Cairo as "Babylon" and to the Egyptian sultan as the "Sultan of Babylon," shows a deliberate choice to use a very charged image.

23. Some pilgrims and crusaders thought he was buried in one of the two main mosques of Jerusalem. Felix Fabri reports, "I have read in some chronicle that the feet and hands of Mahomet are kept there [in the Dome of the Rock mosque], but that the rest of his body was devoured by swine." Felix Fabri, *Felix Fabri's Book of Wanderings,* 2:246. For a bibliography on Felix Fabri, see Ganz-Blätter, *Andacht und Abenteuer,* 387–88.

24. Both quotes in Daniel, *Islam and the West,* 220.

25. Ibid.

26. "Travese muy gran tierra fasta que llegue a la cibdat de al medina donde nasçio Maumat, et dende fuy a Mechan donde esta la ley et el testamento de Mahomat, que esta en un arca de fierro en una casa de piedra calamita. Et por eso esta en el ayre, que nin disciende ayuso nin sube arriba. Et sabet que esta Mechan es cabeça del ymperio de los alarabes" Madrid, Biblioteca Nacional, MS 1997, f34v. Manuscript 9055 contains the same text, though instead of "un arca de fierro," the scribe wrote, "una foja de azero." I have not consulted another manuscript of the text in Salamanca, Biblioteca Universitaria, MS 1890. Thanks to Nancy Marino for bringing this text to my attention.

27. "Nello mezzo di questa chupola era uno vaso ritratto a modo d'una chassetta di ferro pulita istimai di grandezza uno bracco e mezzo e alchuna chosa meno per l'altro verso e istava sospesa e non tochava niente. Allora chonobi lo 'nganno del falso maometto inpero ch'io chonobbi che quella parte di quella falsa c[h]iesa era dal mezzo insu tutta di chalamita la quale ène una pietra marina ch'è di cholore tra nero e bigo e à questa propieta in se ch'ella tira il ferro a sse per la sua frigidezza . . . e questa chagone l'archa di maometto ch'è di ferro ista sospesa perche lla chalamita la tiene, e lla grossa gente sarraina non sanno che chosa sia chalamita chredono che ll'archa che ista in altura istia per miracholo." Text and translation cited are from Allaire, "Portrayal of Muslims" 252–53, 265n53; see Allaire, *Andrea da Barberino.*

28. *Chanson d'Antioche*, vv. 3447–50, 4968–70; *Chanson de Jérusalem,* vv. 7276–87.

29. "Quidam perditionis filius, Machometus pseudopropheta, surrexit, qui per saeculares illecebras et voluptates carnales multos a veritate seduxit; cujus perfidia etsi usque ad haec tempora invaluerit, confidimus tamen in Domino, qui jam fecit nobiscum signum in bonum, quod finis hujus bestiae appropinquat, cujus numerus secundum Apocalypsin Joannis intra sexcenda sexaginta sex clauditur, ex quibus jam pene sexcenti sunt anni completi." Innocent III, *Quia maior* (PL 216, 818). On Innocent's *Quia maior,* see Cole, *The Preaching of the Crusades,* 104–9.

30. Oliver of Paderborn, *The Capture of Damietta,* 50.

31. See Richard, "L'Extrême-Orient légendaire au Moyen-Age"; Richard, five articles in the section "Latins et Mongols" of his *Croisés, missionnaires, et voyageurs.*

32. Matthew Paris, *Chronica maior,* 4:345–46.

33. Ibid., 5:630–31.

34. This is indeed the doctrine of Chingis-Khan, who prided himself on being the lord of the world; see Richard, "The Mongols and the Franks," 48.

35. Matthew of Paris, Additamenta, 6:351

36. Felix Fabri, *Book of Wanderings* 2:251.

37. Ibid., 2:669–70.

38. Thomas Dainero saw the procession in 1501, according to his *Die ordenung zu ofen wider den Thurken gemacht* (1501, 1502). The ritual was also performed 1513, according to a chronicle in manuscript in Budapest. Both of these texts are described by Eckhardt, "Le Cercueil flottant," 86–87.

39. Prideaux, *The True Nature of the Imposture*, 134.

40. Wollstonecraft, *Vindication of the Rights of Woman*, 44.

41. "Un dicton hongrois, 'Il flotte entre ciel et terre comme le cercueil de Mahomet' (Lebeg mint Mohammed koporsója ég és föld között) traduit plaisamment la situation de quelqu'un qui mal assuré de son avenir redoute l'état d'incertitude où il se trouve." Eckhardt, "Le Cercueil flottant," 77. He also tells (87–88) of a nineteenth-century Sicilian peasant who recounted the story of Muhammad's coffin (apparently believing it was true) and said that the way to make the coffin fall down was to put garlic onto it, since garlic is supposed to counter magnetism.

42. Boulainvilliers, *La vie de Mahomed*.

43. Gibbon, *Rise and Fall of the Roman Empire*, 3:75–131.

44. B. Lewis, *Islam and the West*, ch. 5, "Gibbon on Muhammad," 85–98.

45. Even Voltaire, who portrays Muhammad as a lustful, power-hungry fanatic in his play *Mahomet, ou le fanatism*, does so primarily in order to attack the violent fanaticism he sees in the French wars of religion. See Hadidi, *Voltaire et l'Islam*.

Chapter 3. Rhetoric, Polemics, and the Art of Hostile Biography

1. See Fita, "Once bulas"; Fita, "Sobre la bibliografía de San Pedro Pascual." On Pedro Pascual see below, chapter 9. 2. He describes this in his *Disputa contra los Jueus:* many prisoners, he says, "se tornaven a la mala secta dels moros." *Obras*, 3:1.

3. Pedro Pascual, *Sobre la seta Mahometana*, in *Obras* 4:1–357. The only manuscript I have been able to identify for this text is from c. 1500: Biblioteca de El Escorial, Monasterio, MS h.II.25, ff.1r–179r (*Bibliography of Old Spanish Texts*, 292); the manuscript also contains Pedro's *Tratado del libre albedrio contra el fatalismo de los Mahometanos* (ff.179r–199r) and a series of proverbs (199v–200r).

4. *Obras*, 4:106; the transcription contains errors that may be due to subsequent corruption by scribes. In other works he gives quotations in both Arabic and Hebrew. *Obras*, 2:209 (Arabic), 3:38 (Hebrew). On Pedro's use and knowledge of the Mi'râj, see Asin Palacios, *Escatología musulmana de la Divina comedia*, 378–80; Cerulli, *Il libro della scala*.

5. "Translade de latin in romance . . . la historia di Mahomat asi como fallé escripta en nuestros libros . . . y demas de lo que se contiene en esa historia, escrivi algunas otras cosas que me dixeron algunos moros, cuydando alabar su ley, e que fallé escriptas en los libros de los moros." *Obras*, 4:3.

6. Pedro cites the Hadîth in several places, particularly 41–49. He cites al-Kindi by name at 41 and 46. On this well-known work of Christian polemic, probably an anonymous tenth-century text but most frequently referred to as the "Apology of al-Kindî," see Burman, *Religious Polemic;* Burman, "*Tathlîth al-wahdânîyah*"; Abel, "L'Apologie d'Al-Kindi"; Burman, "The Influence of the *Apology of al-Kindî*"; Tolan, *Saracens*.

7. "En quanto entiendo por lo que decían algunos moros en las disputaciones, pésales de los alabanzas que dixo Mahomad de Jhesu Christo, ca manifestamente contra los moros dixo." *Obras,* 4:217.

8. "Los Cristianos *que vieron* a Mahomad, e pugnaron de saber la verdad de su començamiento e de su fin." *Obras,* 4:67 (emphasis mine).

9. *Obras,* 4:67–84. On these legends, see Cambier, "L'épisode des taureaux"; see above, chapter 1.

10. Pedro Pascual, *Obras,* 4:138–42; see above, chapter 2

11. "Semeja que la ystoria sobre dicha escripta es verdadera." *Obras,* 4:142.

12. Daniel, *Islam and the West,* esp. 255–76; he discusses Pedro at 116–18 and 261–64.

13. See Menéndez Pidal, "Cómo trabajaron las escuelas alfonsíes"; Catalán, "El taller historiográfico alfonsí"; this and other studies on Alfonso's historiography are reprinted in his *La estoria de España de Alfonso X*; Fernandez-Ordonez, "La *Estoria de España*." See also Fraker, "Alfonso X"; Cárdenas, "Alfonso's Scriptorium and Chancery"; Linehan, *History and Historians,* 463ff.; Márquez Villanueva, *El Concepto Cultural Alfonsí;* Martin, ed., *La historia alfonsí.*

14. On Ramón Martí's anti-Muslim polemics and his knowledge and use of Arabic texts of philosophy, see Tolan, *Saracens,* 233–74.

15. Burman, *Religious Polemic.*

16. Petrus Alfonsi, *Dialogue against the Jews*; Tolan, *Petrus Alfonsi,* 12–41; Tolan, *Saracens,* 148–67.

17. See Chazan, *Barcelona and Beyond*; Cohen, *The Friars and the Jews,* 108–28.

18. Ramón Martí, *De seta Machometi*; Tolan, *Saracens,* 236–39.

19. This occurs at several points in the debate, according to Hebrew text purporting to be Nachmanides' own record of the disputation. Nachmanides, *The Disputation at Barcelona.*

20. "Quando ceciderit musca in vas, submergite eam ibi, quia in una ala portat venenum et in altera medicinam, ponite ante alam in qua est venenum deinde aliam." *De seta Machometi,* 32. Hernando (at a note to this passage) has identified the source as §LIX, XVI and XVII of al-Bukhârî's *Sahih,* ed. O. Houdas and W. Marçais, in *Les traditions islamiques,* 4 vols. (Paris, 1903–14). On al-Bukhârî's *Sahih,* see J. Robson, "al-Bukhârî, Muhammad b. Ismâ`îl," EI^2 1:1336–37; Robson, "Hadîth," EI^2 3:24–30

21. "Hec autem omnia videntur plus verba stulti vel derisoris quam prophete vel nuntii Dei." Ramon Martí, *De seta,* 32.

22. "Manifeste contra mandatum divinum, contra legem naturalem et contra rationem." Ramon Martí, *De seta,* 44.

23. "Dedit causam et occasionem suis quod quasi sine verecundia et timore multi perpetrent illud scelus." Ramon Martí, *De seta,* 48.

24. Thanks to Gretchen Starr-Lebeau for suggesting this contrast.

25. For the text of Alfonso's *Estoria de España,* I have used the version known as the *Primera crónica general de España.*

26. This is the conclusion of Fraker, "Alfonso X."

27. Márquez Villanueva, *El Concepto Cultural Alfonsí,* 90, 111n13. On the use of the Mi`râj in the texts of Rodgrigo Jiménez de Rada and Alfonso el Sabio, see Miguel Asin Palacios, *La escatología musulmana de la Divina comedia,* 376–78, 384–87.

28. Rodrigo Jiménez de Rada, *Historia Arabum*. Menéndez Pidal lists the sources used by Alfonso, chapter by chapter, in his edition of Alfonso X, *Primera crónica general*, cxxv–cxxvii for the chapters on Muhammad.

29. While it is beyond the scope of this article to offer a full analysis of Rodrigo's treatment of Muhammad, Rodrigo uses material from Hadîth collections: for example, he tells, in *Historia Arabum* § 1, the story of two angels who took out his heart and cleansed it of sin. The legend is well known to Muslim authors; it is reported, for example, by Abû Bakr Ahmad al-Baihaqî in his eleventh-century biography of the Prophet; on this and other such pious legends about the Prophet, see Schimmel, *And Muhammad Is His Messenger*, esp. 68.

Rodrigo also seems to use Christian anti-Islamic polemics and earlier Latin chronicles. He follows the *Crónica mozárabe de 754* in erroneously stating that Muhammad conquered Damascus. *Crónica mozárabe de 754*, 8; on this text, see Wolf, "Christian Views of Islam."

30. Alfonso X el Sabio, *Primera crónica general* §478, p. 265. Lucas de Tuy, *Chronicon mundi*. On Lucas, see Martin, *Les juges de Castille*, 201–49; Linehan, *History and Historians*, 357–58; González Muñoz, "La leyenda de Mahoma en Lucas de Tuy"; Henriet, "Hagiographie léonaise et pédagogie de la foi."

31. See Cárdenas, "Alfonso's Scriptorium"; Márquez Villanueva, *El Concepto Cultural Alfonsí*, 100ff.

32. Typically, Pedro inserts a refutation of Islam into his anti-Jewish *Disputa contra los Jueus sobra la fé Catholica*. *Obras*, 2:203–10.

33. "Fallaredes en él con que vos defendades contra los enemigos de nuestra ley." This is in the epilogue to *Sobre la seta Mahometana*, in Pedro Pascual, *Obras*, 4:348.

34. "Fablillas de romances de amor o de otras vanidades." *Obras*, 4:3.

35. In ch. 8, for example, on the Last Supper and Eucharist, after explaining two Old Testament prophecies, he says, "E estas dos profecias podedes alegar contra los Judios e contra Moros." Pedro Pascual, *Obras*, 4:208.

36. *Disputa, Obras* 2:217. He is following the lead of Petrus Alfonsi; see Tolan, *Petrus Alfonsi*, 14, 112.

37. *Obras*, 4:98, 144. Informal theological dispute was possible in thirteenth-century Spain, as is suggested in texts by Christians, Muslims, and Jews. See van Koningsveld and Wiegers, "The Polemical Works of Muhammad al-Qaysî"; Earlier in the century, Aragonese king James I had expressly prohibited laymen from disputing the faith with infidels, preferring to trust the job to well-schooled Dominican missionaries. Burns, *Muslims, Christians, and Jews*, 90. As usual, if a king has to outlaw it, it must be happening.

38. Many thanks to the National Endowment for the Humanities for providing me with a 1995 Summer Stipend and to the University of North Carolina at Greensboro for the Kohler International Studies Grant and New Faculty Research Grant; this support enabled me to conduct research for this article at the Biblioteca Nacional in Madrid. Thanks also to Horacio Santiago Otero and the other members of the Centro de Estudios Históricos of the Consejo Superior de Investigaciones Científicas who helped make my Madrid visit productive and enjoyable. An earlier version of this paper was presented to the Annual Meeting of the American Historical Association in Atlanta in January 1996.

My thanks to Jodi Bilinkoff, Gretchen Starr-Lebeau, and Thomas Burman for their helpful comments and suggestions at that meeting.

Chapter 4. Peter the Venerable on the "Diabolical Heresy of the Saracens"

1. For the edition of Peter's Latin texts with German translation, see Peter of Cluny [Petrus Venerabilis], *Schriften zum Islam*. On Peter the Venerable and his polemics against Islam, see *Pierre Abélard, Pierre le Vénérable*; Constable and Kritzeck, eds., *Petrus Venerabilis;* D'Alverny, "Deux traductions latines du Coran au Moyen-Age"; D'Alverny, "Pierre le Venerable et la légende de Mahomet"; Kritzeck, *Peter the Venerable and Islam*; Kritzeck, "De l'influence de Pierre Abélard sur Pierre le Vénérable dans ses oeuvres sur l'Islam"; Torrell, "La notion de prophétie et la méthode apologétique dans le *Contra Saracenos* de Pierre le Vénérable"; Lemay, "L'apologétique contre l'Islam chez Pierre le Vénérable et Dante"; Jolivet, "L'Islam et la raison, d'après quelques auteurs latins des IXe [*sic:* should be XIe] et XIIe siècles"; Iogna-Prat, *Ordonner et exclure;* Martínez Gázquez, "Finalidad de la primera traducción latina del Corán."

2. Kritzeck, *Peter the Venerable and Islam,* 15.

3. For criticisms of this image of Peter as a tolerant student of Islam, see Brolis, "La crociata di Pietro il Venerabile"; Kedar, *Crusade and Mission,* 101. Indeed, in order to form this image of a tolerant Peter opposed to crusading, Kritzeck had to willfully overlook the evidence amassed by Berry, "Peter the Venerable and the Crusades." See also two reviews of Kritzeck's book: Richard Lemay in *Middle East Forum* 41 (1965): 41–44, and S. M. Stern in *Medium Aevum* 35 (1966): 248–52. Kritzeck has also been criticized for errors in his editing and translating of Peter's Latin texts.

4. Jean Leclercq, *Pierre le Vénérable;* Torrell and Bouthillier, *Pierre le Vénérable et sa vision du monde,* 3–104.

5. Little, "Intellectual Training," 236.

6. Bredero, "The Controversy between Peter the Venerable and Saint Bernard of Clairvaux"; Torrell and Bouthillier, *Pierre le Vénérable et sa vision du monde,* 92–101 (who give full bibliographical references to other studies on the subject).

7. Heloise, *Epistola* 1, in Peter Abelard, *Historia calamitatum*, appendix, p. 116; Little, "Intellectual Training," 238.

8. Petrus Alfonsi, *Diálogi contra Iudeos*, 98; Petrus Alfonsi, *Dialogue against the Jews,* 156; *Risâlat al-Kindî* [Latin translation], 80–81.

See bibliography for references to the Arabic text of the *Risâlat al-Kindî* and a modern French translation. On the *Risâlat al-Kindî* and its importance to later works of medieval anti-Islamic polemic, see Abel, "L'Apologie d'Al-Kindi"; van Koningsveld, "La Apología de Al-Kindî en la España." On Petrus Alfonsi's *Diálogi,* see Tolan, *Petrus Alfonsi and His Medieval Readers.*

9. Little, "Intellectual Training."

10. Peter of Cluny, *Contra Petrobrusianos hereticos*, 3.

11. Peter of Cluny, *Contra sectam*, in *Schriften zum Islam,* 232; on Kritzeck's (mis)interpretation of this passage, see Brolis, "La crociata di Pietro il Venerabile," and Kedar, *Crusade and Mission*. On this text, see Iogna-Prat, *Ordonner et exclure,* chs. 3–8.

12. Moore, *The Origins of European Dissent,* 102; Châtillon, "Pierre le Vénérable et

les Pétrobrusiens"; see also Fearns, "Peter von Bruis"; Torrell and Bouthillier, *Pierre le Vénérable et sa vision du monde,* 162–71; Moore, "Building Ramparts."

13. Petrus Venerabilis, *Contra Petrobrusianos hereticos*, 4, 165; Torrell and Bouthillier note that the same purpose underlies many of the stories in Peter's *De Miraculis* of visits from ghosts of those who have benefited from the prayers of Cluny's monks. *Pierre le Vénérable et sa vision du monde,* 170–71.

14. Peter of Cluny, *Letters of Peter the Venerable,* §98 (258–59), §115 (303–8), §167 (400–401), §168 (401–2); Torrell and Bouthillier, *Pierre le Vénérable et sa vision du monde,* 89–92; Zerbi, "San Bernardo di Chiaravalle e il concilio de Sens"; Zerbi, "Remarques sur l'*Epistola 98* de Pierre le Vénérable"; Thomas, "Die Persönlichkeit Peter Abaelards."

15. Kritzeck, "De l'influence de Pierre Abélard sur Pierre le Vénérable"; Jolivet, "L'Islam et la raison"; Peter Abelard, *Dialogus inter philosophum iudaeum et christianum.* On this text, see Von Moos, "Les collations d'Abélard."

16. For the dates of composition, see Friedman's introduction to her edition of Peter of Cluny, *Adversus Iudeorum inveteratam duritiem*, lvii–lxx; Torrell and Bouthillier, *Pierre le Vénérable et sa vision du monde,* 172–74; Kniewasser, "Die antijüdische Polemik des Petrus Alphonsi," 59.

17. See Tolan, *Petrus Alfonsi,* 116–17; Friedman's introduction to Peter's *Adversus Iudeorum inveteratam duritiem*, xvii–xviii; Kritzeck, *Peter the Venerable and Islam,* 27n83; Dahan, *Les Intellectuels chrétiens et les Juifs au moyen âge,* 458–59.

18. *Adversus Iudeorum inveteratam duritiem*, v, 126.

19. Ibid., v, 151.

20. "Bouinus intellectus" (Peter, *Adversus Iudeorum inveteratam duritiem,* 43). Yvonne Friedman, in her introduction, cites eleven places where Peter refers to the Jews as animals (viii, note 5).

21. On this trip, see Bishko, "Peter the Venerable's Journey to Spain"; Torrell and Bouthillier, *Pierre le Vénérable et sa vision du monde,* 59–67; Kniewasser, "Die antijüdische Polemik des Petrus Alphonsi"; Kritzeck, *Peter the Venerable and Islam,* 3–14.

22. Peter of Cluny, *Epistola ad Petrum de Joanne contra eos qui dicunt Christum nunquam se in Evangeliis aperte Deum dixisse,* PL 189:487–508. Constable (2:331–43) shows that Petrus de Joanne and Peter of Poitiers are indeed one and the same: Peter the Venerable himself in *De Miraculis* describes how he met the other Peter at the monastery of St. Jean d'Anselmy (hence the de Joanne); Peter of Cluny, *De Miraculis* §I:4.

23. Burman, "*Tafsîr* and Translation."

24. The original manuscript of the collected translations, used by Peter the Venerable as he composed his own anti-Islamic works is conserved in the Bibliothèque de l'Arsenal (MS n° 1162); see D'Alverny, "Deux traductions."

25. See, for example, 57r, in the Koran translation, the reader is referred to the translation of the *Risâlat al-Kindî* ("bonus et doctus Christianus cuius liber in isto codice continetur").

26. For the debate on the identity of the annotator and examples of the variety of the annotations, see Burman, *Religious Polemic,* 85–89. An example of a basic misunderstanding of Muslim practice is one annotator's assertion that Muhammad was buried in Mecca (MS A, 21v).

27. Kritzeck, *Peter the Venerable and Islam,* 115–52.

28. Peter of Cluny, *Summa totius haeresis Saracenorum,* in *Schriften zum Islam,* §3.

29. Kedar, *Crusade and Mission,* 90n.

30. Petrus Alfonsi, *Diálogi* §V, 94–95; *Dialogue,* 151–52. The same material is in the Latin translation of the *Risâlat al-Kindî.* Peter seems to be following Alfonsi's narration of these events rather than that of the *Risâlat,* although he does correct Alfonsi, who identified Sergius as a Jacobite monk (*Dialogi,* 95). Peter (following the *Risâlat* [*Exposición y refutación del Islam,* 100]) identifies Sergius as a Nestorian (Peter the Venerable, *Summa,* 206).

31. Peter of Cluny, *Summa,* §10; Horace, *Ars poetica* 1:1–2.

32. The idea that Porphyry was an apostate Christian has been common in Christian texts since the fifth century. See R. Grant, "Porphyry among the Early Christians"; O'Meara, *Porphyry's Philosophy,* esp. 52ff. Thanks to Bernard McGinn for bringing these works to my attention.

33. One can only be dismayed by Kritzeck's assertion that one of Peter's great achievements was "the dissociation of Mohammed from other heresiarchs" *(Peter the Venerable and Islam,* 27–30); clearly, he is doing precisely the opposite.

34. Peter the Venerable, *Letters of Peter the Venerable,* ed. Constable, §111, p. 295. Another version of this letter is edited by Kritzeck (*Peter the Venerable and Islam,* 212–14); the latter version does not contain Peter's criticisms of the *Risâlat al-Kindî.* Several passages of the text are also common to the *Summa.* For the relationship between these three texts, see *Letters of Peter the Venerable,* ed. Constable, 2:275–84; D'Alverny, "Deux traductions," 72–76; Kritzeck, *Peter the Venerable and Islam,* 27–30.

35. Peter of Poitiers wrote a letter to Peter the Venerable in summer or autumn of 1155 in which he refers to Peter's polemics against Jews and Petrobrusians and rejoices at the fact that he will now undertake to refute the errors of the Saracens. On Peter of Poitiers, see *Letters of Peter the Venerable,* ed. Constable, 2:331–43; Torrell and Bouthillier, *Pierre le Vénérable et sa vision du monde,* 180–83. Torrell and Bouthillier have misunderstood the relationship between the *Summa* and the *Contra sectam*; they refer to the *Summa* as "placée en Préface du *Contra Sarracenos*" (336). In fact, the two texts are completely independent.

36. For Kritzeck, the text is complete as is (*Peter the Venerable and Islam,* 155–56). Torrell and Bouthillier think that he had planned on writing more (*Pierre le Vénérable et sa vision du monde,* 182).

37. *Contra sectam* in *Schriften zum Islam,* here §9.

38. Adelard, *Questiones naturales, Beiträge zur Geschichte der Philosophie und Theologie des Mittelalters* 31, pt. 2, 11. See Burnett, "Adelard of Bath and the Arabs."

39. Peter of Cluny, *Contra sectam,* §29; he quotes the Koranic injunctions at §35. On this, see Kedar, *Crusade and Mission,* 99–104.

40. "Quae uero est natura haec, que substantia, uel essentia? None illa, quae communi uniuersarum gentium more, iuxta proprietatem uniuscuiusque linguae Deus creditur, Deus dicitur? Est igitur natura illa, Deus ille, qui solus increatus est, qui solus creator est." *Contra sectam,* §32. Peter may have taken the identification of *substantia* with God the creator from Petrus Alfonsi, who identifies the creator God the Father and

with *substantia*. Petrus Alfonsi, *Diálogi contra Iudeos* §6, 104–5; *Dialogue*, 165–66; see Tolan, *Petrus Alfonsi*, 36–37.

41. *Risâlat al-Kindî*, Tartar trans., 125–27; Latin trans, 38–39; Petrus Alfonsi, *Diálogi contra Iudeos* §VI, 105–6; *Dialogue*, 166; see Tolan, *Petrus Alfonsi*, 36–39. For other examples of this common ploy, see Burman, *Religious Polemic*, 72–73, 81–82, 163ff; Daniel, *Islam and the West*, 200–209.

42. MS A, 28v; Peter of Cluny, *Contra sectam*, §64–65; see Kritzeck, *Peter the Venerable and Islam*, 177–78.

43. Peter of Cluny, *Contra sectam*, §66–67; *Risâlat al-Kindî*, Tartar trans., 251–53.

44. Peter of Cluny, *Contra sectam*, §97–154; a similar argument is found in the *Risâlat al-Kindî*, Tartar trans., 137–73

45. *Risâlat al-Kindî*, Tartar trans., 137–53; Peter of Cluny, *Contra sectam*, §117, 119.

46. Peter of Cluny, *Contra sectam*, §138; II Timothy 4:3–4.

47. Torrell and Bouthillier, *Pierre le Vénérable et sa vision du monde* (see index, p. 441, "Grégoire le Grand").

48. Torrell and Bouthillier, *Pierre le Vénérable et sa vision du monde*, 308–14.

49. An earlier version of this essay was presented to the seminar "Savoirs et Pouvoirs: Histoire Culturelle de l'Espagne Médiévale," at the Collège d'Espagne in Paris, February, 1997. Thanks to the participants of that seminar for their helpful comments, in particular to the organizer, Adeline Rucquoi, and to Gabriel Martinez-Gros. Thanks also to Robert Bartlett and Thomas Burman for their comments and corrections, and to Bernard McGinn for bibliographical advice.

Chapter 5. The Dream of Conversion: Baptizing Pagan Kings in the Crusade Epics

1. On the use of *chrétienté* as an equivalent of "baptism," see Flori, *"Pur eshalcier sainte crestiënté,"* 178–79.

2. On the image of the Saracen as pagan in the *chanson de geste*, see Tolan, *Saracens*, ch. 5; Bancourt, "Les musulmans dans les chansons de geste du Cycle du roi"; Bancourt, "Le visage de l'Autre"; Daniel, *Heroes and Saracens;* Jacoby, "La littérature française dans les états latins de la Méditerranée à l'époque des croisades, diffusion et création."

3. See Haidu, *The Subject of Violence*; Flori, *"Pur eshalcier sainte crestiënté"*; Bervoc-Huard, "L'Exclusion du sarrasin dans la *Chanson de Roland*"; Payen, "Une poétique de génocide joyeux"; Köhler, *Ideal und Wirklichkeit in der höfischen Epik*; Benton, "'Nostre Franceis n'unt talent de fuïr'"; Morrissey, *L'empereur à la barbe fleurie*, 71–123.

4. Tolan, *Saracens*, ch. 5; Jean Flori, "'Oriens horribilis'"; Flori, "Radiographie d'un stereotype"; Flori, "En marge de l'idée de guerre sainte"; Cole, "'O God'"; S. Loutchitskaja, "*Barbarae nationes*."

5. In the San Silvestro chapel of the Basilica dei Quattro Coronati, the story of the Donation of Constantine is narrated in a series of eight frescoes. They are reproduced by Cesare d'Onofrio, *La papessa Giovanna*, 196–201. On the propaganda about the donation of Constantine, in texts and images from papal and imperial points of view, see Diana M. Webb, "The Truth about Constantine: History, Hagiography, and Confusion"; Stroll, *Symbols as Power*; Louis Réau, *Iconographie de l'Art chrétien*.

6. "Procedit novus Constantinus ad lavacrum, deleturus leprae veteris morbus sordentesque maculas gestas antiquitus recenti latice deleturus. Cui ingresso ad baptismum sanctus Dei sic infert ore facundo: "mitis depone colla, Sigamber; adora quod incendisti, incende quod adorasti." Gregory of Tours, *Historia Francorum* II.31; translation by Lewis Thorpe, *The History of the Franks,* 144 (modified here). "Mitis depone colla" is often translated as "bow your head in meekness" (Thorpe trans.), but Michel Rouche has shown that Gregory is probably referring to the talismanic *colla* or *collaria* worn by Germanic kings and priests. Rouche, *Clovis,* 280–81. On the exploitation of Clovis baptism in the French royal ideology of the thirteenth and fourteenth centuries, see Beaune, *Naissance de la Nation France,* 75–100.

7. Wood, "Gregory of Tours and Clovis"; Daly, "Clovis: How Barbaric, How Pagan?"

8. This is the solution proposed by Wood, "Gregory of Tours and Clovis," 251. For Constantine as a heretic in the writings of Jerome, see his *Chronicon,* ed. Helm, *Eusebius Werke,* 7:228–34; in the writings of Isidore, see the *Chronica majora,* ed. T. Mommsen, MGH AA 11:2, 391–506, 334.

9. Vatican, MS Vat. Lat. 1960 (fourteenth century) contains two nearly identical images, depicting the baptisms of Clovis (f. 171) and of the king of the Bretons (f. 205). Apart from the superior position of the bishop Remigius, the elements that often distinguish medieval representations of Clovis's baptism are Queen Clothilde (normally depicted to the king's right) and the dove that brings the sacred ointment from heaven for the anointing of the king. For a ninth-century example, see the image that figures among the scenes of the life of St. Remigius on an ivory plaque now at the Musée de Picardie (Amiens), analyzed by Jean-Claude Bonne, "Les ornements de l'histoire (à propos de l'ivoire carolingien de saint Rémi)," esp. 55–58.

10. Peter of Cluny, *Liber contra secta sive haeresim Saracenorum,* 100–102.

11. Alfonso X el Sabio, *Cantigas de Santa Maria,* ed. Mettmann, *Cantiga* 28, "como Santa Maria deffendeu Costantiobre dos mouros que a conbatian e a cuidavan fillar." The sultan is not named, but is called "mouro Soldan" (v. 50); he arrives before Constantinople "con oste de pagãos" (17). The bibliography concerning the text, illumination, and music of the *Cantigas* is considerable. See Katz et al., eds., *Studies on the Cantigas de Santa Maria: Art, Music, and Poetry.* On the image of the Muslims in the *Cantigas,* see Mercedes García-Arenal, "Los moros en las *Cantigas* de Alfonso el Sabio."

12. Petrus Tudebodus, *Historia de Hierosolymitano itinere,* 112; cf. *Gesta Francorum et aliorum Hierosolimitanorum,* ed. Bréhier, 154.

13. See Flori, "Des chroniques à l'épopée . . . ou bien l'inverse?"; Riley-Smith, *The First Crusade and the Idea of Crusading,* 135–52; *Chanson d'Antioche,* ed. Duparc-Quioc; J. and L. Hill, introduction to their edition of Petrus Tudebodus, *Historia de Hierosolymitano itinere*; France, *Victory in the East,* 374–82.

14. See *Chanson d'Antioche,* 226–34.

15. On the relations between these texts and on their complex manuscript tradition, see *Chanson d'Antioche,* 43–80; Bender and Kleber, *Les épopées romanes,* vol. 3, tome 1/2, fascicule 5; Cook and Crist, *Le Deuxième cycle de la Croisade,* esp. 80. The texts are published in the ten volumes of the OFCC (Old French Crusade Cycle, 1977–95). On the ideology of these texts, see Kleber, "Pèlerinage, vengeance, conquête: la conception

de la première croisade dans le cycle de Graindor de Douai," Au Carrefour des routes d'Europe: La Chanson de Geste. Xe Congrès international de la Société Rencesvals pour l'étude des épopées romanes, Strasbourg, 1985, Senefiance 21 (1987): 757–75. Kleber, "Graindor de Douai: remanieur-auteur-mécène?"; Cook, "Crusade Propaganda in the Epic Cycles of the Crusade"; Duparc-Quioc, *Le cycle de la croisade*; Cahen, "Le premier cycle de la croisade (Antioche-Jérusalem-Chétifs): Notes brèves à propos d'un livre (récent)"; Hatem, *Les Poèmes épiques des croisades*. On the use of this cycle by aristocratic families, see Duparc-Quioc, "Recherches sur l'origine des poèmes épiques de croisade et sur leur utilisation éventuelle par les grande familles nobles"; Graboïs, "La bibliothèque du noble d'*Outremer* à Acre dans la seconde moitié du XIIIe siècle." On the *Chanson d'Antioche,* see also Deschaux, "Le merveilleux dans la *Chanson d'Antioche*"; Cook, *"Chanson d'Antioche," chanson de geste: le cycle de la croisade est-il épique?;* Darbishire, "The Christian Idea of Islam in the Middle Ages, According to the *Chanson d'Antioche*"; Gosman, "La Propagande de la croisade et le rôle de la chanson de geste comme porte-parole d'une idéologie non-officiel"; Sumberg, "Au confluent de l'histoire et du mythe: la *Chanson d'Antioche*, chronique en vers de la première croisade."

16. See Grillo, introduction to his edition of the *Chrétienté Corbaran*, xv–xlviii; Grillo, "Les redactions de la *Chrétienté Corbaran*, première branche des continuations du cycle de la croisade," *Au Carrefour*, 585–600; Bender, "La fin du premier cycle de la croisade ou le retour à l'histoire"; *Chanson d'Antioche,* 59–66.

17. The infidels decapitate a priest performing mass in a church; the decapitated priest, unperturbed, completes the mass. *Chanson d'Antioche,* vv. 544–57.

18. "De Mieke briseront les murs et le palis, / Si trairont Mahomet de la forme u est mis, / Et les deus candelabres qu'illuec sont assis" (*Chanson d'Antioche*, vv. 4968–70). Compare with the prophecy earlier in the poem: "Et briseront de Mecke le mur et le pali, / S'en trairont Mahomet et Appolin aussi, / S'en donront l'or a cels qui Jhesu ont servi. / Benoite soit li terre u il furent norri!" (vv. 3447–50).

19. *Chanson d'Antioche*, vv. 3447–50, 4968–70; *Chanson de Jérusalem,* ed. Thorpe, vv. 7276–87.

20. *Chanson d'Antioche,* vv. 6620–21.

21. "VII.[xx]. ans ot la vielle passés." *Chanson d'Antioche*, v. 5257; according to MS B she is 700 years old.

22. She appears three times in the *Chanson d'Antioche,* where her name is Calabre: vv. 766–73, 5252–68, and 6838–6956. According to Duparc-Quioc (105–6), the first passage is an addition by Graindor de Douai, whereas the second is by Richard le Pèlerin.

23. For example, Charlemagne asks Baligant to convert in the *Chanson de Roland* (vv. 3596–99).

24. *Chanson d'Antioche,* 57n48.

25. Ibid., vv. 170–81, 205–13; on the attribution of this passage to Graindor rather than to Richard, see *Chanson d'Antioche,* 100–102.

26. Ibid., vv. 9570–79.

27. Kedar, *Crusade and Mission,* 57–65.

28. Graindor's text, as it exists in the extant manuscripts, has been modified subsequently; in particular, a series of passages announcing the subject of the *Chrétienté*

Corbaran have been added, according to Geoffrey Myers, "*Les Chétifs:* Étude sur le développement de la chanson," and Myers, ed., *Les Chétifs*; cf. U. Holmes and W. McLeod, "Source Problems of the *Chétifs*, a crusade *Chanson de geste*." In Graindor's original version, Corbaran may have been the relatively clement pagan jailer of the Christian heroes, but he showed no disposition for conversion to Christianity. The reworked version, in contrast, anticipates the events of the *Chrétienté Corbaran*, with announcements such as the following: "La fist rois Corbarans molt grant cevalerie / Saciées que Dex l'ama, li fils sainte Marie, / Puis en fu baptiziés en sa cité antie, / O lui .XX. mile Turc de le gent paienie / Sa mere en fu dolante, Calabre li florie, / Tel duel en ot la vielle tolir li valt la vie. / Puis en mut si grant gerre, que que nus vos en die, / Ke toute paienime en fu puis estormie / Il meismes assis a molt grant ost banie / La dedans Oliferne en sa cité antie." *Les Chétifs* 2764–73; cf. vv. 2933–49, 3053–61. See Myers, "*Les Chétifs:* Étude," 74–75.

29. "L'esvesque de Matran ont el Temple trové, / L'esvesque de Foroiz et de Fescam l'abbé, / Et le riche clergié dont il i ot plenté / Qui en Jherusalem estoient demoré . . . / Premiers ont Corbaran baptizié et levé, / Godefrois le leva, li roys de la cité, / Et Remons de Saint Gille qui le poil ot mellé." *Les Chétifs*, vv. 224–27, 230–32.

30. See Grillo, "Les rédactions de la *Chrétienté Corbaran*." While Bender ("La fin du premier cycle de la croisade") qualifies the Continuations as a "retour à l'histoire," this is only true of the second brand of the Continuations and not for the *Chrétienté Corbaran*, which (as Grillo shows) represents a return to the world of the *chansons de geste*. On the Continuations, see also Grillo, "Considérations sur la version de Londres-Turin des continuations du premier cycle de la croisade"; Bender, "Royauté et chevalerie dans les Continuations du Cycle de la Croisade"; Bender, "The Saladin Material in the Continuations of the First Crusade Cycle."

31. The artists who painted the illuminations were from the same workshop as those who produce the sumptuous "Old Testament Picture Bible" (New York, Pierpont Morgan Library MS 638); this at least is the conclusion of Allison Stones, "Sacred and Profane Art: Secular and Liturgical Book-Illumination in the Thirteenth Century," 106–7; see also her article "Secular Manuscript Illumination in France."

32. These two conversions take place only in the Arsenal manuscript, v. 243v.; see *Chrétienté Corbaran*, ed. Grillo, 37, 86–87.

33. Corbaran is the first pagan king to accept baptism in the crusade cycle, but there is the example of Balan, a Saracen baron in the *Chanson d'Aspremont*, who converts to Christianity. Balan is indeed convinced by the Franks' military prowess, but also by their customs and religion. Balan brings no military aid to the Franks, but his conversion represents a moral victory. The *Chanson d'Aspremont* may have been composed between Saladin's capture of Jerusalem in 1187 and the Third Crusade and may have been used as propaganda to recruit crusaders. Already, it seems, some Europeans dreamed not only of conquering the infidels but also of converting them. See Bancourt, "Le visage de l'Autre: étude sur le sens de la *Chanson d'Aspremont*"; DLF, 106–7.

34. See Grillo, "Royauté et chevalerie," 316–17.

35. OFCC, vol. 7, *The Jérusalem Continuations*, ed. Peter Grillo, pt. 2, vv. 2130–42.

36. The lineage of these kings of Jerusalem is simplified in the branch, which makes the infant Baudouin the great-nephew of Godfrey of Bouillon.

37. Gilles de Corbeil, *Ierapigra ad purgandos prelatos*, f. 39v. Gaston Paris published a brief passage of this text, which he dates c. 1215 ("La légende de Saladin," 294–95). On the medieval legends concerning Saladin, see below, chapter 6.

38. *Récits d'un ménestrel de Reims au treizième siècle*, ed. Natalis de Wailly, § 21. On this text, see Le Goff, *Saint Louis*, 377–87; Grossel, "Le même et l'autre: la croisade dans les *Récits d'un ménestrel de Reims*." *Le Roman de Saladin* repeats roughly the same version of his self-baptism. *Roman de Saladin*, ed. Crist, 168–69.

39. An earlier version of this chapter was presented to the seminar "Histoire comparée de phénomènes de conversion: la conversion au Moyen Âge" at the Centre de Recherches Historiques, École des Hautes Études en Sciences Sociales, Paris, May 1996, organized by Charles Amiel. Thanks to Michelle Szkilnik and Peter Grillo for their comments and corrections.

Chapter 6. Mirror of Chivalry

1. Voltaire, *Essai sur les mœurs*, 1:862.

2. Ibid., 1:580.

3. As far as possible, I will use "Salâh al-Dîn" to refer to the historical Sultan and "Saladin" to refer to his incarnation in European legend.

4. Dante, *Inferno*, 4:129.

5. Ibid., 12:107.

6. On the legend of Saladin, see Zeibi, "Saladin de l'histoire à la légende"; Berriot, "Le mythe de Saladin"; G. Paris, "La légende de Saladin"; Möhring, "Der andere Islam"; Jubb, *The Legend of Saladin*.

On the historical Salâh al-Dîn, see Lyons and Jackson, *Saladin;* Ehrenkreutz, *Saladin*; Gibb, *Saladin*; Regan, *Saladin and the Fall of Jerusalem;* Möhring, *Saladin und der dritter Kreuzzug*; Housley, "Saladin's Triumph." See also Dajani-Shakeel, "Some Aspects." Two modern novelized biographies are Ali, *The Book of Saladin* and Chauvel, *Saladin: Rassembleur de l'Islam*.

The legend of Saladin lives on in modern cinema. See Halim, "The Signs of Saladin."

7. Gilles le Bouvier (1386–1455, also called Le Héraut Berry), *Armorial de France*, ed. Auguste Vallet de Viriville (Paris, 1866), 199–210; on this text see DLF, 539–40, and Zeibi, "Saladin de l'histoire à la légende, 267–68, 433–51. The name has continued until the twentieth century: Bernard Saladin d'Anglure is author of *La vie changée en pierre: vie et oeuvre de Davidaluk Alasuaq, artiste inuit du Québec* (Quebec, 1978).

8. "Quis dabit capiti meo aquam, et oculis meis fontem lacrymarum, et plorabo interfectos populi mei?" Petrus Blessensis, *De hierosolymitana peregrinatione accelerenda*, PL, 207:1057. Peter is citing (and slightly altering) Jeremiah 9:1, which in the Vulgate reads "interfectos filiae populi mei?"

9. On the ideology of the chroniclers of the First Crusade, see Riley-Smith, *The First Crusade*; Tolan, *Saracens*, ch. 5; Cole, "O God."

10. Gregory VIII, *Audita tremendi*, PL, 202:1539–42.

11. Rostagnus, monk of Cluny, echoes Gregory in seeing dissension and sin as having called down God's retribution; God gave the city to the new Philistines, Saladin and his

"barbarous people." Rostagnus, *Tractatus exceptionis capitis Sancti Clementis Papae et Martyris ab Constantinopoli ad Cluniacum translati,* PL, 209:907–8.

12. PL, 207:1063.

13. Paris, "Un poème latin contemporain sur Saladin." Paris dates the poem to shortly after 1187; Jean Richard argues for a later date ("L'arrière plan," 15n).

14. "Occurent hodie menti fletus Jheremie." This is the incipit to the *Carmen de Saladino.* Paris, "Un poème latin," 437.

15. *Carmen de Saladino*, vv. 28–44; Paris, "Un poème latin," 438.

16. *Carmen de Saladino*, vv. 44–56, 61–71; Paris, "Un poème latin," 438–39.

17. "Vult magis atque magis nostris accedere pagis." *Carmen de Saladino*, v. 74; Paris, "Un poème latin," 439.

18. "Nostraque victorem Saladinum culpa vocavit / Sex vicibus victus vice septena superavit." *Carmen de Saladino*, vv. 86–87; Paris, "Un poème latin," 439.

19. *The Jerusalem Continuations*, ed. Peter Grillo, OFCC, volume 7, part 2, 140–70, vv. 5649–6778. The story of Saladin's rise to power in Egypt is vv. 5655–5759. On the place of the *Jerusalem Continuations* in the crusade cycle, see Grillo's introduction (vol. 7, part 1). See also K. Bender and H. Kleber, eds., *Les épopées romanes*; K. Bender, ed., *Les épopées de la Croisade*; Cook and Crist, *Le Deuxième cycle de la Croisade.*

For other versions of the story, see *Chronique d'Ernoul et de Bernard le Trésorier*, 40–41; *Roman de Saladin*, 23–28; G. Paris, "La légende de Saladin," 284–89.

20. Cole, "'O God,'" 105; cf. her discussion of similar accusations of Saladin's pollution of the Cross by Henry of Albano in 1188 (109–10).

21. *De expugnatione Terrae Sanctae per Saladinum libellus,* in Ralph of Coggeshall, *Chronicon Anglicanum*, ed. J. Stevenson, *Rolls Series* 66 (London, 1875, 1965), 209–62; Cole, "'O God,'" 107–8.

22. "Vir acris ingenii, armis strenuus et supra modicum liberalis." William of Tyre, *Chronicon,* book 20, ch. 11. "Vir consilio providus, armis strenuus et supra modicum liberalis." Ibid., 21, 6. William repeats the accusations that Salâh al-Dîn murdered the Shiite caliph (20, 11) and that he usurped the rule of Damascus from Nûr al-Dîn's son, but this does not detract much from William's largely positive portrayal of him—indeed, it is precisely on these two occasions that he gives the two assessments quoted above. William frequently expressed admiration for the Christians' bitterest enemies: he describes Nûr al-Dîn as "maximus nominis et fidei christiane persequutor, princeps tamen iustus, vafer et providus et secundum gentis sue traditiones religiosus" (20, 31).

23. William of Tyre, *Chronicon,* 21, 6.

24. On the complex textual history of the French translations and continuations to William of Tyre, see Pryor, "The *Eracles* and William of Tyre"; Morgan, *The Chronicle of Ernoul and the Continuations of William of Tyre* (Oxford, 1973); *La Continuation de Guillaume de Tyr; Chronique d'Ernoul et de Bernard le Trésorier*; DLF, 414, 648–49; RHC Occ. 1–2. On the *Estoires d'outremer et de la naissance Salehadin,* see Jubb, "Citry de la Guette."

25. See, for example, Benedictus de Accoltis, *Historia Gotefridi,* RHC Occ., 5:620.

26. The dramatic story of his capture and beheading by Salâh al-Dîn has been told too many times to need retelling here. For the Arabic accounts, see Gabrieli, *Arab Historians*

of the Crusades, 111–12, 123–24, 134. Western writers also vilified Reynald, with the exception of Peter of Blois, who makes him into a martyr in his *Passio Reginaldi Princeps olim Antiocheni* (PL, 207:957–76).

27. For chronicler Benedictus de Accoltis, Saladin was "blessed with great courage and genius"; his Egyptian subjects appreciated "magno animo atque ingenio praeditus . . . ejus clementiam, liberalitatem, et animi magnitudinem." Benedictus de Accoltis, *Historia Gotefridi*, RHC Occ., 5:619. For Jacques de Vitry, bishop of Acre in the early thirteenth century, Saladin had been both a divine scourge and a skilled and clever ruler. Jacques de Vitry, *Historia orientalis*.

28. See, for example, the *Conti di Antichi Cavalieri*, § 13; *La Continuation de Guillaume de Tyr*, 71–72.

29. This is the assessment of Saladin by the *Récits d'un ménestrel de Reims*, ch. 7; English translation by Stone in *Three Old French Chronicles of the Crusades*, 267.

30. *Historia et gesta Ducis Gotfridi seu Historia de obsidione Terrae Sanctae*, ch. 47; RHC Occ., 5:524. This assessment is echoed by Jacques de Vitry in his *Historia orientalis*.

31. Ambroise, *L'Estoire de la guerre sainte*; English translation by Stone in *Three Old French Chronicles of the Crusades*. On the *Estoire*, see DLF, 415–16; Bancourt, "De l'image épique à la représentation historique"; Bancourt, "De l'imagerie au réel." Jean Richard (*Encyclopedia Britannica* 1:722) says that Ambroise is probably the author of a now lost firsthand account that was used as a model for both the *Estoire* and the *Itinerarium regis Ricardi*.

32. Ambroise, *Estoire de la guerre sainte*, chs. 10–11; Stone, trans., 19–21.

33. Ambroise, *Estoire de la guerre sainte*, ch. 19; Stone, trans., 33.

34. Ambroise, *Estoire de la guerre sainte*, ch. 48; Stone, trans., 115–16.

35. Ambroise, *Estoire de la guerre sainte*, ch. 35; Stone, trans., 79.

36. Bancourt, "De l'image épique à la représentation historique," 226–28.

37. Ambroise, *Estoire de la guerre sainte*, chs. 38–39; Stone, trans., –94. On this battle, see Lyons and Jackson, *Saladin*, 336–39.

38. Ambroise, *Estoire de la guerre sainte*, ch. 40; Stone, trans., 95.

39. Ambroise, *Estoire de la guerre sainte*, ch. 45; Stone, trans., 109.

40. McGinn, "Iter Sancti Sepulchri."

41. Ambroise, *Estoire de la guerre sainte*, ch. 48; Stone, trans., 115.

42. Ambroise, *Estoire de la guerre sainte*, ch. 57; Stone, trans., 144.

43. Ambroise, *Estoire de la guerre sainte*, ch. 58; Stone, trans., 151.

44. Ambroise, *Estoire de la guerre sainte*, ch. 59; Stone, trans., 153.

45. Ambroise, *Estoire de la guerre sainte*, ch. 59; Stone, trans., 153. According to Ibn Shaddad, it was Badr al-Dîn Dildirim who played the role of go-between for Richard; see Lyons and Jackson, *Saladin*, 359.

46. Ambroise, *Estoire de la guerre sainte*, ch. 61; Stone, trans., 159.

47. Ambroise, *Estoire de la guerre sainte*, ch. 61; Stone, trans., 157.

48. Ambroise, *Estoire de la guerre sainte*, ch. 61; Stone, trans., 158.

49. Ambroise, *Estoire de la guerre sainte*, ch. 61; Stone, trans., 158.

50. Tyerman, *England and the Crusades*, 117; Tristram, *English Medieval Wall Painting*, 2:15–17, 70–71, 73, 106–7, 110–11, 130–32, 184–85, 215.

51. See Loomis, "The *Pas Saladin* in Art and Heraldry"; Cook and Crist, *Le Deuxième cycle de la Croisade*. Crist (134–42) compares the characters in various versions (written and plastic) of the *Pas*. While G. Paris (491–94) speculates that this scene might be based on Richard's relief of Jaffa, Loomis shows that there is little evidence for this theory. Crist, while showing that Ambroise's catalogue of twelve knights has nothing in common with those mentioned in the *Pas*, nevertheless illogically concludes that Ambroise's list of knights is the basis for the later story of the *Pas*.

52. *Pas Saladin*, ed. F. E. Lodeman, in *Modern Language Notes* 12 (1897): 21–34, 84–96, 209–29, 273–81; on this text, see DLF, 1098.

53. Jean Froissart, *Chroniques*, book 4, ch. 1; see Loomis, "The *Pas Saladin* in Art and Heraldry," 88.

54. GP;*R*2

55. The *Récits d'un ménestrel de Reims* are a series of short, dramatic legends and anecdotes about historical figures from the twelfth and thirteenth centuries: French kings and knights, Emperor Frederick II, and crusaders. A number of the stories revolve around the third crusade and Saladin. On this text see DLF, 1247; Grossel, "Le même et l'autre."

56. *Récits d'un ménestrel de Reims*, ch. 9; Stone, trans., 270–72; ch. 24; trans., 309–12.

57. The *Roman de Saladin* survives only in a fifteenth-century prose version, part of the cycle of *Jean d'Avesnes*. On the two epic cycles of the Crusade, see DLF, 356–58; K. Bender and H. Kleber, *Les épopées romanes*; H. Bender, ed., *Les épopées de la Croisade*; Cook and Crist, *Le Deuxième cycle de la Croisade;* OFCC.

58. Petrarch, *Trionfo della fama*, 2:148–50, in *Rime e Trionfi*.

59. *Conti di Antichi Cavalieri* §12; the Italian text with a French translation and introduction by Gérard Genot and Paul Larivaille is found in *Novellino*. I disagree with the interpretation of the tale given by Genot and Larivaille in their introduction to the text (11–13); they stress that Saladin is Bertran's "disciple" in this story, wheras he becomes morally autonomous in the later stories. Yet this is true only as regards love (as we will see below); in his manner of ruling, Saladin from the beginning shows his superiority to Christian kings.

60. *Conti di Antichi Cavalieri*, §15.

61. Ibid., §14. There are many versions of this, the earliest being that of Ambroise's *Estoire de la Guerre Sainte*. Ambroise tells us that it was Saphadin (i.e., al-'Âdil, Salâh al-Dîn's brother), who brought two magnificent steeds to Richard during the heat of battle, urging him to take them as a testimony to his prowess and valor and hinting that if Richard survived the battle he would find a way to repay Saphadin. In later versions (including the *Conti*) it becomes Saladin himself who gives Richard the horse. *Novellino* (§76) tells the same story, but adds a different ending: Richard, not trusting Saladin, orders one of his servants to mount the horse. When he does, the horse takes off at a gallop and does not stop until it reaches Saladin's tent. "Thus a man should never trust in the friendly gestures of an enemy." The *Roman de Saladin* (124–25) has a version similar to that of *Conti*. For other versions, see *Chronique d'Ernoul et de Bernard le Trésorier*, 281–82; G. Paris, . "La légende de Saladin," 489–91.

62. *Récits d'un ménestrel de Reims*, ch. 21; Stone, trans., 299–300.

63. *Récits d'un ménestrel de Reims*, ch. 21; Stone, trans., 301–2.

64. The story is told by Jacques de Vitry, Étienne de Bourbon, and other medieval preachers in their sermons; it is also used by several Italian authors, including Bosone da Gubbio (see G. Paris, "La légende de Saladin," 299n).

Fernán Perez de Guzman, writing in the first half of the fifteenth century, tells of the death of Saladin in 1123 [*sic*] and calls him "varón muy usado notable in armas, muy franco e muy liberal, mucho verdadero e cierto en sus palabras." When Saladin dies, he tells his pennant-bearer to go around with his shroud and proclaim, "Ved aqui el señor de todo oriente! Que toda su potencia y gloria no lieva consigo sino este pobre y vil paño." Perez de Guzman, *Mar de Histórias*, 140.

Voltaire retells the story in *Essai sur le mœurs*, 1:580: "Il avait fait porter dans sa dernière maladie, au lieu du drapeau qu'on élevait devant sa porte, le drap que devait l'ensevelir; et celui qui tenait cet étendard de la mort criait à haute voix: 'Voilà tout ce que Saladin, vainqueur de l'Orient, remporte de ses conquêtes.'"

65. *Récits d'un ménestrel de Reims*, ch. 21; Stone, trans., 299.

66. *Conti di Antichi Cavalieri*, §12; a slightly different version of the story is told in the *Roman de Saladin*.

67. G. Paris, "Un poème latin," 434.

68. *Récits d'un ménestrel de Reims*, ch. 2; Stone, trans., 258–59. The legend of Eleanor's liaison with Saladin was still known to Voltaire in the eighteenth century. "On dit même qu'elle oubliait toutes les fatigues d'un si cruel voyage avec un jeune Turc d'une rare beauté, nommé Saladin." Voltaire, *Essai sur les mœurs*, 1:573.

69. Bosone da Gubbio, *Avventuroso Ciciliano;* Boccaccio, *Decameron*, 10:9. See G. Paris, "La légende de Saladin," 428–32.

70. Gabrieli, *Arab Historians of the Crusades*, 101.

71. See Colombo-Timelli, "Entre littérature et vie," 31ff.

72. It also circulated widely in a later prose version, *Ordene de chevalerie*. See also Keen, *Chivalry*, 6–8; Crist, 124–32; DLF, 1087. On other versions of the dubbing story, see G. Paris, "La légende de Saladin," 290–91.

73. On the complex relations between dubbing rituals and liturgy, see Flori, "Chevalerie et liturgie"; Flori, "Du nouveau sur l'adoubement."

74. *Roman de Saladin*, 131.

75. According to the romance *Baudouin de Sebourc*, the captive "dame de Ponthieu" is the mother of Saladin; he is her great-grandson according to *La fille du comte de Ponthieu*. See also *Le Bâtard de Bouillon*, 323–24; Crist, 120–24; *La fille du comte de Ponthieu*; Danielle Quéruel, "Le Cycle de la fille du comte de Ponthieu," in Quéruel, *Splendeurs de la cour de Bourgogne*, 371–479; DLF, 132, 445–46.

76. "Salehadins l'a mout voluntiers esgardé
E dist a soi meïsmes: 'Frans sont plain d'onesté!'" vv. 6307–8

"Mout les [i.e., the priests singing the mass] a volentiers li amiraus oïs
Et dist entre ses dens: 'Par Mahom Goumelis,
Hounerablement est li dix des Frans servis.'" vv. 6313–15.

Another branch of the *Jerusalem continuations* makes Saladin into a renegade Christian, according to *La Chanson d'Antioche: Étude critique*, ed. Duparc-Quioc, 256n.

77. *Récits d'un ménestrel de Reims*, ch. 21; Stone, trans., 302.

78. *Roman de Saladin*, 168–69.

79. Cf. Gregory of Tours, *Historia Francorum*, 2:31; see above, chapter 5.

80. Gilles de Corbeil, *Ierapigra ad purgandos prelatos*, Paris, Bibliothèque Nationale MS Nouv. Acq. 138; passage discussed is at f. 39v. Gaston Paris (294–95) publishes an extract of the text, which he dates to c. 1215.

A collection of tales in Italian from the late thirteenth century, *Novellino*, tells how Saladin asked the Christians for a truce, so that he could come to their camp, see how they lived, and—if he approved of their lifestyle—convert to Christianity. He went and found that the kings were eating in luxury at a sumptuous table, the nobles were eating well at a richly laid table, and the poor were eating meager scraps and sitting on the ground. He chastised the Christians for not taking better care of their poor and went away. He then invited the Christians to his camp, where he had prepared a special tent, whose floor was covered with a rich cloth embroidered all over with crosses. When he saw that the Christians walked on this cloth and spat on it, he chastised them: "How can you call yourselves protectors of the cross, when you do not even show it the barest respect." He announced that the truce was over, and the next day he again attacked the Christians. *Novellino*, §25.

81. "Sed sobrietas Mahometicorum hodie superat subrietatem Christianorum. Unde eorum pincipes [*sic*] Saladinus, audiens Christianos esse tribus ferrulis, vel quatuuor, ait, tales non esse terra dignos." Petrus Cantor, *Verbum abbreviatum*, PL, 205:328. I have found no definition for "ferrulis" that makes sense in this context.

82. *Conti di Antichi Cavalieri*, § 16.

83. Here again I disagree with the interpretation of the tale given by Genot and Larivaille in their introduction to the text (13); I do not see in this tale "la déprécation de l'Islam vis-à-vis du Christianisme." What is deprecated, rather, is theocracy and fanaticism of any sort.

84. On the various versions of this story, see G. Paris, "La légende de Saladin," 296–98.

85. "On dit qu'il laissa par son testament des distributions égales d'aumônes aux pauvres mahométans, juifs et chrétiens; voulant faire entendre que tous les hommes sont frères, et que pour les secourir il ne faut pas s'informer de ce qu'ils croient, mais de ce qu'ils souffrent." Voltaire, *Essai sur les mœurs*, 1:580.

86. *Novellino* §73. In this version, the question is a trap set by Saladin to trick the Jew into insulting Islam and giving him a pretext for taking his riches from him; Saladin is humbled by the Jew's reply and lets him go unharmed. According to Boccaccio, who retells the story in the *Decameron* (1:3) Saladin confessed his evil intentions to the Jew and then showered gifts upon him, making him a special counselor and close friend.

87. The tale is told in the *Gesta romanorum*, in Bosone da Gubbio's *Avventuroso Ciciliano*, and in the Hebrew *Schebet Jehuda* (G. Paris, "La légende de Saladin," 296–98). The *Dit du Vrai Aniel* (composed between 1270 and 1285) is an allegorical poetic version of the tale, which concludes that Christianity is the true religion, given miraculous powers of the Christian "ring"; see DLF, 387. In 1779, Gotthold Ephraim Lessing used the tale as the basis for his play *Nathan der Weise*.

88. Ginzburg, *The Cheese and the Worms*, 50–51.

89. Jean de Joinville, *Histoire de Saint Louis,* ch. 63, p. 137.

90. *Chronique d'Ernoul et de Bernard le Trésorier,* 172, 234–35.

91. Ibid., 216–17.

92. I wish to thank the American University of Cairo for the generous support that made possible my participation in the Second Annual Conference on Cross Cultural Encounters in the Mediterranean. I particularly wish to extend my thanks to David Blanks for inviting me to participate, to all the American University faculty members who extended a warm welcome to me during my visit, and to the other conference participants for a stimulating and rewarding exchange.

Chapter 7. *Veneratio Sarracenorum*

1. See Tolan, *Saracens,* ch. 8.

2. On Burchard, see Scheffert-Boichorste, "Der Kaiserliche Notar"; Worstbruck, "Burchard von Straßburg"; *Repertorium fontium historiae medii aevi* 2:607–8.

3. On Burchard's mention of the pyramids, see Cannuyer, "Les Pyramides d'Egypte dans la littérature médio-latine."

4. Scheffert-Boichorste, "Der Kaiserliche Notar," 231.

5. *Epistola ad Nicolaum abbatem Sigesbergensiam* [Siegburg, dioc. Köln] *de legatione sua Aquileiam, Salzburgum et in Hungariam anno 1161,* in Burchard, *Epistolae.*

6. *Epistola alia ad Nicolaum de victoria Friderici I imperatoris et de excidio Mediolanensi a. 1162,* in Burchard, *Epistolae.*

7. *Chronica regia coloniensis,* 110–11. Scheffert-Boichorste ("Der Kaiserliche Notar," 230) posits that Burchard might be the author of the chronicle of Cologne in which the letter concerning Milan is inserted.

8. Scheffert-Boichorste, "Der Kaiserliche Notar," 233 ; MGH 2:130; st. 4191, 4192, 4222, 4248.

9. Laurent, "Burchard von Strassburg," 145.

10. "Illis diebus legati regis Babyloniae ad imperatorem venerunt, rara et preciosa munera deferentes. Legatio talis erat, quod idem rex peteret ut filio suo filia imperatoris matrimonio iungeretur, ea conditione ut ipse rex cum filio et omni regno suo christianitatem susciperet et omnes captivos relaxaret. Imperator vero eosdem legatos per dimidium fere annum secum detinuit, et sigulas civitates et ritus diligenter notare et inspicere concessit." *Annales coloniensis maximi,* anno 1173, p. 786

11. "In nativitate sancti Iohannis Ratisponam venit, ubi nuncii regis Grecorum iterum adierunt pro coniunctione filiae eius filio imperatoris. Imperator legatos regis Babliloniae cum magno honore et multis donis remittit." *Annales coloniensis maximi,* anno 1174, p. 787. In 1188, Frederick sent another embassy to Saladin, this time no doubt on a more bellicose mission, in preparation for the crusade (*Chronica regia coloniensis,* 140; Scheffert-Boichorste, "Der Kaiserliche Notar," 246).

12. Lyons and Jackson, *Saladin,* 81.

13. Burchard of Strasbourg, *Itinerarium,* 67 ; Arnold of Lübeck, *Chronica Slavorum,* 239. P. Peeters ("La légende de Saïdnaia," 140–41), who refers only to Arnold's text, sees this description of a "terra . . . in angustum ducta" as anachronistic, proof of the text's

inauthenticity, since Busrâ was a flourishing city until its destruction by an earthquake in 1202. But Burchard himself does not mention the name of Busrâ; his description could in fact refer to the region south of Damascus, which had been ravaged by razzias between the rulers of Jerusalem and Damascus during the twelfth century.

14. Lyons and Jackson, *Saladin*, 115.

15. The three manuscripts of Burchard's text are Rome, Bibl vat. lat. 1058, f. 108r–112r (13th c.) (see Pelzer, ed., *Biblothecae Apostolicae*, 603–12); München, Universitätsbibliothek 76 (manuscript burned in 1944), base manuscript of the edition by Lehmann and Glauning, who describe it (Burchard, *Itinerarium*, 61–62); Wien, Österreichisches Staatsbibliothek cod. 362, f. 36r–38v (14th c.), described in *Tabulae codicum manuscriptorum*, 54–55. Lehmann and Glauning's edition of the text is based on the Munich manuscript with corrections from the other two manuscripts.

16. Arnold of Lübeck, *Chronica Slavorum;* Burchard's text is inserted at 235–41.

17. Burchard of Strasbourg, *Itinerarium*, 64; Arnold of Lübeck, *Chronica Slavorum*, 236.

18. Burchard of Strasbourg, *Itinerarium*, 64; Arnold of Lübeck, *Chronica Slavorum*, 236–37.

19. Burchard of Strasbourg, *Itinerarium*, 65; Arnold of Lübeck, *Chronica Slavorum*, 237.

20. Ibid.

21. Burchard of Strasbourg, *Itinerarium*, 67; Arnold of Lübeck, *Chronica Slavorum*, 239.

22. "Hic ortus habet fontem, unde irrigatur, quia alia aqua non potest irrigari. Nota, quod nusquam terrarum nisi in hoc loco balsamus crescit. Ad hunc quidem fontem beata virgo cum filio suo Herodis persecucionem fugiens per aliquod tempus ibi latitabat, lavans ad fontem illum pannos pueri. Quapropter usque in hodiernum diem fons ille a Sarracenis in veneracione habetur, cereos et incensum illuc deferentes, quando ibi se lavant. In Epyphania vero maxima multitudo illic convenit de omni confinio et lavat se cum aqua predicta." Burchard of Strasbourg, *Itinerarium*, 65; Arnold of Lübeck, *Chronica Slavorum*, 237–38.

23. Zanetti, "Matarieh," cites numerous texts concerning the presence of pilgrims at Matariyya ; Burchard is the earliest of these texts. On this sanctuary, see also Milwright, "The Balsam of Matariyya."

24. Cited by Zanetti, "Matarieh," 36.

25. Burchard of Strasbourg, *Itinerarium*, 66; Arnold of Lübeck, *Chronica Slavorum*, 238.

26. Zilio-Grandi, "La Vierge Marie dans le Coran," 63–72; Qur'ân 19:22–27.

27. See Tolan, *Saracens*, 126–34.

28. "A Damascho ad quatuor miliaria est locus quidam in montibus situs, qui Sardencia <Saydaneia-Arnold> vocatur et a Christianis inhabitatur, et est ibi ecclesia in rupe sita in honore beate Marie dedicata, in qua XII moniales virgines et VIII monachi deo et beate virgini serviunt. In qua ecclesia vidi tabulam ligneam ad mensuram unius ulne longam et latam ad modum dimidie retro altare positam in muro, que patens videbatur

per fenestram et ferreo laqueari cancellatim fuit firmata. In qua effigies beate Marie depicta resplenduit, sed nunc, quod dictu mirabile est, pictura super lignum est incarnata et oleum odoriferum super odorem balsami incessanter emanat. Per quod multi Christiani et homines ceteri diversis languoribus oppressi sanantur oleumque illud numquam minuitur, quantumque inde accipitur. Tablua predicta a quoquam tangi nunquam audetur, videri autem omnibus conceditur. Item oleum a Christiano religioso servatum augmentatur et pro quacunque infirmitate cum devocione et fide sincera sumptum fuerit pro honore beate virginis cum missarum sollempntitatibus indubitanter impetrabitur. Ad illum locum in assumpcione et in nativitate gloriose virginis omnes Sarraceni terre illius una cum Christianis causa orandi confluunt. Sarraceni quoque sua cerimonialia illic offerunt cum maxima devocione. Hec tabula primum Constantinopoli facta fuit et depicta in honore beate virginis, inde a quodam patriarcha Iherusalem transducta. Tunc tempois quidam abbatissa loci supradicti graci orandi descendit Iherusalem et, inpetrata a patriarcha prefata tabula, eam secum ad ecclesiam sibi commissam gaudens deportavit. Fuit autem hoc anno incarnacionis dominice C° et LXXVIII <8709–Arnold>. Sed postea per multa tempora cepit oleum sacrum ex ea manare." Burchard of Strasbourg, *Itinerarium,* 68; Arnold of Lübeck, *Chronica Slavorum,* 239–40. For the date of the icon's arrival at Saydnaya, I follow Arnold, since the date given in Burchard's texts (1178) is obviously a copyist's error.

29. On Saydnâyâ, see Baraz, "The Incarnated Icon of Saidnaya Goes West"; Devos, "Les premières versions occidentales de la légende de Saïdanaia"; Kedar, "Convergences of Oriental Christian, Muslim and Frankish Worshippers"; Pringle, *The Churches of the Crusader Kingdom* 2:219–21; Meri, *The Cult of Saints,* 210–12.

30. "Credunt enim Sarraceni beatam virginem per angelum concepisse Jesum Christum et post partum virginem permanisse. Hunc virginis filium prophetam fuisse dicunt et adeo mirabiliter cum anima et corpore in celum assumptum fuisse, celebrantes eius nativitatem, sed negant eum dei filium et baptizatum, crucifixum, mortuum et sepultum. Credunt eciam legem Christi habere et apostolorum, qui circumcisi sunt, nos vero minime. Credunt eciam apostolos, prophetas fuisse et plures martires et confessores in veneracione habent." Burchard of Strasbourg, *Itinerarium,* 66; Arnold of Lübeck, *Chronica Slavorum,* 238.

31. "Item credunt Sarraceni se habere paradysum in terra, in quem post hanc vitam sint transituri. In quo credunt esse quatuor flumina, unum de vino, secundum de lacte, tercium de melle, quartum de aqua et omne genus fructuum ibidem nasci dicunt ibique pro velle suo comedent et bibent et unusquisque eorum omni die pro voluptatis explecione nove virgini possit commisceri et, si quis in prelio a Christiano interfectus fuerit credit se in paradyso X virginibus debere abuti. Sed quid de illis mulieribus contingat, que cottidie secundum eos corrumpuntur, michi respondere nesciebant." Burchard of Strasbourg, *Itinerarium,* 66–67; Arnold of Lübeck, *Chronica Slavorum,* 238–39.

32. See, for example, Daniel, *Islam and the West,* 172–76.

33. "Apud Kayr <Ahir> est publicum prostibulum [sodomitarum] <meretricum>. Mulieres Sarracenorum linthiaminibus velate et cooperte incedunt ; numquam templa <eorum> ingrediuntur ; in maxima custodia eunuchorum habentur ita, quod maiores domine numquam domicilia sua egrediantur nisi per percepta dominorum suorum et

nec frater nec alius propinquuus viri vel mulieris sine consensu domini ad mulierem suam audeat ingredi. Viri quoque V vicibus infra diem et noctem ad templum vadunt orare et loco campane precone utuntur. Religiosi autem Sarraceni ad quamlibet horam se lavant sive lavare solent cum aqua, incipientes a capite usque ad pedes et postea vadunt orare. Numquam vero, ut dicitur, sine venia orant. Credunt enim in deum creatorem omnium, et Mahometh prophetam fuisse dicunt <sanctissimum> eorumque legis auctorem, quem eciam frequentare solent in peregrinacionibus suis. Habent insuper alios sue legis auctores in veneracione. Unicuique Sarraceno licet ducere uxores VII legittime simul et cuilibet illarum divisim expensas condictas et commissas a contractu nupciarum providet. Insuper, quotquot habuereit sclavas vel servas, cum illis licenter peccat, quasi inde non habeat peccatum. Quarum ancillarum, si aliqua conceperit, statim <a dominio Domini> libera erit. Et quemcumque filiorum suorum sive de ancilla sive de libera heredem constituere potest secundum velle suum. Multi tamen sunt Sarraceni adeo religiosi, quod non habent tantum nisi unam uxorem. Infra VII uxores licet habere, sed non ultra nisi in concubinis, ut dictum est." Burchard of Strasbourg, *Itinerarium*, 69; Arnold of Lübeck, *Chronica Slavorum*, 240–41.

34. "Qui vivunt et regnant cum dyabolo in secula seculorum. Amen." Burchard of Strasbourg, *Itinerarium*, 69.

35. "Quid inter ista considerandum nisi immensa clementia Redemptoris, que nec iustum, nec impium dono sue pietatis patitur esse expertem. Iustum quidem, humilem et quietum, et trementem sermones suos, premium viter eterne concedens, summo bono, quod ipse est, et aspectu sue claritatis beaficat. Impium autem quandoque in hac mortali vita temporalibus bonis eternaliter dampnandum exuberare permittit. Inde est, quod ipsi reprobi optimas regiones tenentes, frumento vino et oleo abundent, auro, argento gemmis vestivus quoque sericis exultent, aromatibusque pigmentis et balsamis luxurient, et nichil, quod oculis concupiscant, intemptatum relinquant. Impletur enim in illis prophetia Ysaac, qui cum Iacob speciali dono benedixisset, dixit Esau : In pinguedine terre et in rore celi desuper erit benecitio tua. Hec de verbis Domini propare possumus, dicentis : Diligite inimicos vestros, benefacite his, qui oderunt vos, ut sitis filii patris vestri, qui in celis est, qui solem suum oriri facit super bonos et malos, et pluit super iustos et inuiustos. Et David : Ecce, inquit, ipsi peccatores et abundantes in seculo optinuerunt divitias. Cum tamen hoc loco per terram et rorem terrenas divitias accipiamus, per rorem alibi gratia Spiritus sancit intelligitur, ut idem David dicit : Descendet sicut pluvia in vellus, factum plane Geneonis exprimens, ubi per rorem gratia Spiritus sancit, et per vellus intemerata virgo Maria accipitur, que concipiendo seu gignendo Dei filium, mater et virgo permansit. Terra etiam dedit fructum suum, quando eadem virgo benedictum fructum ventris sui, Christum, mundi salvatorem, benedicta generavit.

Hec de statu gentilium sive ecclesie, quam iner ipsos mirabiliter Deus conservarre dignatur, dicta sufficiant. Nunc ad oardinem historie prosequendum revertamur." Arnold of Lübeck, *Chronica Slavorum*, 241.

Chapter 8. Saracen Philosophers Secretly Deride Islam

1. Giordano da Pisa, *Quaresimale fiorentino* §75, p. 361: "Tutti i filosofi che fuoro grandi filosofi, dico quelli che fuoro diritti filosofi e maggiori, non pòttero amare le cose

del mondo, e dannaro la legge de' saracini anzi ch'ella fosse, ch'aspettano i diletti mondani. E se dicessi: "or non ha tra lloro filosofi?" Dico che ssì: Avicenna fu saracino, e fu filosofo e si fece beffe de la legge sua, e schernila. Se v'ha nullo filosofo o grande savio, e' medesimi scherniscono la legge loro e fànnosine beffe."

2. Gardet, *Dieu et la destinée de l'homme*, 278, citing Fakhr al-Dîn al-Râzî, *Muhassal*. See Georges Anawati, "Fakhr al-Dîn al-Râzî," EI[2] 2:751. Fakhr al-Dîn al-Râzî is not to be confused with the better-known philosopher and physician Abû Bakr Muhammad Zakariyyâ' al-Râzî, who lived in the ninth and tenth centuries.

3. See Louis Gardet, "Allâh," EI[2] 1:106; Adang, *Islam frente a Judaísmo*, 77–78; Tolan, *Petrus Alfonsi*, 22–24.

4. See Gardet, "*Djanna*," EI[2] 2:447; Gardet, "Kiyâma," EI[2] 5:235.

5. See Smith and Haddad, *The Islamic Understanding of Death and Resurrection*; Gardet, *Dieu et la destinée de l'homme*.

6. Ibn Sînâ, *Risâlat adhawiyya fi amr al-ma'âd*, cited by Gardet, "Djanna." On this subject, see the extensive treatment given by Michot, *La destinée de l'homme selon Avicenne*. On the specific problem of bodily resurrection, see Michot, "Avicenne et la destinée humaine." On Avicenna and his thought more generally, see A. Goichon, "Ibn Sînâ," EI[2] 3:941; Goodman, *Avicenna*; S. Inati, 'Ibn Sînâ,' in Nasr and Leaman, eds., *History of Islamic Philosophy*, 231–46; Janssens, *An Annotated Bibliography on Ibn Sînâ*.

7. These are summarized by Michot, *La destinée*, 13–14n58.

8. Ibn Sînâ, *Epistola sulla vita futura*, 94–97; Michot, "Avicenne et la destinée humaine," 471–74.

9. The relevant passage of the *Kitâb al-Najât* is translated by Arberry, *Avicenna on Theology*, 64–76. On this work, see Janssens, *An Annotated Bibliography*, 22–24.

10. Ghazâlî, *al-Durra al-Fâkhira*. For a discussion of this text, see Smith and Haddad, *The Islamic Understanding of Death and Resurrection*, 31–61.

11. Gardet, *Dieu et la destinée de l'homme*, 17, 281.

12. Janssens, "Al-Ghazzâlî's *Tahâfut*"; al-Ghazâlî, *The Incoherence of the Philosophers*; W. Montgomery Watt, "Al-Ghazâlî, Abû Hâmid b. Muhammad b. Muhammad al-Tûsî," EI[2] 2:1038; Massimo Campanini, "Al-Ghazzali," in Nasr and Leaman, eds., *History of Islamic Philosophy*, 258–74.

13. Al-Ghazâlî, *Incoherence*, conclusion, 1–3.

14. Ibid. §20:24–25.

15. Salman, "Algazel et les Latins."

16. D'Alverny, "Algazel dans l'Occident latin."

17. See Van Riet, "The Impact of Avicenna's Philosophical Works in the West"; Janssens, *Annotated Bibliography*, 237–52. The impact of specific works of Avicenna on specific Latin writers will be discussed below.

18. For an introduction to the vast bibliography on this subject, see Rashed et al., *Histoire des sciences arabes*; Burnett, *The Introduction of Arabic Learning*; Burnett, "The Translating Activity in Medieval Spain"; Micheau, "La transmission à l'Occident chrétien."

19. Tolan, "Reading God's Will in the Stars."

20. Peter of Cluny, *Contra sectam*, §20.

21. Peter of Cluny, *Contra Petrobrusianos hereticos*, 4, 165.

22. Peter of Cluny, *Summa totius haeresis Saracenorum* §10, in *Schriften zum Islam*; Horace, *Ars poetica* 1:1–2.

23. Peter of Cluny, *Contra sectam*, §29.

24. "Quae uero est natura haec, que substantia, uel essentia? None illa, quae communi uniuersarum gentium more, iuxta proprietatem uniuscuiusque linguae Deus creditur, Deus dicitur? Est igitur natura illa, Deus ille, qui solus increatus est, qui solus creator est." *Contra sectam*, §32. Peter may have taken the identification of *substantia* with God the creator from Petrus Alfonsi, who identifies the creator God the Father and with *substantia*. Petrus Alfonsi, *Diálogi contra Iudeos*, §6, 104–5; *Dialogue against the Jews*, 165; see Tolan, *Petrus Alfonsi*, 36–37.

25. On Ramon Martí, see above, chapter 3; Tolan, *Saracens*, ch. 10.

26. Ramon Martí, *Explanatio symboli Apostolorum*, 491.

27. Ramon Martí, *Explanatio symboli Apostolorum*, 493: "Quod autem in errorem induxit sapientes sarracenorum ut non crederent resurrectionem corporum videtur processisse ex Alcorano; quum ibi contineatur quod post resurrectionem habebunt delectationes corporales, ut delectatio cibi, potus, et coitus; que, in veritate, si in alia vita essent, intellectum a cogitatione et dilectione summi boni impedierent: Unde, quia visum est eis hoc esse inconveniens, sicut est in veritate, negaverunt corporum resurrectionem, ponentes tamen beatitudinem hominis in anima, non intelligentes quod corpus humanum posset vivere sine cibo."

28. Ramon Martí, *Explanatio symboli Apostolorum*, 493; he cites "Avicenna in libro de scientia divina, tractatu IX capite VII, loquens de felicitate anima." According to Cortabarria, "La connaissance de l'Islam," 281), this is a reference to Avicenna's *al-Shifâ'* (*Book of Healing of the Soul*, a long work on which Avicenna's shorter *Kitab al-Najât* is based). Abraham Ibn Daud composed a partial Latin translation of this text in the mid-twelfth century: *Avicenna latinus liber de De anima seu Sextus de Naturalibus: édition critique de la traduction latine médiévale*, ed. S. Van Riet, 2 vols. (Leuven, 1968, 1972).

29. Ramon Martí, *Explanatio symboli Apostolorum*, 494; Cortabarria, "La connaissance," 280–84.

30. Roger Bacon, *Opus maius, pars septima*. On Roger Bacon, see Hackett, ed., *Roger Bacon and the Sciences*; Hackett, "Philosophy and Theology in Roger Bacon's *Opus Maius*"; Crombie and North, "Bacon, Roger"; Southern, *Western Views of Islam*, 52–61; Sidelko, "The Condemnation of Roger Bacon"; Tolan, *Saracens*, ch. 9; Salman, "Algazel et les Latins," 111–18.

31. "Avicenna dicit in Radicibus moralium quod Machometus non dedit nisi gloriam corporum, non animarum, nisi in quantum anima condelectatur corpori." Bacon, *Opus maius, pars septima*, 206; Burke translation, 801.

32. "Nam Avicenna in nono Metaphisice redarguit Machometum propter hoc, quod solum posuit delicias corporales et non spirituales." Bacon, *Opus maius, pars septima*, 215; Burke translation, 808.

33. "Avicenna et philosophi ceteri contradicunt plebi et sacerdotibus; ostendunt enim quod non solum est gloria corporum, set animarum propria et maior, et determinat quod secto illo cito destruetur." Bacon, *Opus maius, pars septima*, 208; Burke translation, 803.

34. Bacon, *Opus maius, pars septima,* 266; translated and discussed by Tolan, *Saracens,* ch. 9.

35. "Dicit Avicenna in Moralibus quod Machometus solum loqutus est de gloria corporis; sed nos scimus, ut ait, quod maior est gloria animarum, quia non sumus asini reputantes tantum corporis delicias; et ideo suum legis latorem Avicenna reprehendit, et vult alium investigare, qui non solum corporum promittit gloriam, sed magis animarum." Bacon, *Opus maius, pars septima,* 22; Burke translation, 649.

36. These arguments are discussed in Tolan, *Saracens,* ch. 9.

37. On the condemnations, particularly those of Paris in 1210, 1270 and 1277, see Wippel, "The Condemnations of 1270 and 1277 at Paris"; E. Grant, "The Condemnation of 1277"; Duhem, *Le Système du monde.* For a translation of the condemnation of 1277, see E. Grant, *A Source Book in Medieval Science,* 45–50.

38. Sidelko, "The Condemnation of Roger Bacon."

39. Here are a few of the more recent and useful items from the considerable bibliography concerning Llull's writings on Islam: Beattie, "*'Pro exaltatione sanctae fidei catholicae'*"; Burman, "The Influence of the *Apology of al-Kindi*"; Colomer, "Raimund Lulls Stellung"; Courcelles, *La parole risquée;* Johnston, "Ramon Lull and the Compulsory Evangelization of Jews and Muslims"; Johnston, *The Spiritual Logic of Ramon Llull;* Lohr, "Ramon Lull and Thirteenth-Century Religious Dialogue"; Tolan, *Saracens,* ch. 11; For English translations of some of Llull's key works, see Ramon Llull, *Doctor Illuminatus* and *Selected Works of Ramon Llull.*

40. Hillgarth, *Ramon Lull and Lullism,* 21–22; Lavajo, "The Apologetical Method of Ramon Marti"; Cortabarria, "Connaissance de l'Islam."

41. Lavajo, "The Apologetical Method of Raymond Marti," 159.

42. "Et ideo ego, qui sum verus Catholicus, non intendo probare Articulos contra Fidem, sed mediante Fide." *Liber de convenientia fidei et intellectus in objecto,* cited by Burman, "The Influence of the *Apology,*" 216n97.

43. Llull composed the tract in 1271–72, first in Arabic, then in Catalan, according to Colomer, "Raimund Lulls Stellung." For Llinares and Bonner, he composed it between 1274 and 1276 (Llinares, introduction to his French translation of Ramon Llull, *Le Livre du Gentil et des trois sages,* 7n1; Bonner in Ramon Llull, *Doctor Illuminatus,* 81).

44. "Veritat és que enfre nós som diverses a creure la glòria de paradís, car alcuns la creeen haver segons que jo t'he recontat; e açò entenen segons exposició literal, la qual prenen de l'Alcorà, qui és nostre lig, e dels proverbis de Mafumet e de les gloses dels exponedors de l'Alcorà e dels proverbis. Mas altres gents són enfre nos qui entenen la glòria moralment, e exponen-la espiritualment, e dien que Mafumet parlava per semblança a les gents qui eren pegues e sens enteniment; e per ço que.ls pogués enomorar de Déu, lur recontava la glòria damunt dita. E per açò aquells que han aquesta creença dien que en paradís non haurà glòria de menjar ni de jaer ab fembra ni de les altres coses damunt dites; e aquests aitals són naturals e grans clergues, e són hòmens qui en alcunes coses no serven bé los manaments de nostra lei, e per açò nós los havem enfe nós quaix a heretges; a qual heretgia són venguts per oir lògica e natures. E per açò és feit establiment enfre nosaltres que públicament null home nos gos legis lògica ne na-

tures." *Libre del gentil et dels tres savis*, (c. 1275) in Ramon Llull, *Obres essencials*, 2 vols. (Barcelona: Selecta, 1957–60); translation in Ramon Llull, *Selected Works* 1:292–93.

45. The same conclusion is reached by Courcelles, *La Parole risquée*, 160–65.

46. "Tants són vils fets e sutzes, cels que féu Mafumet, e tant se desconvenen ses paraules e sos fets a sentedat de vida e de propheta, que majorment aquels sarra_ns qui saben molt e han sotill engín, e que han elevat enteniment, non crehen que Mafumet sia profeta; e per açò han fet establiment los sarra_ns que nul home no gos mostrar lògica de natures enfre ells, per ço que agen rudi enteniment, per lo qual sien en oppinió que Mafumet sia propheta. Amable fill, aytals sarra_ns qui han sobtill enteniment e qui no creen que Mafumet sia propheta, serien leugers a convertir a la fe cathòlica, si era qui la fe lus demostràs e·ls pre_càs." *Doctrina pueril* (1282–3), 164–65.

47. "Illi maxime litterati, quia de illis in Macometo pauci credunt, ex eo quia bene cognoscunt, quod ipse peccator homo fuit, et quod in eorum lege posuit multas trufas. Et de hoc sunt experti aliqui arabici christiani; unus inter quos possum dici. Conuersis autem maioribus Saracenis minores conuerterentur per consequens per maiores." Llull, *Liber de fine*, CCCM, 35:256.

48. "Sarraceni bene litterati non credunt vere quod Machometus sit propheta. Nam in alcoranus, in quo est lex eorum, inueniunt multa inconuenientia contra sanctitatem et veram prophetiam." Llull, *De acquisitione Terre Sancte* (1309), quoted from MS by Beattie, "'*Pro exaltatione*,'" 119n.

49. On Ghazâlî's logical works, see Watt, "al-Ghazâlî"; on Llull's use of Ghazâlî, see Johnston, *Spiritual Logic*, 31–44.

50. Dominique Urvoy, "Les causes laïques de l'occultation du fait arabe dans l'histoire de la pensée occidentale," in Clément, Pondevie, and Tolan, eds., *Culture arabe et culture européenne*, 203–21.

51. For Riccoldo's biography, see Panella, "Ricerche su Riccoldo da Monte di Croce." For Riccoldo's works, see bibliography. On Riccoldo, see also Tolan, *Saracens*, ch. 10.

52. "Sapientes eorum incipiebant notabiliter execrari peruersitatem legis et quia euacuari poterat tam per libros prophetarum quam per legem Moysi quam etiam per ueridicos libros philosophorum, ideo Califfe de Baldacco ordinauerunt quod nullum aliud esset studium in Baldacco nisi de alcorano et indeo inuenimus eos ualde modicum scire tam de ueritate theolgie quam de suptilitate philosophye. Nichilominus tamen sapientes eorum nullam fidem adhibent dictis alcorani, sed ipsum derident in secreto; tamen in publico timore aliorum honorant." *Peregrinatio*, 186–88.

53. "Surrexerunt autem contra utrosque Saraceni quidam periti in philosophia et ceperunt legere in libris Aritotilis et Platonis et inceperunt contempnere omnes sectas Saracenorum et ipsum Alchoranum.

Quod aduertens quidam Calipha de Baldacco nomine [name left blank in manuscript] Edificauit in Baldacco Nadamyam et Mestanzeriam, scolas solemnissimas et reformauit studium Alcorani et ordinauit quod de quibuscumque prouinciis uenirent in Baldaccum ad studium Alchorani, studentes haberent cellas et stipendia necessaria de comuni, et ordinauit quod Saraceni et attendentes ad Alchoranum nullo modo studerent in philosophia; nec reputant eos bonos Saracenos qui philosophie intendunt pro eo quod omnes tales contempnunt Alchoranum." *Libellus contra legem Saracenorum*, ch. 13, p. 121.

54. Dante, *Inferno,* 4:143–44; on this passage see Tolan, "Du sage arabe au Sarrasin irrationnel."

55. An earlier version of this paper was presented to the International Medieval Congress at Kalamazoo, May 2000.

Chapter 9. Walls of Hatred and Contempt

1. See above, chapter 3; Tolan *Saracens*, ch. 7.

2. Juan Manuel, *Libro de los estados,* 248–49.

3. See Mirrer, *Women, Jews, and Muslims;* Nirenberg, *Communities of Violence.*

4. Mettmann rejects the authenticity of several other works, including the *Disputa contra los Jueus.* Mettmann, *Die volkssprachliche apologetische Literatur*, 21–24. On the (dubious) authenticity of the Catalan texts attributed to Pedro Pascual, see also Riera i Sans, "L'invencio literaria de Sant Pere Pasqual."

5. To accentuate the difference between the Christian "Us" and the Muslim "Other," Eulogius and Alvarus also deploy animal metaphors, asserting that the "Chaldeans" are savages, beasts, not humans like us. See Millet-Gérard, *Chrétiens mozarabes*, 95–122, 145–48.

6. If this reference is authentic, this would suggest a previous period of captivity in Granada, *before* he was named bishop in 1296.

7. "Com yo Religios, e Bisbe per la gracia de Deu de la Ciutat de Jaen del Regne Castella, e assi no anomenat, com per mia ventura fos pres en poder del Rey de Granada, e veent molts dels Christians esser catius, no sabents lettres ne be de la fe dels Christians, tot die, qui un qui altre se tornaven a la mala secta dels Moros." He describes this in his *Disputa contra los Jueus:* many prisoners, he says, "se tornaven a la mala secta dels moros." Pedro Pascual, *Obras,* 3:1.

8. Pedro Pascual, *Sobre la seta Mahometana,* in *Obras,* 4:1–357; Pedro himself gives the date (235–36). The unique MS dates c. 1500: Biblioteca de El Escorial, Monasterio, MS h.II.25, ff.1r–179r (Faulhaber et al., eds., *Bibliography of Old Spanish Texts*, 292; this MS contains another text by Pedro, the *Tratado del libre albedrio contra el fatalismo de los Mahometanos* (ff.179r–199r); and a series of Proverbs (199v–200r). On Pedro Pascual, see Fita, "Once bulas"; Fita, "Sobre la bibliografía de San Pedro Pascual"; Saiz Muñoz, "Críticas contra el profeta Muhammad"; Riera i Sans, "L'invencio literaria de Sant Pere Pasqual."

9. "No quiero que el pecador muera en sus malos pecados, mas que se convierta, e que viva [Ezek. 23:11]; e por ende veyendo yo que muchos en este cativerio por razon que se enbuelvan en grandes pecados, e desesperan de la misericordia de Dios, como Cayn que mató a su hermano Habel, e desesperó e fuè perdido; e como Judas que truxo a su Señor, e desesperó e enforcóse; e por razon de mengua de entendimiento, que no saben la ley de los christianos, ni la de los moros, a quien engañò Mahomat, e ellos toman plazer en engañar christianos e sacar de su ley. Veyendo yo esto, ove dolor de las ánimas de nuestros christianos, que veya perderse por no saber ni conoscer la verdad; e por ende . . . trasladé de latin en romançe llana mente, no por rimas, ni por concordanças, por razon que los rimadores suelen añadir o menguar en la verdad, la historia di Mahomat ai

como fallè escripta en nuestros libros, que fueron en el tiempo que començó mahomat, y demás de lo que se contiene en esa historia, escrivi algunas otras cosas que me dixeron algunos moros, cuydando alabar su ley, e que fallé escriptas en los libros de los moros. E despues escrivi algunas cosas de lo que fallè escripto en los Evangelios, e en las Epistolas, e en libros auténticos, que se leen en la santa Iglesia." Pedro Pascual, *Obras,* 4:2–3.

10. "Fallaredes en él con que vos defendades contra los enemigos de nuestra ley." This is in the epilogue to *Sobre la seta,* 348.

11. "Los que iacemos en tal lugar . . . Amigos, esforzadvos, e aved consolación en nuestro Señor Jhesu Christo, por cuyo nombre çufris fierros, e cárceres, fambre, sed, e muchas otras lazerias, e penas, e sosaños." *Obras,* 4:350.

12. "Fablillas de romances de amor o de otras vanidades." *Sobre la seta,* 3 .

13. "Un sancto obispo, que fué uno de los mas letratos que ovo en el mundo fasta el dia de hoy, e fué en Africa obispo ante que comenzase la secta de Mahomad, e este ovo nombre Sant Augustin, e scribió muchos libros." *Sobre la seta,* 258 .

14. "Los moros dizen que no veen, ni entienden como oviesse Dios podido salvar a nos en otra manera, sino si muriesse en cruz por nos, ca pudo mandar otro omo o ángel que nos redimiesse e nos salvase muriendo, o non muriendo; e a esta razón la primera respuesta esta es." *Sobre la seta* 4:14, p.182 .

15. "Los moros e los judios dizen que pues Jhesu Christo, de quien nos deçimos que es nuestro Salvador, fue tajado e circumcidado, que nos, pues no nos tajamos, que non podemos ser salvos." *Sobre la seta,* 186–87.

16. Ibn `Abdun, *Hisba,* 109.

17. "Si no viessen la cruz e las ymágenes, no se acordarían tan muchas vezes, ni se moverian los corazones a piedad; e por estas razones son puestas las cruzes e las ymágenes en las yglesias, e no porque nos creamos que en las piedras, ni en los maderos ay deydad, ni divinidad ninguna, ni que nos puedan ayudar ni desayudar." *Sobre la seta,* 288.

18. *Sobre la seta,* 241.

19. Ibid., 288–89.

20. He introduces (often with formulas such as "podedes responder"), defensive arguments concerning the Eucharist (210), the Trinity (307–8), crucifixes and images (241–42, 287–90), and the divinity of Jesus (313).

21. *Sobre la seta,* 144.

22. "Esta razon dixe yo a algunos moros que se tienen por sabidores, e yo nunca fallé quien me respondiese a ella." *Sobre la seta,* 1:8:242, p. 144.

23. *Sobre la seta,* 224.

24. "E en quanto entiendo por lo que decian algunos moros en las disputationes, pésales de los alabanzas que dixo Mahomad de Jhesu Christo, ca manifiesta mente contra los moros dixo." *Sobre la seta,* 217; see p. 158 (on the incarnation) and p. 210 (on bodily resurrection).

25. He is no doubt referring to Petrus Comestor's *Historia Scolastica.* On the *Apocalypse of Pseudo-Methodius,* see Tolan, *Saracens,* 46–50; Flori, *L'Islam et la fin des temps,* 133–41.

26. *Sobre la seta* 1:8, pp. 69–71.

27. *Apocalypse of Pseudo-Methodius,* §V, p. 130; §X, p. 139.

28. Paulus Alvarus, *Indiculus luminosus,* § 21, in CSM, 293–95; on this passage, see chapter 1; Southern, *Western Views of Islam,* 23; Wolf, *Christian Martyrs in Muslim Spain,* 91–95.

29. "Dad loor a Dios, e reconoscedvos por pecadores. E que vos merescistes, e merescedes esto que çufrides e mas; e en todo bendecid el nombre de Dios, ca asi facio Job, e los Apóstoles, e los sanctos Padres, e los Confessores, que fueron encarcerados, e en mas graves cárceres, e en peores prissiones que nos somos, asi como aparesçe manifiestamente por las historias." *Sobre la seta,* 204–5.

30. On Pelagius, see Tolan, *Saracens,* 94, 106–7.

31. On the Franciscan martyrs of Ceuta (1227), see Tolan, *Saracens,* ch. 9.

32. "Con espada començaron, e con espada mantienen su seta maldita, e por ende razon es que con espada fenezcan su vida." *Sobre la seta,* 61 .

33. "El Soldan dixole vete a buena ventura, que no te quiero facer mártir, que te fagan fiesta después los christianos" [204]. See Tolan, *Le Saint Chez le Sultan.*

34. *Sobre la seta,* 1:1:36, pp. 16–17; this notion is already found in the Midrash and in the writings of Jerome. See Ginzberg, *Legends of the Jews,* 1:237–40, 263–69; 5:230–33, 246–47. Thanks to Alan Corre for these references.

35. "Estos pueblos siempre fizieron persecuçion e guerra a los fijos legitimos que descendieron de Abraham, que son dichos pueblos de Israel, *e aun no cesan,* e asi cumplen la profecia que le fué dicha a su padre Ismael, que devia seer cruel, e robador, e sus manos contra todos los omes, e las manos de todos contra él, e fincarán tiendas contra sus hermanos; e la letra del hebrayco dize que devia ser *velut onager,* conviene a saber, asno silvestre." *Sobre la seta,* 1:8:8, p. 69.

36. See Shahîd, *Rome and the Arabs;* Rotter, *Abendland und Sarazenen.*

37. Pedro Pascual, *Sobre la seta,* 1:8:4, p. 68.

38. "E después echanlo a las vezes por las bocas, a las vezes por de yuso, e por ende nos los de España, dezimosles *moros,* asi como en denuesto, porque les fazen echar el oro por el peor lugar; onde moro tanto diz como *meante oro.*" *Sobre la seta,* 72–73.

39. "E yo digo que es muncho mayor bestia que bestia, el que lee los libros de tu seta, o Mahomat, et los tus dichos, et los tus fechos, et te cree." "maldita seta e suzia." *Sobre la seta,* 1:8:206, 132

40. Ferreiro, "Jerome's Polemic."

41. "Labamiento de dentro en las corazones." *Sobre la seta,* 88.

42. *Sobre la seta,* 208; 2 Cor 3:6.

43. "E estos dos profecias podedes alegar contra los Judíos e contra moros." *Sobre la seta,* 208.

44. See Iogna-Prat, *Ordonner et exclure;* above, chapter 4.

45. See above, chapter 3.

46. "El en mal dia naszido." *Sobre la seta,* 46.

47. "Fablillas, mentiras, vanidades, contrariedades, chufas, eregia, neçedad, denuestas a Dios, baviquias." *Sobre la seta.*

48. "E por ende mala bez o nunca fallarédes moro sabio en philosophia, que no sea erege en su ley, ca conosce manifiesta mente que Mahomat fue neçio, e no sopo que dixo

en esto, e en otras muchas cosas, asi como ome sin letras e que no sabia que se deçia. . . . Onde escarnio façen de Mahomat los sabios de su ley misma." *Sobre la seta*, 145; see above, chapter 8.

49. *Castigos e documentos para bien vivir*, 126–33. Thanks to María Jesús Lacarra for drawing my attention to this text.

Chapter 10. A Dreadful Racket

1. W. 'Arafat, "Bilâl b. Rabâh," EI[2] 1:1215; T. Juynboll, "Adhân," EI[2] 1:187; Bloom, *Minaret*, 21–35.

2. σήμαντρον, derived from de σῆμα, sign, designates first a visual sign, second a seal, and third an object in wood or metal used to call monks or faithful to prayer. See Lampe, *A Patristic Greek Lexicon*, 1231; Stephanus, *Thesaurus graecae linguae*, 7:181–82.

3. H. Farmer, "Sandj," EI[2] 9:9.

4. Hillenbrand, *Islamic Architecture*, 129–71; Hillenbrand et al, "Manâra," EI[2] 6:361. Bloom, *Minaret*, affirms that it is in Abbâsid Iraq that the first minarets were built.

5. Based on the French translation of Fattal, *Le Statut légal*, 66, 204–5.

6. Fattal, *Le Statut légal*, 204–5.

7. For the example of Kûfa in the eighth century, see Fattal, *Le Statut légal*, 206.

8. Fattal, *Le Statut légal*, 60–69.

9. Ibid., 62.

10. Ibid., 64.

11. Ibid.

12. Ibid., 206–7.

13. Ibid., 205.

14. Ibid., 206.

15. C.Hillenbrand, "Mayyâfârikîn," EI[2] 6:928a.

16. Zanetti, "Matarieh," 35.

17. For other examples, see M. Canard, "al-Hakim, Bi-Amr Allâh," EI[2] 3:76 (for the prohibitions against ringing the *nâqûs* during the reign of the Fatimid Caliph al-Hakim). For the evidence concerning the ringing of bells in Tiflis (Georgia) under the Il-Khânids, see V. Minorsky and C. Bosworth, "Tiflis," EI[2] 10:478.

18. Fattal, *Le Statut légal*, 185.

19. See Gabrieli, *Arab Historians of the Crusades*, 168–73.

20. G. Deverdun, "al-Karawiyyîn (masdjid)," EI[2] 4:632.

21. Fattal, *Le Statut légal*, 79. The text may have been altered by later authors, as Fattal notes, 77n21.

22. Ibid., 83.

23. B. Heller, "Sîrat 'Antar," EI[2] 1:518.

24. R. Traini, "Rûmiya," EI[2] 8:612.

25. Al-Maqqarî, *Nafh al-tîb min ghusn al-Andalus al-ratîb*, cited by Vanoli, "Immagini dell''Altro' nelle fonti arabo-spagnole," 49; Dodds, *Architecture and Ideology*, 104.

26. There is a large bibliography concerning the martyrs of Cordoba; for a synopsis of works up to 1970, see Wolf, *Christian Martyrs in Muslim Spain*, 36–47. See also Mil-

let-Gérard, *Chrétiens mozarabes et culture islamique*; Lapiedra Gutiérrez, "Los mártires de Córdoba"; Coope, *The Martyrs of Córdoba;* Herrera Roldán, *Cultura y lengua latina*; Wolf, "Christian Views of Islam"; Tolan, "Mahomet et L'Antéchrist dans l'Espagne du IXe siècle"; Wolf, "Muhammad as Antichrist"; Tolan, "Réactions chrétiennes aux conquêtes musulmanes"; Tolan, *Saracens*, ch. 4.

27. "Mox ut illectum superstitione mendaci uulgus clangorem tinnientis metalli aure captauerit, in omnem maledictionem et spurcitiam linguam admouere non differt. Ergo non incongrue maledicuntur, qui tanto odio aduersus Dei sortem sequipedas suos informant." Eulogius of Córdoba, *Memoriale sanctorum* §21, in CSM, 386.

28. "Set quum uaselice signum, hoc est, tinnientis eris sonitum, qui pro conuentum eclesie adunandum horis homnibus canonicis percutitur, audiunt, derisione et contemtui iniantes, mobentes capita infanda iterando congeminant, et omnem sexum universamque etatem totiusque Christi Domini gregem non uniformi subsannio, set milleno contumiarum infamio maledice inpetunt et deridunt." Paulus Alvarus, *Indiculus luminosus* §6, in CSM, 278–79.

29. "Sed et alia inaudita uanitatis scelera praedicans adinuentione ueripellis, a quo obsidebatur, inuenta, qui se eidem transfigurauit in angelum luci, delubra in quibus pessimum dogma suum coleretur extruxit, constituens in ultimo idolatriae situ turrem altiori pinnaculo ceteris aedibus prominentem, ex qua populis ueneno nequitiae suae illectis sacrilegi furoris contionaretur decretum; quod hodie suae impietatis sacerdotes ab illo edocti obseruant, ita ut more aselli dissutis mandibulis impurisque patentibus labiis horrendum praeconium non prius emittant quam obseratis utroque digito auribus: quod aliis exequendum annuntiant, quasi quoddam edictum sceleris idem ipse eorum propheta audire non patitur. Quem impietatis ruditum dum diuae memoriae auus meus Eulogius aure captaret, ferunt continuo uexillo crucis frontem praemuniens cum gemitu hunc psalmum solitum fuisse cantare: "Deus, quis similis tibi? Ne taceas neque sileas, Deus, quoniam ecce inimici tui, Domine, sonuerunt et qui te oderunt leuauerunt caput" (Ps. 82:2–3). Nos autem mox ut fallentis uocuem praeconis audimus confestim oramus: "Salua nos, Domine, ab auditu malo et nunc et in aeternum," et iterum: "Confundantur omnes qui adorant sculptilia et qui gloriantur in simulacris" (Ps. 96:7)." Eulogius of Córdoba, *Liber apologeticus martyrum* §19, in CSM, 487.

30. Jonathan Bloom affirms that Eulogius and Alvarus make no mention of minarets, yet Bloom has not consulted their texts but simply cites a few passages in translation that he had found principally in Dodds, *Architecture and Ideology*, 103. Bloom, "Mosque Towers and Church Towers," 363.

31. See Millet-Gérard, *Chrétiens mozarabes et culture islamique*, 104–8.

32. "Ecce et cotidie horis diurnis et nocturnis in turribus suis et montibus caligosis Dominum maledicunt, dum uatem impudicum, periurum, rabidum et iniquum, una cum Dominum testimonii voce extollunt." Paulus Alvarus, *Indiculus luminosus*, §6, in CSM, 278.

33. On the name Moazim, see Millet-Gérard, *Chrétiens mozarabes et culture islamique*, 41n79.

34. "Quod iste in fumosis turribus cotidie barritu inormi et monstruoso hac ferarum rictu, dissolutis labiis et faucium iatu aperto ut cardiaci uociferant hac vocife-

rando uelut furiosi preconant, ut muniant Maozim cum Deo alieno quem cognouit, id est ut Maozim, quem illi Cobar uocant, hoc est maiorem, cum Deo alieno, ide est, demone illo qui ei sub persona Gavrihelis apparuit, uno uenerationis nomine muniat, ut per hoc herrorem euum in corda credentium tegat, dum nomine maioris Dei ritum uociferantionis extollit et supprestitioso conatu, nefando spiritu, nobilium animas inficit. Set ne uidear hoc enigmatice et non proprie dici et magis reputer ingenio humano quesita quam diuino spiritu enucleata proferre, apertiora inducenda sunt probamenta. Ecce enim eodem ritui dediti dies illos, quibus insaniam in domo idoli consecrant, eodem uocabulo actenus in pleraque nomina ab Ebrayco discrepat, Almozem ipse ferie apellantur, ipsoque tempore quo iam dicto idolo antiquitus ipsa gens in gentilitas posita ex uniuersis partibus concurrebat, nunc eadem perdita turba magnitudine extirpato, perenniter serbiunt. Maozim in loco suo, ut profeta spiritu diuino retulit, usque odie incolunt, quando et in ipsos dies solito nuncupant nomine et mensem illum quem Almoarram uocitant, ut cultores idolatrie olim sustollebant, ita hii odie habundantiori perfectione, ut siui uidentur, celo tenus perferunt. Paulus Alvarus, *Indiculus luminosus,* §25, in CSM, 298–99; on this passage see Millet-Gérard, *Chrétiens mozarabes et culture islamique,* 39–45.

35. Some Greek authors associate *akbar* (often deformed as *koubar)* with a god worshiped by the "Hagarenes," without mention of Maozim. See, for example, Georges the Monk (PG 110:873); on this author, see Ducelier, *Chrétiens d'Orient et Islam au Moyen Age,* 161–64. For another Greek text mentioning "Koubar," see Meyendorff, "Byzantine Views of Islam," 118–19.

Adelphus, a Latin author of the twelfth century, affirms, "I have often heard the Saracens invoke that horrible monster Muhammad with their voices, so that they can adore him in their bacchanal rites, calling on him and worshipping him as a god." Adelphus, *Vita Machometi,* 113. See Tolan, *Saracens,* ch. 6.

36. Millet-Gérard, *Chrétiens mozarabes et culture islamique,* 43; Wolf, "Muhammad as Antichrist," 12–13.

37. See Millet-Gérard, *Chrétiens mozarabes et culture islamique,* 45.

38. "Basilicarum turres euerteret, templorum arces dirueret et excelsa pinnaculorum prosterneret." Eulogius of Córdoba, *Liber apologeticus martyrum* §22, in CSM, 488–89. Cf. Eulogius, *Memoriale sanctorum* 3:3, in CSM, 441.

39. Dodds, *Architecture and Ideology,* 103; Bloom, *Minaret,* ch. 7, "Minarets as Signs of Conflict in the Magrheb"; Hernández Giménez, *El alminar de 'Abd al-Rahmân III;* Torres-Balbás, *La Mezquita de Córdoba*; Bloom, "Mosque Towers and Church Towers."

40. "Et heu et ue huic tempori nostro sapientie Christi egeno, zelo zabolico pleno, in quo nullus inuenitur qui iuxta iussum Domini tonantis etherei super montes Bablionie caligosasque turres superbie crucis fidei adtollat uexillum, sacrificium Deo offerens uespertinum." Paulus Alvarus, *Indiculus luminosus,* §6, in CSM, 278.

41. On Al-Mansûr, see Sénac, "Al-Mansûr et la reconquête"; Chalmeta, "Al-Mansûr billah," EI[2] 6:430; Lévi-Provençal, *Histoire de l'Espagne musulmane,* 2:197–272. On the expedition to Santiago, see Jean-Pierre Molénat, "*Sh*ant Yâkub," EI[2] 9:304, who gives a bibliography of sources and studies; to the latter we can now add Pérez de Tudela Velasco, "Guerra, violencia y terror."

42. Ibn Darrâj, *Dîwân*, poems 77, 102, 120, 128; Makki, "La España cristiana en el *Dîwân* de Ibn Darrây."

43. Ibn 'Idhârî, *Kitâb al-Bayân al-Mughrib* 2:295–97; Fagnan, trans. 2:493–95; reproduced in Bresc et al., *La Méditerranée*, 19–21.

44. Ibn Khaldûn, *'Ibar*, French translation in Dozy, *Recherches sur l'histoire et la littérature*, 1:101.

45. Al-Maqqarî, *Nafh al-tib*, 2:193–196, 1:227–28.

46. Sampiro, *Cronica*, inserted in the *Historia Silense*, ed. Justo Perez de Urbel and Atilano Gonzalez Ruiz-Zorilla (Madrid: CSIC, 1959), 172. Sampiro does not mention the fact that Vermudo had given one of his daughters to Al-Mansûr in marriage. On Sampiro, see Deswarte, *De la destruction à la restauration*, 29. See also Huete Fudio, *La Historiografía latina*.

47. *Historia Silense*, 175; on this chronicle, see Deswarte, *De la destruction à la restauration*, 29.

48. "Interim rex Alcorexi cum multis Agarenorum militibus Portugalensi regionem intrauit, Galletiam et Compostella uenit et totam terram predauit. Ad ecclesiam ergo siue ad sepulcrum Beati Iacobi apostoli destruendum uenire disposuit, set Deo annuente territus rediit et confussus." *Chronica Najerensis*, 2:33.

49. "Interea Rudericus Velasqui et pater prefati episcopi cum ceteris consulibus huius terre Sarracenos cum duce eorum Almezor in partes istas duxit. Qui Compostellam uenientes maiorem partem parietum beati Iacobi ecclesie preter eius sanctissimum altare penitus destruxerunt. Igitur beatissimus Iacobus uolens ne ab ecclesia sua, quam ipsi tante superbie calce oppreserant, impune euaderent, tanto dissenterie morbo eos percussit, quod, mortuis eorum quam pluribus, perpauci ad propria redierunt. Cum que dux eorum Almezor interna consideratione tante ultionis periculo suos acrius percuti conspiceret, quisnam esset ille, cuius aula eorum impetu iam fere destructa esset, sui itineris ductores fertur consuluisse. Quorum nimirum responsione, Iacobum scilicet, unum ex discipulis Filii Marie Virginis, cuius nomen apud eos "ecce Mariam" nuncupatur, ibidem certissime tumulari comperiens ac tante audacie penitudinem gerens fugam obstinate iniit et in fugiendo repentino languore percussus apud Metinacelim, ubi sepultus est, animam suam sinui Mafometh infeliciter commendauit." *Historia Compostellana* 1:2.

50. Lucas de Tuy, *Miracula Sancti Isidori*, cited by Patrick Henriet, "Xénophobie et intégration isidoriennes," 52.

51. "Ad sepulchrum vero beati Iacobi Apostoli, ut illud frangeret, audacter {sic} sed territus quadam fulguratione rediit." "Tulit autem barbarus Almazor campanas minores ecclesiae sancti Iacobi, et ob insigne fecit eas Cordubem deduci, et in oratorio suo pro lampadibus suspendit eas." Lucas de Tuy, *Chronicon mundi*. On Lucas de Tuy, see Martin, *Les juges de Castille;* Linehan, *History and Historians*, 357–58; Henriet, "Hagiographie et Politique"; Henriet, "Xénophobie et intégration"; Henriet, "Hagiographie léonaise"; Henriet, ed., "Chroniqueur, hagiographe, théologien."

52. "Inuentae sunt ibi campanae quas ob insigne ab Ecclesia Sancti Iacobi Apostoli Rex Cordubensis olim detulerat Almanzor et Rex Catholicus Fernandus fecit eas Sarracenorum humeris ad Ecclesiam S. Iacobi repartari. Capta est ciuitas Cordubensis era MCCLXXIV & reuersus est inclytus Rex Fernandus Toletum cum victoria et gloria

magna. O quam beatus iste Rex qui abstulit opprobrium Hispanorum, euertens solium barbarorum, et restituens Ecclesiae Sancti Iacobi Apostoli campanas suas cum magno honore, quae multo tempore fuerant Cordubae, ob iniuriam et opprobrium nominis Christi." Lucas de Tuy, *Chronicon mundi.*

53. "Tunc precepit ut in turribus ubi consueuerant campane pulsari, Sarracenus quispiam proclamaret sicut et adhuc hodie proclamatur a cultoribus secte sue." Rodrigo Jiménez de Rada, *Historia Arabum,* §3, p. 7.

54. Based on the French translation by Guichard, *L'Espagne et la Sicile musulmanes,* 123.

55. Burns, *Islam under the Crusaders,* 187.

56. "In locis ubi suffraganei pontiffices sacrificia sancta Ihesu Christo quondam offerebant, nunc pseudo-prophete nomine extollitur, et in turribus ecclesiarum in quibus olim tintinabula releuabant, nunc quedam prophana preconia fidelium aures insurdant." D'Alverny and Vajda, "Marc de Tolède," 267. On Mark of Toledo, see also Tolan, "Las traducciones y la ideología de reconquista."

57. "De nocte ascitis militibus christianis maiorem mezquitam ingressus est Toletanam, et eliminata spurcicia Machometi erexit altaria fidei christiane et in maiore turri campanas ad conuocationem fidelium collocauit." Rodrigo Jiménez de Rada, *Historia de rebus Hispaniae.*

58. Here is the full text of Jiménez de Rada's description of the raid of Santiago: "Cum que ad maritima peruenisset, etiam ciuitatem et ecclesiam beati Iacobi deuastauit, set fulgure territus ab eo loco, ubi esse corpus apostoli credebatur, abstinuit, quod tamen proposuerat uiolare. Nichilominus tamen campanas minores in signum uictorie se cum tulit et in mezquita Cordube pro lampadibus collocauit, que longo tempore ibi fuerunt. Almançor autem cum suo exercitu percussus a Domino pro scelere sacrilegii dignam sustinuit ultionem, nam qui sanctum locum apostoli prophanarat, inmunda sui plaga, scilicet, dissenteria, fere totus exercitus est consumptus; reliqui morte subitanea perierunt. Quod audiens rex Veremudus misit multitudinem peditum expeditam, qui imbelles et infirmitate consumptos in montanis de facili trucidarunt. Et sic Almançor coactus peste ad propria est reuersus." Rodrigo Jiménez de Rada, *De rebus Hispaniae,* 5:16.

59. "Arabes exierunt, et in festo apostolorum Petri et Pauli a sordibus Machometi patricia ciuitas expurgatur. Set rex in turri maiori, ubi solebat nomen perfidi inuocari, precepit lignum crucis uiuifice exaltari, et ceperunt omnes cum gaudio et lacrimis Deus adiuua conclamare, et subsequenter regale uexillum iuxta crucem dominicam collocari, et cepit in iustorum tabernaculis gaudii et leticie uox audiri, clero cum pontificibus aclamante: Te Deum laudamus, te Dominum confitemur.

Et tunc uenerabilis Iohannes Oxomensis episcopus, regalis aule cancellarius, cum Gundisaluo Conchensi, Dominico Beaciensi, Adam Placentinensi, Sancio Cauriensi episcopis mezquitam ingressus est Cordubensem, que cunctas mezquitas Arabum ornatu et magnitudine superabat. Et quia uenerabilis Iohannes, de quo diximus, Roderici Toletani primatis uices gerebat, qui tunc temporis apud sedem apostolicam morabatur, eliminata spurcicia Machometi et aqua lustrationis perfusa, in ecclesiam comutauit et in honore beate Virginis erexit altare et missam sollempniter celebrauit. . . .Et cum in oprobrium populi christiani campane Sancti Iacobi, quas, ut diximus, Almançor detulerat in Cordubensi mezquita, dependerent functe officio lampadarum, rex Fernandus easdem campanas fecit ad ecclesiam beati Iacobi reportari, et ecclesie beati Iacobi restitute sunt." Rodrigo Jiménez de Rada, *Historia de rebus Hispaniae,* 9:16–17.

60. Jaume I, *Llibre dels feyts,* §445.

61. See Burns, *Islam under the Crusaders,* 187–91, who shows that even after 1311, the muezzin continued to call out the *adhân* in many Muslim communities in the peninsula. Thanks to Jean-Pierre Molénat and Michelle Szkilnik for their comments and corrections of an earlier version of this article.

Bibliography

Sources

Actus Petri cum Simone. Edited by R. A. Lipisius and M. Bonnet. In *Acta Apostolorum Apocrypha*, 1:5–130. Leipzig: Hermannum Mendelssohn, 1891.

Adelard of Bath. *Questiones naturales. Beiträge zur Geschichte der Philosophie und Theologie des Mittelalters* 31, pt. 2.

Adelphus. *Vita Machometi*. Edited by B. Bischoff. In "Ein Leben Mohammeds (Adelphus?) (Zwölftes Jahrhundert)." *Anecdota Novissima: Texte des vierten bis sechzenten Jahrhundert* (1984): 106–22.

Alexandre du Pont. *Roman de Mahomet*. Edited by Yvan Lepage. Paris: Klincksieck, 1977.

Alfonso X el Sabio. *Primera crónica general de España*. Edited by Ramón Menéndez Pidal. Madrid: Gredos, 1955, 1977.

———. *Cantigas de Santa Maria*. 2 vols. Edited by Walter Mettmann. Vigo: Edicións Xerais de Galicia, 1981.

Ambroise. *L'Estoire de la guerre sainte*. Edited by Gaston Paris. Paris: Imprimerie nationale, 1897.

Annales colonienses maximi. MGH SS 17.

Apocalypse of Pseudo-Methodius. Edited and translated by Francisco J. Martinez. "Eastern Christian Apocalyptic in the Early Muslim Period: Pseudo-Methodius and Pseudo-Athanasius." PhD diss., Catholic University of America, 1985.

The Apocryphal New Testament. J. K. Elliot, trans. Oxford: Oxford University Press, 1993.

Arnold of Lübeck. *Chronica Slavorum*. Edited by G. Pertz. In MGH SS 21. Munich, 1869; reprint, 1988.

Bacon, Roger. *Opus maius, pars septima: moralis philosophia*. Edited by E. Massa. Zürich, 1953.

———. *The Opus Majus of Roger Bacon*. Translated by Robert Burke. 2 vols. New York, 1962.

Le Bâtard de Bouillon. Edited by Robert Cook. Geneva: Droz, 1972.

Bernard of Clairvaux. *The letters of St Bernard of Clairvaux.* Bruno Scott James & Beverly Mayne Kienzle, eds. & trans. Kalamazoo: Cistercian Publications, 1998

Bosone da Gubbio. *L'avventuroso siciliano.* Roberto Gigliucci, ed. Rome: Bulzoni, 1989.

Burchard of Strasbourg. *Epistolae.* Edited by F. Güterboeck. "Le lettere del notaio imperiale burcardo intorno alla politica del Barbarossa nello schismo ed alla distruzione di milano." *Bolletino dell'Istituto storico per il medio evo e Archiv. Murator* 66 (1949): 1–65.

———. *Itinerarium.* Edited by P. Lehmann and O. Glauning. In "Mittelalterliche Handschriftenbruchstücke der Universitätsbibliothek und des Georgianum zu München." *Zentralblatt für Bibliothekswesen,* Beiheft 72 (1940): 61–73.

Castigos e documentos para bien vivir ordenados por le rey don Sancho IV. Edited by Agapito Rey. Bloomington: Indiana University Press, 1952.

Chanson d'Antioche. Edited by Suzanne Duparc-Quioc. Paris: Geuthner, 1976.

Chanson de Jérusalem. Edited by Nigel Thorpe. Old French Crusade Cycle 6 (1992).

Chanson de Roland. Edited by Ian Short. Paris: Lettres gothiques, 1990.

Chrétienté Corbaran. Edited by Peter Grillo. Old French Crusade Cycle 7 (1984).

Chronica Najerensis. Edited by J. A. Estévez Sola. In *Chronica Hispana saeculi XII* CCCM 71A (1995).

Chronica regia coloniensis. MGH SS Rerum Germ. in Usum Scholarum 18 (1880).

Chronique d'Ernoul et de Bernard le Trésorier. Edited by L. de Mas-Latrie. Paris, 1871.

Conti di Antichi Cavalieri. Edited by A. Del Monte. Milan: Cisalpino-Goliardica, 1972.

La Continuation de Guillaume de Tyr (1184–97). Edited by Margaret R. Morgan. Paris: Académie des Inscriptions et Belles-Lettres, 1982.

Crónica mozárabe de 754. Edited by José Eduardo Lopez Pereira. Zaragoza: Anubar, 1980.

Dainero, Thomas. *Die ordenung zu ofen wider den Thurken gemacht.* 1501, 1502.

Embrico of Mainz. *La vie de Mahomet.* Edited by Guy Cambier. *Collection Latomus* 52 (Brussels, 1961).

Eulogius of Córdoba, *Liber apologeticus martyrum.* CSM 475–495.

Felix Fabri. *Evagatorium in Terrae Samctae, Arabiae, et Egypti peregrinationem.* Edited by K. D. Hassler. 3 vols. Stuttgart, 1843–49.

———. *Felix Fabri's Book of Wanderings.* Anonymous English translation. 2 vols. *The Library of the Palestine Pilgrims' Text Society,* vols. 7–8 and 9–10. London, 1887–97; reprint, New York, 1971.

Fidentius of Padua. *Liber recuperationis terrae sanctae.* Edited by G. Golubovich. In *Biblioteca bio-bibliographica della terra santa e dell' oriente francescano* 2 (Florence, 1927): 1–60

La fille du comte de Ponthieu: Version du XIIIe et XVe siècles. Paris, 1923.

Froissart, Jean. *Chroniques.* Paris: Lettres Gothiques, 2004.

Gauthier de Compiègne. *Otia de Machomete.* Edited by R. B. C. Huygens. In Alexandre du Pont, *Roman de Mahomet.* Paris: Klincksieck, 1977.

Gesta Francorum et aliorum Hierosolimitanorum: Histoire *anonyme de la première Croisade.* Edited by Louis Bréhier. Paris: Champion, 1924.

al-Ghazâlî. *al-Durra al-Fâkhira.* Edited by M. Gautier. Leipzig, 1877.

———. *The Precious Pearl.* Translated by Jane Smith. Missoula, Mont.: Scholar's Press, 1979.

———. *The Incoherence of the Philosophers: Arabic Text with Parallel English Translation.* Edited and translated by M. Marmura. Provo: Brigham Young University Press, 1997.

Ghâzi Ibn al-Wâsitî. *Radd 'alâ ahl al-dhimma wa man tabi'ahum.* Edited and translated R. Goththeil. "An Answer to the Dhimmis." *Journal of the American Oriental Society* 41 (1921): 383–457.

Gilles le Bouvier, *Armorial de France*, ed. Auguste Vallet de Viriville. Paris, 1866.

Giordano da Pisa. *Quaresimale fiorentino.* Edited by Carlo Delcorno. Florence: Sansoni, 1974.

Gregory of Tours. *The History of the Franks.* Translated by Lewis Thorpe. London: Penguin, 1974.

Guibert de Nogent. *Dei Gesta per Francos.* Edited by Robert Huygens. Turnholt: Brepols, 1996.

———. *The Deeds of God through the Franks: A Translation of Guibert de Nogent's Gesta Dei per Francos.* Translated by Robert Levine. Rochester, N.Y.: Boydell Press, 1997.

Guillaume le Breton. *Philippide.* In *Oeuvres de Rigord et de Guillaume le Breton,* vol. 2, ed. H. Delaborde. Paris, 1885.

Historia Compostellana. Edited by E. Falque Rey. CCCM 70 (1988).

Historia monachorum in Aegypto. Greek text edited by A. Festugière. *Subsidia hagiographica* 34 (Brussels, 1961).

Historia Silense. Edited by Justo Perez de Urbel and Atilano Gonzalez Ruiz-Zorilla. Madrid: CSIC, 1959.

Ibn 'Abdun. *Hisba (Traité sur la vie urbaine et les corps de métiers).* Translated by E. Lévi-Provençal. *Séville musulmane au début du XIIe siècle.* Paris: Librairie Orientaliste Paul Geuthner, 1947.

Ibn Darrâj. *Dîwân.* Spanish translation by Margarita La Chica Garrido. *Almanzor en los poemas de Ibn Darrây.* Zaragoza: Anúbar, 1979.

Ibn 'Idhârî, *Kitâb al-Bayân al-Mughrib.* Edited by G. Colin and E. Lévi-Provençal. *Histoire de l'Espagne de la conquête au XIe siècle.* 2 vols. Beruit: Dar al-Sakifa, 1948.

———. *Histoire de l'Afrique et de l'Espagne intitulée al-Bayano'l-Mogrib.* 2 vols. French translation by E. Fagnan. Algiers, 1904.

Ibn Sînâ. *Risâlat adhawiyya fi amr al-ma'âd.* Edited and translated by F. Lucchetta. *Epistola sulla vita futura.* Padua: Antenore, 1969.

Isidore of Seville. *Chronica majora.* Edited by T. Mommsen. MGH AA.

Jacobus de Voragine. *Legenda Aurea.* Edited by T. Graesse. Dresden, 1890; Osnabrück, 1969.

Jacques de Vitry. *The Historia Occidentalis of Jacques de Vitry: A Critical Edition.* Edited by J. F. Hinnebusch. Fribourg: Spicilegium Friburgense, 1972.

———. *La traduction de l'Historia Orientalis de Jacques de Vitry.* Edited by Claude Buridant. Paris: Klincksieck, 1986.

———. *Lettres.* Edited by R. Huygens. Leiden: Brill, 1960.

Jaume I. *Llibre dels feyts.* Edited by Ferrán Soldevilla. Barcelona: Edicions 62, 1982.

Jean de Joinville, *Vie de Saint Louis.* J. Monfrin, ed. Paris: Garnier, 1995.

Jerome. *Chronicon.* Edited by Rudolf Helm. *Eusebius Werke,* 7:228–34. Berlin: Akademie, 1956.

Juan Manuel. *Libro de los estados*, in *Obras completas*, ed. José Manuel Blecua, 1:191–502. Madrid, 1982–83.

Liber Nycholay. Edited and translated into Spanish by Fernando González Muñoz. "*Liber Nycholay*, la leyenda de Mahoma y el cardenal Nicolás." *Al-Qantara* 25 (2004): 5–43.

Lucas de Tuy. *Chronicon mundi*. Edited by Emma Falque. CCCM 74 (2003).

Al-Maqqarî. *Nafh al-tib*. Translated by Pascal Gayangos. *The History of the Mohammedan Dynasties in Spain*. 2 vols. London: Oriental Translation Fund, 1840–43.

Matthew Paris. *Chronica maior*. Edited by H. R. Luard. Rolls series (*Rerum britannicarum medii aevi*), no. 57. 7 vols. London, 1872–83.

———. *Chronica maior*. Partial translation by J. A. Giles, *Matthew Paris's English History from the Year 1235 to 1273*. London: Bell, 1852; reprint, New York: AMS Press, 1968.

Nachmanides. *The Disputation at Barcelona*. Translated by Charles Chavel. New York: Shilo, 1983.

Novellino, suivi de Contes de chevaliers du temps jadis. Edited and translated by Gérard Genot and Paul Larivaille. Paris: 10/18, 1988.

Oliver of Paderborn. *Historia damiatina*. Edited by O. Hoogeweg. In *Die Schriften des Kölner Domscholasters, spätern Bischofs von Paderborn und Kardinal-Bischofs von S. Sabina Oliverus, Bibliothek des litterarischen Vereins in Stuttgart* 202 (1894).

———. *Historia damiatina*. English translation by John J. Gavigan. *The Capture of Damietta*. Philadelphia: University of Pennsylvania Press, 1948.

Ordene de chevalerie. Edited and translated by Keith Busby. In *Raoul de Houdenc: le Roman des Eles; the Anonymous Ordene de Chevalerie*. Amsterdam, 1983.

Pas Salhadin. Edited by F. E. Lodeman. In *Modern Language Notes* 12 (1897): 21–34, 84–96, 209–29, 273–81.

Paulus Alvarus, *Indiculus luminosus*. CSM 270–315.

Pedro Pascual. *Obras de San Pedro Pascual*. Edited by P. Armegon Valenzuela. 4 vols. Rome, 1907–8.

Perez de Guzman, Fernán. *Mar de Histórias*. Edited by Joaquín Rodriguez. Madrid: Ediciones Atlas, 1944.

Peter Abelard. *Dialogus inter philosophum iudaeum et christianum*. Edited by Rudolf Thomas. Stuttgart: Bad Cannstatt, 1970.

———. *Dialogue of a Philosopher with a Jew and a Christian*. Translated by Pierre Payer. Toronto: Pontifical Institute of Medieval Studies, 1979.

———. *Historia calamitatum*. Edited by Jacques Monfrin. Paris: Vrin, 1967.

———. *Historia calamitatum*. Translated by B. Radice. In *The Letters of Abelard and Heloise*. London: Penguin, 1974.

Peter of Cluny [Petrus Venerabilis]. *Adversus Iudeorum inveteratam duritiem*. Edited by Yvonne Friedman. CCCM 58 (1985).

———. *Contra Petrobrusianos hereticos*. Edited by James Fearns. CCCM 10 (1968).

———. *De Miraculis*. Edited by D. Bouthillier. CCCM 83 (1988)

———. *The Letters of Peter the Venerable*. Edited by Giles Constable. 2 vols. Cambridge: Harvard University Press, 1967.

———. *Contra sectam*. In *Schriften zum Islam*. Edited by R. Glei. Corpus Islamo-Christianum, series latina 1. Alternberg: CIS, 1985.

———. *Summa totius haeresis Saracenorum*. In *Schriften zum Islam*. Edited by R. Glei. Corpus Islamo-Christianum, series latina 1. Alternberg: CIS, 1985.

Petrarch, Francesco. *Rime e Trionfi di Francesco Petrarca*. Edited by Ferdinando Neri. Turin: Unione Tipogr.-Ed. Torinese, 1960.

Petrus Alfonsi (Pedro Alfonso). *Diálogi contra Iudeos,* Latin text by K. Mieth with Spanish translation by E. Ducay. *Diálogo contra los Judíos*. Zaragoza: Larumbe, 1996.

———. *Dialogue against the Jews*. Translated by Irven Resnick. Washington: Catholic University of America Press, 2006.

Petrus Tudebodus. *Historia de Hierosolymitano itinere*. Edited by J. and L. Hill. Paris, 1977.

Qur'ân. Translated by N. Dawood. *The Koran*. London: Penguin, 1956.

Ramon Llull. *Doctor Illuminatus: A Ramon Llull Reader*. Edited and translated by A. Bonner. Princeton: Princeton University Press, 1993.

———. *Doctrina pueril*. Edited by Gret Schib. Barcelona: Barcino, 1972.

———. *Liber de fine*. CCCM, 35

———. *Le Livre du Gentil et des trois sages*. Armand Llinares, trans (into French). Paris: Cerf, 1993

———. *Obres essencials*. 2 vols. Barcelona: Selecta, 1957–60.

———. *Selected Works of Ramon Llull*. Edited and translated by A. Bonner. 2 vols. Princeton: Princeton University Press, 1985.

Ramon Martí. *De seta Machometi o De origine, progressu, et fine Machometi et quadruplici reprobatione prophetiae eius*. Edited and translated into Spanish by Josep Hernando i Delgado, in *Acta historica et archaeologica medievalia* 4 (1983): 9–51.

___. *Explanatio simboli Apostolorum*. J. March y Battles, ed., "En Ramon Martí y la seva Explanatio simboli Apostolorum,"in *Annuari de l'Institut d'Esudis Catalans* (1908), 443–96.

Récits d'un ménestrel de Reims. Edited by Marie-Geneviève Grossel. Valenciennes: Presses universitaires de Valenciennes, 2002.

Riccoldo da Montecroce. *Epistolae V de perditione Acconis 1291*. Edited by R. Röhricht. In *Archives de l'orient latin* 2 (1884): 258–96.

———. *Libelli ad nationes orientales* (electronic edition of Latin text with introduction by Kurt Jensen. www.ou.dk/hum/kuj/riccoldo.

———. *Libellus contra legem Saracenorum*. Edited by J. Merigoux. In *Memorie domenicane*, n.s. 17 (1986): 1–144.

———. *Pérégrination en terre sainte et au Proche Orient et lettres sur la chute de Saint-Jean d'Acre,* Latin edition and French translation by René Kappler. Paris: Champion, 1997.

Risâlat al-Kindî. Risâlat 'Abd Allâh Ibn Ismâ'îl al-Hâshimî ilâ 'Abd al-Masî Ibn Isâq al-Kindî wa-Risâlat al-Kindî ilâ al-Hâshimî (*The Apology of El-Kindi: A Work of the Ninth Century, Written in Defence of Christianity by an Arab)*. Edited by A. Tien. London, 1885.

———. [medieval Latin translation] *Exposición y refutación del Islam: La versión latina de las epístolas de al-Hašimi y al-Kindi*. Edited by Fernando González Muñoz. La Coruña: Universidade da Coruña, 2005.

———. [modern French translation] Translated by Georges Tartar. *Risâlat al-Kindî (Dialogue islamo-chrétien sous le Calife al-Ma'mûn (813–834): Les épîtres d'al-Hashimî et d'al-Kindî.* Paris: Nouvelles Éditions Latines, 1985.

Rodrigo Jiménez de Rada. *Historia Arabum.* Edited by J. Lozano Sanchez. Seville: Publicaciones de la Universidad de Sevilla, 1974.

———. *Historia de rebus Hispaniae.* CCCM 72 (1987).

Roman de Saladin. Edited by Larry S. Crist. Geneva: Droz, 1972.

Thomas of Cantimpré, *Vita Sanctae Lutgardis virginis cistercensae,* ch. 4 (Acta Sanctorum Jun. IV, p. 209); *Supplementum ad vitam Sanctae Mariae Oigniacensis* (Acta Sanctorum Jun. V, p. 578–81).

Toledoth Yeshu. English translation by Hugh Schonfield. *According to the Hebrews, a new translation of the Jewish life of Jesus (the Toldoth Jeshu), with an inquiry into the nature of its sources and special relationship to the lost Gospel according to the Hebrews.* London: Duckworth, 1937.

La vida de Santa María Egipciaca, traducida por un juglar anónimo hacía 1215. Edited by María Soledad de Andres. Madrid: Imprenta Silverio Aguirre Torre, 1964.

La vie de Sainte Marie l'Égyptienne. Edited by Peter Dembowski. Geneva: Droz, 1977.

Voltaire, *Essai sur les mœurs.* 2 vols. Paris: Garnier, 1963.

Studies

Abel, Armand. "L'Apologie d'Al-Kindi et sa place dans la polémique islamo-chrétien." *Atti del covegno internazionale sul tema: L'oriente cristiano nella storia della civiltà,* 501–23. Rome, 1964.

Adang, Camila. *Islam frente a Judaísmo: La polémica de Ibn Hazm de Córdoba.* Madrid: Aben Ezra, 1994.

Ali, Tariq. *The Book of Saladin.* London: Verso Books, 1998.

Allaire, Gloria. Allaire. *Andrea da Barberino and the Language of Chivalry.* Gainesville: University Press of Florida, 1997.

———. "Portrayal of Muslims in Andrea da Barberino's *Guerrino il Meschino.*" In *Christian Perceptions of Islam,* ed. John Tolan, 243–68.

Altman, Charles F. "Types of Opposition and the Structure of Latin Saints' Lives." *Medievalia et Humanistica* 6 (1975): 1–11.

Arberry, Arthur. *Avicenna on Theology.* London: J. Murray, 1951; reprint, Westport, Conn.: Hyperion, 1979.

Asin Palacios, Miguel. *La escatología musulmana de la Divina comedia.* 4th ed. Madrid: Hiperión, 1984.

Bancourt, Paul. "De l'image épique à la représentation historique du Musulman dans *L'estoire de la Guerre Sainte* d'Ambroise (*L'estoire* et la *Chanson d'Aspremont*)." *Au Carrefour des routes d'Europe: La Chanson de Geste.* Aix: CUERMA, 1987.

———. "De l'imagerie au réel: l'exotisme oriental d'Ambroise." Senefiance 11 (1982): 27–39.

———. "Les musulmans dans les chansons de geste du Cycle du roi." Thesis, Université de Provence, Aix-en-Provence, 1982.

———. "Le visage de l'Autre: étude sur le sens de la *Chanson d'Aspremont.*" *De l'étranger à l'étrange ou la conjointure de la merveille, Senefiance* 25 (1988): 45–56.

Baraz, Daniel. "The Incarnated Icon of Saidnaya Goes West: A Re-examination of the Motif in the Light of New Manuscript Evidence." *Le Muséon* 108 (1995): 181–91.

Barceló, Miquel, and José Martínez Gázquez, éds. *Musulmanes y cristianos en Hispania durante las conquistas de los siglos XII y XIII.* Bellaterra: Universidad Autónoma de Barcelona, 2005.

Beattie, Pamela Drost. "'*Pro exaltatione sanctae fidei catholicae*': Mission and Crusade in the Writings of Ramon Llull." In *Iberia and the Mediterranean World*, ed. Simon, 113–29.

Beaune, C. *Naissance de la Nation France.* Paris: Gallimard, 1985.

Bender, Klaus, ed. *Les épopées de la Croisade.* Edited by Karl-Heinz Bender. *Zeitschrift für französische Sprache und Literatur*, Beiheft N.F. 11 (Stuttgart, 1987).

Bender, "La fin du premier cycle de la croisade ou le retour à l'histoire." In *Histoire et littérature au Moyen Age,* ed. D. Buschinger, 29–38. Göppinger, 1991.

Bender, Klaus, and H. Kleber. *Les épopées romanes: Grudriss der romanischen Literaturen des Mittelalters.* Vol. 3. Heidelberg, 1986.

Benton, John F. "'Nostre Franceis n'unt talent de fuïr': The *Song of Roland* and the Enculturation of a Warrior Class." *Olifant* 6 (1979): 237–58.

Berriot, François. "Le mythe de Saladin dans la littérature médiévale." In Berriot, *Spiritualités, hétérodoxies et imaginaires: Études sur le Moyen Âge et la Renaissance,* 159–71. Saint Étienne: Publications de l'Université de Saint-Etienne, 1994.

Berry, Virginia. "Peter the Venerable and the Crusades." In *Petrus Venerabilis, 1156–1956,* ed. Constable and Kritzeck, 141–62.

Bervoc-Huard, Carole. "L'Exclusion du sarrasin dans la *Chanson de Roland:* Vocabulaire et idéologie." In *Exclus et systèmes d'exclusion dans la littérature et la civilisation médiévales,* 345–61. Paris: Champion, 1978.

Bishko, Charles. "Peter the Venerable's Journey to Spain." In *Petrus Venerabilis, 1156–1956,* ed. Constable and Kritzeck, 163–75.

Bloom, Jonathan. *Minaret: Symbol of Islam.* Oxford: Oxford University Press, 1989.

Bonne, Jean-Claude. "Les ornements de l'histoire (à propos de l'ivoire carolingien de saint Rémi)." *Annales HSS* 51 (1996): 37–70.

———. "Mosque Towers and Church Towers in Early Medieval Spain." In *Künstlerischer Austausch: Akten des XXVIII internationalen Kongresses für Kunstgeschichte,* d. T. Gaehtgens, 361–71. Berlin: Akademie, 1993.

Boulainvilliers, Henri de. *La vie de Mahomed.* Amsterdam: Chez P. Humbert, 1730.

———. *The Life of Mahomet.* London: W. Hinchliffe, 1731; reprint, Piscataway: Gorgias Press, 2002.

Boyer, Regis. *L'epopée: Typologie des sources du moyen âge occidental,* fasc. 49. Turnhout: Brepols, 1988.

Bredero, A. H. "The Controversy between Peter the Venerable and Saint Bernard of Clairvaux." In *Petrus Venerabilis, 1156–1956,* ed. Constable and Kritzeck, 53–71.

Bresc, Henri, et al. *La Méditerranée entre pays d'Islam et monde latin (milieu Xe siècle–milieu XIIIe siècle).* Paris: Sedes, 2001.

Brolis, M. "La crociata di Pietro il Venerabile: guerra di arma o guerra di idee?" *Aevum* 61 (1987): 327–54.

Burman, Thomas. "The Influence of the *Apology of al-Kindî* and *Contrarietas Alfolica* on Ramon Lull's Late Religious Polemics, 1305–1313." *Medieval Studies* 53 (1991): 197–228.

———. *Religious Polemic and the Intellectual History of the Mozarabs.* Leiden: Brill, 1994.

———. "*Tafsîr* and Translation: Robert of Ketton, Mark of Toledo, and Traditional Arabic Qur'ân Exegesis." *Speculum* 73 (1998): 703–32.

———. "*Tathlîth al-wahdânîyah* and the Twelfth-Century Andalusian-Christian Approach to Islam." In *Medieval Christian Perceptions of Islam*, ed. Tolan, 109–28.

Burnett, Charles. "Adelard of Bath and the Arabs." In *Rencontres de cultures dans la philosophie médiévale: traductions et traducteurs de l'antiquité tardive au XIVe siècle,* ed. Jacqueline Hamesse et al., 89–107. Louvain la Neuve: Universite´ catholique de Louvain, 1990.

———. *The Introduction of Arabic Learning into England.* London: British Library, 1998.

———. "The Translating Activity in Medieval Spain." In *The Legacy of Muslim Spain*, ed. Jayyussi, 1036–58.

Burns, Robert. *Islam under the Crusaders: Colonial Survival in the Thirteenth-Century Kingdom of Valencia.* Princeton: Princeton University Press, 1973.

———. *Muslims, Christians, and Jews in the Crusader Kingdom of Valencia.* Cambridge: Cambridge University Press, 1984.

Cahen, Claude. "Le premier cycle de la croisade (Antioche-Jérusalem-Chétifs): Notes brèves à propos d'un livre (récent)." *Le Moyen Age* 63 (1957): 311–28.

Cambier, Guy. "Embricon de Mayence (1010?–1077) est-il l'auteur de la *Vita Mahumeti*?" *Latomus* 16 (1957): 468–79.

———. "L'épisode des taureaux dans *La legende de Mahomet* (ms. 50, Bibliothèque du Séminaire de Pise)." *Hommage à Léon Herrmann, Collection Latomus* 44 (1960): 228–36.

Cannuyer, Christian. "Les Pyramides d'Egypte dans la littérature médio-latine." *Revue belge de philologie et d'histoire* 62 (1964): 673–81.

Cárdenas, Anthony J. "Alfonso's Scriptorium and Chancery: Role of the Prologue in Bonding the *Translatio Studii* to the *Translatio Potestatis.*" In *Emperor of Culture: Alfonso X the Learned of Castile and His Thirteenth-Century Renaissance,* ed. Robert I. Burns, 90–108. Philadelphia: University of Pennsyvania Press, 1990.

Catalán, Diego. "El taller historiográfico alfonsí: métodos y problemas en el trabajo compilatorio." *Romania* 84 (1963): 354–75.

———. *La estoria de España de Alfonso X: Creación y evolución.* Madrid: Universidad Autónoma, 1992.

Cerulli, Enrico. *Il libro della scala e la questione delle fonti arabo-spagnole della Divina commedia.* Rome: Vatican, 1949.

Châtillon, Jean. "Pierre le Vénérable et les Pétrobrusiens." In *Pierre Abélard, Pierre le Vénérable,* 165–76.

Chauvel, Geneviève. *Saladin: Rassembleur de l'Islam.* Paris: Librairie générale française, 1991.

Chazan, Robert. *Barcelona and Beyond: The Disputation of 1263 and Its Aftermath.* Berkeley: University of California Press, 1992.

Clément, Francois, Malika Pondevie, and J. Tolan, eds. *Culture arabe et culture européenne: L'inconnu au turban dans l'album de famille.* Paris: L'Harmattan, 2006.

Cohen, Jeremy. *The Friars and the Jews.* Ithaca: Cornell University Press, 1984.

Cole, Penny J. "'O God, the Heathen Have Come into Your Inheritance' (Ps. 78.1): The Theme of Religious Pollution in Crusade Documents, 1095–1188." In *Crusaders and Muslims in Twelfth-Century Syria,* ed. Maya Schatzmiller, 84–111. Leiden: Brill, 1993.

———. *The Preaching of the Crusades to the Holy Land, 1095–1270.* Cambridge: Harvard University Press, 1991.

Colombo-Timelli, Maria. "Entre littérature et vie: le jeu chevaleresque dans la Bourgogne de Philippe le Bon." *Rencontres médiévales en Bourgogne* 2 (1992): 27–44.

Colomer, Eusebio. "Raimund Lulls Stellung zu den Andersgläubigen: Zwischen Zwie- und Streitsgerspräch." In *Religionsgespräche im Mittelalter,* ed. Lewis and Niewohner, 217–36.

Constable, Giles, and James Kritzeck, eds., *Petrus Venerabilis, 1156–1956: Studies and Texts Commemorating the Eighth Centenary of His Death.* Studia Anselmiana 40. Rome: Herder, 1956.

Cook, Robert F. "Crusade Propaganda in the Epic Cycles of the Crusade." In *Journeys toward God: Pilgrimage and Crusade,* ed. Barbara N. Sargent-Bauer, 157–75. Kalamazoo: Western Michigan University, 1992.

———. *"Chanson d'Antioche," chanson de geste: le cycle de la croisade est-il épique?* Amsterdam: J. Benjamins, 1980.

Cook, Robert F., and Larry S. Crist. *Le Deuxième cycle de la Croisade: Deux études sur son développement.* Geneva: Droz, 1972.

Coope, Jessica. *The Martyrs of Córdoba: Community and Family Conflict in an Age of Mass Conversion.* Lincoln: University of Nebraska Press, 1995.

Cortabarría Beitia, Angel. "La connaissance des textes arabes chez Raymond Martin, O.P. et sa position en face de l'Islam," *Cahiers de Fanjeaux 18 (1983), Islam et Chrétiens du Midi,* 279–324.

Courcelles, Dominique de. *La parole risquée de Raymond Lulle.* Paris: Vrin, 1993.

Crombie, A. and J. North. "Bacon, Roger." *Dictionary of Scientific Biography* 1 (1970): 377–85.

Dahan, Gilbert. *Les Intellectuels chrétiens et les Juifs au moyen âge.* Paris: Cerf, 1990.

Dajani-Shakeel, Hadia. "Some Aspects of Muslim-Frankish Christian Relations in the Shâm Region in the Twelfth Century." In *Christian-Muslim Encounters,* ed. Yvonne and Wadi Haddad, 193–209. Gainesville: University Press of Florida, 1995.

D'Alverny, Marie-Thérèse. "Algazel dans l'Occident latin." In *Académie du royaume de Maroc, session de novembre, 1985,* 125–46. Rabat, 1986. Reprinted in D'Alverny, *La transmission des textes.*

———. *Connaissance de l'Islam dans l'Occident médiévale.* Aldershot: Variorum, 1994.

———. "Deux traductions latines du Coran au Moyen-Age." *Archives d'histoire doctrinale et littéraire du Moyen Age* 16 (1947–48): 69–131. Reprinted in D'Alverny, *Connaissance.*

———. "Pierre le Venerable et la légende de Mahomet." *Congrès international des sciences historiques à Cluny* (Dijon, 1950), 161–70. Reprinted in D'Alverny, *Connaissance.*

———. *La transmission des textes philosophiques et scientifiques au Moyen Âge.* Aldershot: Variorum, 1994.

D'Alverny, Marie-Thérèse, and Georges Vajda. "Marc de Tolede, traducteur d'Ibn Tumart." *Al-Andalus* 16 (1951): 99–140, 259–307.

Daly, William M. "Clovis: How Barbaric, How Pagan?" *Speculum* 69 (1994): 619–64.

Daniel, Norman. *Islam and the West: The Making of an Image.* 2nd ed. Oxford: Oneworld, 1993.

———. Heroes and Saracens: An Interpretation of the Chansons. Edinburgh: Edinburgh University Press, 1984.

Darbishire, Robert S. "The Christian Idea of Islam in the Middle Ages, According to the *Chanson d'Antioche.*" *Moslem World* 28 (1938): 114–24.

de Ghellinck, Joseph. *L'essor de la littérature latine au XIIe siècle.* Brussels: Desclée de Brouwer, 1955.

degl'Innocenti, A. *L'opera agiografica di Marbodo di Rennes.* Spoleto: Biblioteca di Medioevo Latino, 1990.

Deschaux, Robert. "Le merveilleux dans la *Chanson d'Antioche.*" *Au Carrefour des routes d'Europe: La Chanson de Geste* (Aix: CUERMA, 1987), 431–43.

Deswarte, Thomas. *De la destruction à la restauration: L'idéologie du royaume d'Oviedo-Léon (VIIIe-XIe siècles).* Turnhoult: Brepols, 2003.

Deswarte, Thomas, and Philippe Sénac, eds. *Guerre, pouvoirs et idéologies dans l'Espagne chrétienne aux alentours de l'an mil.* Turnhoult: Brepols, 2005.

Devos, Paul. "Les premières versions occidentales de la légende de Saïdanaia. *Analecta Bollandiana* 65 (1947): 243–78.

Diaz y Diaz, Manuel, and Isabel B. Ceinos, "Los textos antimahometanos más antiguos en codices españoles." *Archives d'histoire doctrinale et littéraire du Moyen Age* 37 (1970): 149–68.

Dodds, Jerrilynn. *Architecture and Ideology in Early Medieval Spain.* University Park: Pennsylvania State University Press, 1990.

d'Onofrio, Cesare. *La papessa Giovanna: Roma e papato tra storia e leggenda.* Rome: Romana Societa` Editrice, 1979.

Dozy, Reinhart. *Recherches sur l'histoire et la littérature de l'Espagne pendant le Moyen Âge.* 2 vols. Leiden: Brill, 1849–1850.

Ducelier, Alain. *Chrétiens d'Orient et Islam au Moyen Age.* Paris: Armand Colin, 1996.

Duhem, Pierre. *Le Système du monde: Histoire de doctrines cosmologiques de Platon à Copernic.* 10 vols.; Paris: A. Hermann, 1913–59.

Duparc-Quioc, Suzanne. *Le cycle de la croisade.* Paris: Champion, 1955.

———. "Recherches sur l'origine des poèmes épiques de croisade et sur leur utilisation éventuelle par les grande familles nobles." In *Atti del convegno internazionale sul tema: La poesia epica e la sua formazione,* 771–96. Rome: Accademia nazionale dei Lincei, 1970.

Eckhardt, Alexandre. "Le Cercueil flottant de Mahomet." In *Mélanges de philologie ro-*

mane et de littérature médiévale offerts à E. Hoepffner: Publications de la Faculté des Lettres de l'Université de Strasbourg, fasc. 113 (1949): 77–88.

Eddé, Anne-Marie and Françoise Micheau, *L'Orient au temps des Croisades*. Paris: Flammarion, 2002.

Ehrenkreutz, Andrew. *Saladin*. Albany: State University of New York Press, 1972.

Emmerson, Richard. *Antichrist in the Middle Ages*. Seattle: University of Washington Press, 1981.

Fattal, Antoine. *Le Statut légal des non-musulmans en pays d'Islam*. Beirut: Dar el-Machreq, 1958, 1995.

Faulhaber, Charles B. et al., eds. *Bibliography of Old Spanish Texts*. 3rd ed. Madison: Hispanic Seminary of Medieval Studies, 1984.

Fearns, James. "Peter von Bruis und die religiöse Bewegung des 12 Jahrhunderts." *Archiv fur Kulturgeschichte* 48 (1966): 313–17.

Fernandez-Ordonez, Ines. "La *Estoria de España*, la *General estoria* y los diferentes criterios compilatorios." *Revista de Literatura* 50 (1988) 15–35.

Ferreiro, Alberto. "Jerome's Polemic against Priscillian in his *Letter* to Ctesiphon." *Revue des études augustiniennes* 39 (1993): 309–32.

Fita, Fidel. "Once bulas de Bonifacio VIII inéditas y biográficas de San Pedro Pascual, Obispo de Jaén y Mártir." *Boletin de la Academia de la Historia* 20 (1892): 32–61.

———. "Sobre la bibliografía de San Pedro Pascual." *Boletin de la Academia de la Historia* 46 (1905): 259–69.

Flint, Valerie. *The Rise of Magic in Early Medieval Europe*. Princeton: Princeton University Press, 1991.

Flori, Jean. "Chevalerie et liturgie." *Le Moyen Âge* 84 (1978): 247–78, 404–42.

———. "Des chroniques à l'épopée . . . ou bien l'inverse?" *Perspectives médiévales* 20 (1994): 36–43.

———. "Du nouveau sur l'adoubement des chevaliers (XIe-XIIIe siècles)." *Le Moyen Âge* 91 (1985): 201–26.

———. *L'Islam et la fin des temps: l'interprétation prophétique des invasions musulmanes dans la chrétienté médiévale*. Paris: Seuil, 2007.

———. "'Oriens horribilis' . . . Tares et défauts de l'Orient dans les sources relatives à la première croisade." In *Orient und Okzident in der Kultur des Mittelalters; Monde oriental et monde occidental dans la culture médiévale, Wodan: Greifswalder Beiträge zum Mittelalter* 68 (1997): 45–56.

———. "Radiographie d'un stéréotype: la caricature de l'islam dans l'Occident chrétien: sens et contresens." *Revue Maroc-Europe: Histoires, Economies, Sociétés* 3 (1992): 91–109.

———. "En marge de l'idée de guerre sainte: l'image des musulmans dans la mentalité populaire en occident (XIe–XIIe siècles)." In *L'occident musulman et l'occident chrétien au moyen âge*, 209–21. Rabat: Publications de la Faculté des Lettres et des Sciences Humaines, 1995.

———. "Pur eshalcier sainte crestiënté: Croisade, guerre sainte et guerre juste dans les anciennes chansons de geste françaises." *Le Moyen Age* 97 (1991): 171–87.

Fraker, Charles. "Alfonso X, the Empire, and the *Primera Crónica*." *Bulletin of Hispanic Studies* 55 (1978): 95–102.

France, John. *Victory in the East: A Military History of the First Crusade*. New York: Cambridge University Press, 1994.

Frassetto, Michael, ed. *Heresy and the Persecuting Society in the Middle Ages: Essays on the Work of R.I. Moore*. Leiden: Brill, 2006.

Gabrieli, Francesco. *Arab Historians of the Crusades*. Berkeley: University of California Press, 1984.

Ganz-Blätter, Ursula. *Andacht und Abenteuer: Berichte europäischer Jerusalem- und Santiago-Pilger (1320–1520)*. Tübingen: Narr, 1990.

García-Arenal, Mercedes. "Los moros en las *Cantigas* de Alfonso el Sabio." *Al-Qantara* 6 (1985): 133–51.

Gardet, Louis. *Dieu et la destinée de l'homme*. Paris: J. Vrin, 1967.

George, Judith. *Venantius Fortunatus: A Latin Poet in Merovingian Gaul*. Oxford: Clarendon, 1993.

Gervers, Michael, and Ramzi J. Bikhazi, eds. *Conversion and Continuity: Indigenous Christian Communities in Islamic Lands, Eighth to Eighteenth Centuries*. Toronto: Pontifical Institute of Medieval Studies, 1990.

Gibb, H. *Saladin: Studies in Islamic History*. Beirut: Arab Institute for Research and Publishing, 1964.

Gibbon, Edward. *The Decline and Fall of the Roman Empire*. 3 vols. New York: Modern Library, 2003.

Ginzburg, Carlo. *The Cheese and the Worms: The Cosmos of a Sixteenth-Century Miller*. Translated by John and Anne Tedeschi. London: Penguin, 1982.

Ginzberg, Louis. *Legends of the Jews*. 7 vols. Philadelphia: Jewish Publication Society of America, 1909–38.

González Muñoz, Fernando. "La leyenda de Mahoma en Lucas de Tuy." In *Actas del III Congreso Hispánico de Latín Medieval*, ed. M. Pérez González, 347–58. León: Universidad de León, 2002.

Goodman, L. *Avicenna*. London: Routledge, 1992.

Gosman, Martin. "La Propagande de la croisade et le rôle de la chanson de geste comme porte-parole d'une idéologie non-officiel." *Olifant* 13 (1988): 212–13.

Graboïs, Aryeh. "La bibliothèque du noble d'*Outremer* à Acre dans la seconde moitié du XIIIe siècle." *Le Moyen Age* 103 (1997): 53–66.

Gransden, Antonia. *Historical Writing in England c. 550 to c. 1307*. Ithaca: Cornell University Press, 1974.

Grant, Edward. "The Condemnation of 1277, God's Absolute Power, and Physical Thought in the Late Middle Ages." *Viator* 10 (1979): 211–44.

———. *A Source Book in Medieval Science*. Cambridge: Harvard University Press, 1974.

Grant, Robert M. "Porphyry among the Early Christians." In W. der Boer et al., eds., *Romanitas et Christianitas: Studia Iano Henrico Waszink*. Amsterdam: North Holland, 1973.

Grillo, Peter. "Considérations sur la version de Londres-Turin des continuations du premier cycle de la croisade." In *Les épopées de la croisade*, ed. Bender, 91–97.

"Les redactions de la *Chrétienté Corbaran*, première branche des continuations du cycle de la croisade," *Au Carrefour des routes d'Europe: La Chanson de Geste* (Aix: CUERMA, 1987), 585–600

———. "Royauté et chevalerie dans les Continuations du Cycle de la Croisade." *Actes du XIe Congrès International de la Société Rencesvals, Memorias de la Real Academia de Buenas Letras de Barcelona* 21 (1990): 307–19.

———. "The Saladin Material in the Continuations of the First Crusade Cycle." In *Aspects de l'épopée romane: mentalité, idéologies, intertextualités*, ed. Hans van Dijk and Willem Noomen, 159–66. Groningen, 1995.

Grossel, Geneviève. "Le même et l'autre: la croisade dans les *Récits d'un ménestral de Reims*." In *La Méditerranée et ses cultures*, ed. Evelyne Berriot-Salvadore. Paris: Cerf, 1996.

Guichard, Pierre. *L'Espagne et la Sicile musulmanes aux XIe et XIIe siècles*. Lyon: Presses Universitaires de Lyon, 1990, 2000.

Hackett, Jeremiah. "Philosophy and Theology in Roger Bacon's *Opus Maius*." In *Philosophy and the God of Abraham: Essays in Memory of James A. Weisheipl, OP*, ed. James Long, 55–69. Toronto: Pontifical Institute of Mediaeval Studies, 1991.

———, ed. *Roger Bacon and the Sciences: Commemorative Essays* (Leiden: Brill, 1997); Hackett,

Hadidi, Djavâd. *Voltaire et l'Islam*. Paris: Association Langues et civilisations, 1974.

Haidu, Peter. *The Subject of Violence: The Song of Roland and the Birth of the State*. Bloomington: University of Indiana Press, 1993.

Halim, Hala. "The Signs of Saladin: A Modern Cinematic Rendition of Medieval Heroism." *Alif: Journal of Comparative Poetics* 12 (1992): 78–94.

Hatem, A. *Les Poèmes épiques des croisades*. Paris: P. Geuthner, 1932.

Henriet, Patrick. "Hagiographie et Politique à León au début du XIIIe siècle: les chanoines réguliers de Saint-Isidore et la prise de Baeza." *Revue Mabillon* n.s. 8 (1997): 53–82.

———. "Hagiographie léonaise et pédagogie de la foi: Les miracles d'Isidore de Séville et la lutte Contre l'hérésie (XIe-XIIIe siècles)." In *L'enseignement religieux dans la couronne de Castille. Incidences spirituelles et sociales (XIIIe-XVIe siècles)*, ed. D. Balou, 1–28. Madrid, 2003 (Collection de la Casa de Velázquez, 79)..

———. "Xénophobie et intégration isidoriennes à León au XIIIème siècle: le discours de Lucas de Tuy sur les étrangers." In *L'Étranger au Moyen Âge, Actes du XXXe congrès de la SHMESP*, 37–58. Paris: Publications de la Sorbonne, 2000.

———, ed. "Chroniqueur, hagiographe, théologien: Lucas de Tuy dans ses œuvres." *Cahiers de linguistique et de civilisation hispaniques médiévales* 24 (2001): 249–78.

Hernández Giménez, Félix. *El alminar de 'Abd al-Rahmân III en la Mezquita Mayor de Córdoba: génesis y repercusiones*. Granada: Patronato de la Alhambra, 1975.

Herrera Roldán, Pedro. *Cultura y lengua latina entre los mozárabes de Córdoba del siglo IX*. Córdoba: Universidad de Córdoba, 1995.

Hillenbrand, Robert. *Islamic Architecture: Form, Function and Meaning*. Edinburgh: Edinburgh University Press, 1994, 2000.

Hillgarth, Jocelyn. *Ramon Lull and Lullism in Fourteenth-Century France*. Oxford: Oxford University Press, 1971.

Holmes, U., and W. McLeod. "Source Problems of the *Chétifs*, a Crusade *Chanson de geste.*" *Romanic Review* 28 (1937): 99–108.

Housley, Norman. "Saladin's Triumph over the Crusader States: the Battle of Hattin." *History Today* 37 (1987): 17–23.

Huete Fudio, Mario. *La Historiografía latina medieval en la península ibérica (siglos VIII-XII): fuentes y bibliografía.* Madrid: Universidad Auto'noma de Madrid, 1997.

Iogna-Prat, Dominique. *Ordonner et exclure: Cluny et la société chrétienne face à l'hérésie, au judaïsme et à l'islam.* Paris: Aubier, 1998. English translation: *Order and Exclusion: Cluny and Christendom Face Heresy, Judaism, and Islam, 1000–1150.* Ithaca: Cornell University Press, 2002.

Jackson, W. "Hildebert of Lavardin." In *Dictionary of the Middle Ages,* 4:225–27. New York: American Council of Learned Societies, 1982–89.

———. "Marbod of Rennes." *Dictionary of the Middle Ages,* 8:122–24.

Jacoby, D. "La littérature française dans les états latins de la Méditerranée à l'époque des croisades, diffusion et création." *Essor et fortune de la Chanson de geste dans l'Europe et l'Orient latin: Actes du 9e congrès international de la Société Rencesvals* 2 (Modena: Mucchi, 1984): 617–46.

Janssens, Jules. *An Annotated Bibliography on Ibn Sînâ (1970–1989).* Leuven: University of Leuven Press, 1991.

———. "Al-Ghazzâlî's *Tahâfut*: Is It Really a Rejection of Ibn Sînâ's Philosophy?" *Journal of Islamic Studies* 12 (2001): 1–17.

Jayyussi, Salma ed. *The Legacy of Muslim Spain.* Leiden: Brill, 1992.

Johnston, Mark. "Ramon Lull and the Compulsory Evangelization of Jews and Muslims." In *Iberia and the Mediterranean World,* ed. Simon, 3–37.

———. *The Spiritual Logic of Ramon Llull.* Oxford: Clarendon, 1987.

Jolivet, Jean. "L'Islam et la raison, d'après quelques auteurs latins des IXe [*sic:* should be XIe] et XIIe siècles." In *L'art des confins: Mélanges offerts à Maurice Gandillac,* ed. A. Cazenave and J. Lyotard, 153–64. Paris, 1985.

Jubb, Margaret. "Citry de la Guette, Translator or *Remanieur?* A Seventeenth-Century Adaptation of a Medieval Chronicle." *Modern Language Review* 85 (1990): 35–49.

———. *The Legend of Saladin in Western Literature and Historiography.* Lewiston: Edwin Mellen Press, 2000.

Katz, I., et al., eds. *Studies on the Cantigas de Santa Maria: Art, Music, and Poetry.* Madison: Hispanic Seminary of Medieval Studies, 1987.

Kedar, Benjamin Z. "Convergences of Oriental Christian, Muslim and Frankish Worshippers: The Case of Aydnâyâ and the Knights Templar." In *The Crusades and the Military Orders Expanding the Frontiers of Medieval Latin Christianity,* ed. Zsolt Hunyadi and József Laszlovszky, 89–100. Budapest: Central European University, 2001.

———. *Crusade and Mission: European Approaches toward the Muslims.* Princeton: Princeton University Press, 1984.

———, ed. *The Horns of Hattin.* Jerusalem: Yad Izhak Ben-Zvi; London: Variorum, 1992.

Keen, Maurice. *Chivalry.* New Haven: Yale University Press, 1984.

Kleber, Hermann. "Graindor de Douai: remanieur-auteur-mécène?" In Karl-Heinz

Bender, *Les Épopées de la croisade*, ed. Karl-Heinz Bender, 66–75. Stuttgart: F. Steiner, 1987.

———, "Pèlerinage, vengeance, conquête: la conception de la première croisade dans le cycle de Graindor de Douai," Au Carrefour des routes d'Europe: La Chanson de Geste. Xe Congrès international de la Société Rencesvals pour l'étude des épopées romanes, Strasbourg, 1985, Senefiance 21 (1987): 757–75.

Kniewasser, Manfred. "Die antijüdische Polemik des Petrus Alphonsi (getauft 1106) und des Petrus Venerabilis von Cluny (+1156)." *Kairos*, n.s., 2 (1980): 34–76.

Köhler, Erich. *Ideal und Wirklichkeit in der höfischen Epik.* Tübingen: Niemeyer, 1956, 1970.

Kritzeck, James. "De l'influence de Pierre Abélard sur Pierre le Vénérable dans ses œuvres sur l'Islam." In *Pierre Abélard, Pierre le Vénérable*, 205–14.

———. *Peter the Venerable and Islam.* Princeton: Princeton University Press, 1964.

Kunze, Konrad. *Die Legende der heiligen Maria Aegyptiaca. Ein Beispiel hagiographischer Überlieferung in 16 unveröffentlichen deutschen, nierländischen und lateinischen Fassungen.* Berlin: E. Schmidt, 1978.

———. *Studien zur Legende der heiligen Maria Aegyptiaca im deutschen Sprachgebiet, Philologische Studien und Quellen* 49. Berlin, 1969.

Lampe, G. *A Patristic Greek Lexicon.* Oxford: Clarendon Press, 1961.

Landbert, Malcolm. *Medieval Heresy: Popular Movements from the Gregorian Reform to the Reformation.* 2nd ed. Oxford: Blackwell, 1992.

Lapiedra Gutiérrez, Eva. "Los mártires de Córdoba y la política anticristiana contemporánea en Oriente." *Al-Qantara* 15 (1994): 453–63.

Laurent, J. "Burchard von Strassburg." *Serapeum: Zeitschrift für Bibliothekwissenschaft, Handschriftenkunde und ältere Literatur* 19 (1858): 145–54; 20 (1859): 174–76.

Lavajo, Joachim. "The Apologetical Method of Ramon Marti, according to the Problematic of Ramon Lull." *Islamochristiana* 11 (1985): 155–76.

Lemay, Richard. "L'apologétique contre l'Islam chez Pierre le Vénérable et Dante." *Mélanges offerts à René Crozer* 2 (Poitiers, 1966): 755–64.

Leclercq, Jean. *Pierre le Vénérable.* Abbaye Saint-Wandrille, 1946.

Le Goff, Jacques. *Saint Louis.* Paris, 1996.

Lévi-Provençal, Evariste. *Histoire de l'Espagne musulmane.* 2 vols. Paris: Maisonneuve et Larose, 1950, 1999.

Lewis, Bernard. *Islam and the West.* Oxford: Oxford University Press, 1993.

Lewis, Bernard, and F. Niewohner, eds. *Religionsgespräche im Mittelalter.* Wiesbaden: Harrassowitz, 1992

Lewis, Suzanne. *The Art of Matthew Paris in the Chronica Maior.* Berkeley: University of California Press, 1987.

Linehan, Peter. *History and Historians of Medieval Spain.* Oxford: Clarendon Press, 1993.

Little, Lester. "Intellectual Training and Attitudes towards Reform." In *Petrus Venerabilis, 1156–1956*, ed. Constable and Kritzeck, 235–49.

Lohr, Charles. "Ramon Lull and Thirteenth-Century Religious Dialogue." In *Diálogo filosófico-religioso*, ed. Santiago Otero, 117–29.

Loomis, Roger. "The *Pas Saladin* in Art and Heraldry." In *Studies in Art and Literature for Belle da Costa Greene*, ed. Dorothy Miner, 83–91. Princeton: Princeton University Press, 1954.

Loutchitskaja, S. "*Barbarae nationes:* les peuples musulmans dans les chroniques de la Première croisade." In *Autour de la première croisade,* ed. Michel Balard, 99–107. Paris: Publications de la Sorbonne, 1996.

Lyons, Malcolm, and D. Jackson. *Saladin: the Politics of Holy War.* Cambridge: Cambridge University Press, 1982.

McGinn, Bernard. "Iter Sancti Sepulchri: the Piety of the First Crusaders." In *The Walter Prescott Webb Lectures: Essays in Medieval Civilization,* ed. Bede Karl Lackner and Kenneth Roy Philip, 33–70. Austin: University of Texas Press, 1978.

Makki, Mahmud Ali. "La España cristiana en el *Dîwân* de Ibn Darrây." *Boletín de la Real Academia de Buenas Letras de Barcelona* 30 (1964): 63–104.

Mancini, Alessandro. "Per lo studio della leggenda di Maomette in Occidente." *Rendiconti della R. Accademia Nazionale dei Lincei,* serie sexta, 10 (1934): 325–49.

Manitius, Max. *Geschichte der lateinischen Literatur des Mittelalters.* 3 vols. Munich: C.H. Beck'sche Verlagsbuchhandlung, 1911–1931.

Márquez Villanueva, Francisco. *El Concepto Cultural Alfonsí.* Madrid: Mapfre, 1994.

Martin, Georges, ed. *La historia alfonsí: el modelo y sus destinos (siglos XIII-XV).* Madrid: Casa de Velázquez, 2000.

———. *Les juges de Castille: Mentalités et discours historique dan l'Espagne médiévale. Annexes des Cahiers de linguistique hispanique médiévale,* 6. Paris: Klincksieck, 1992.

Martínez Gázquez, José. "Finalidad de la primera traducción latina del Corán." In *Musulmanes y cristianos en Hispania,* ed. Barceló and Martínez Gázquez, 71–77.

Menéndez Pidal, Gonzalo. "Cómo trabajaron las escuelas alfonsíes." *Nueva revista de filología hispánica* 5 (1951): 363–80.

Meri, Josef. *The Cult of Saints among Muslims and Jews in Medieval Syria.* Oxford: Oxford University Press, 2003.

Mettmann, Walter. *Die volkssprachliche apologetische Literatur auf der Iberischen Halbinsel im Mittelalter.* Opladen: Westdeutscher Verlag, 1987.

Meyendorff, John. "Byzantine Views of Islam." *Dumbarton Oaks Papers* 18 (1964): 115–32.

Meyerson, Mark and Edward English, éds. *Christians, Muslims, and Jews in Medieval and Early Modern Spain.* Notre Dame: University of Notre Dame Press, 2000.

Micheau, Françoise. "La transmission à l'Occident chrétien: les traductions médiévales de l'arabe au latin." In J.-C. Garcin et al., *Monde musulman médiéval: X*ème *-XV*ème *siècles,* 2:399–419. Paris: Presses Universitaires de France, 1995–2000.

Michot, Jean. "Avicenne et la destinée humaine: à propos de la résurrection des corps." *Revue philosophique de Louvain* 79 (1981): 453–83.

———. *La destinée de l'homme selon Avicenne.* Leuven: Peeters, 1986.

Milwright, Marcus. "The Balsam of Matariyya: An Exploration of a Medieval Panacea." *Bulletin of the School of Oriental and African Studies* 66 (2003): 193–209.

Millet-Gérard, Dominique. *Chrétiens mozarabes et culture islamique dans l'Espagne des VIII*e*-IX*e *siècles,* Paris: Études augustiniennes, 1984.

Mirrer, Louise. *Women, Jews, and Muslims in the Texts of Reconquest Castile*. Ann Arbor: University of Michigan Press, 1996.

Möhring, Hannes. "Der andere Islam: Zum Bild vom toleranten Sultan Saladin und neuen Propheten Schah Ismail." In O. Engels and P. Schreiner, eds., *Die Begegnung des Westens mit dem Osten. Kongreßakten des 4. Symposions des Mediävistenverbandes in Köln 1991 aus Anlaß des 1000. Todesjahres der Kaiserin Theophanu*. Sigmarigen: Thorbecke, 1993.

———. *Saladin und der dritter Kreuzzug: Aiyubidische Strategie und Diplomatie im vergleich vornehmlich der arabischen mit den lateinischen Quellen*. Wiesbaden, 1980.

Moore, Robert I. "Building Ramparts: Heresy and Social Change in the Time of Peter the Venerable." In *Musulmanes y cristianos en Hispania*, ed. Barceló and Martínez Gázquez, 41–49.

———. *The Formation of a Persecuting Society*. Oxford: Blackwell, 1987.

———. *The Origins of European Dissent*. Oxford: Blackwell, 1978, 1985.

Morgan, Margaret R. *The Chronicle of Ernoul and the Continuations of William of Tyre*. Oxford: Oxford University Press, 1973.

Morrissey, Robert. *L'empereur à la barbe fleurie: Charlemagne dans la mythologie et l'histoire de France*. Paris: Gallimard, 1997.

Myers, Geoffrey. "*Les Chétifs*: Étude sur le développement de la chanson." *Romania* 105 (1984): 63–87.

———, ed. *Les Chétifs*. Old French Crusade Cycle, vol. 5. 1981.

Nasr, S. H., and O. Leaman, eds. *History of Islamic Philosophy*. London: Routledge, 1996.

Niermeyer, J. F. *Mediae Latinitatis lexicon minus*. Leiden: Brill, 1976.

Nirenberg, David. *Communities of Violence: Persecution of Minorities in the Middle Ages*. Princeton: Princeton University Press, 1996.

Olsen, Alexandra H. "De Historiis Sanctorum: A Generic Study of Hagiography." *Genre* 13 (1980): 407–30.

O'Meara, John J. *Porphyry's Philosophy from Oracles in Augustine*. Paris: Études Augustiniennes, 1959.

Panella, Emilio. "Ricerche su Riccoldo da Monte di Croce." *Archivum Fratrum Praedicatorum* 58 (1988): 5–85.

Paris, Gaston. "La légende de Saladin." *Journal des savants* (1893): 284–99, 354–65, 428–38, 487–98.

———. "Un poème latin contemporain sur Saladin." *Revue de l'Orient latin* 1 (1893): 433–44.

Payen, Jean-Charles. "Une poétique de génocide joyeux: devoir de violence et plaisir de tuer dans la *Chanson de Roland*." *Olifant* 6 (1979): 226–36.

Peeters, P. "La légende de Saïdnaia," Analecta Bollandiana 25 (1906): 137–157.

Pelzer, Augustus, ed. *Biblothecae Apostolicae Vaticanae codices manu scripti recensiti*. Rome: Vatican, 1931.

Pérez de Tudela Velasco, María Isabel. "Guerra, violencia y terror: las destrucción de Santiago de Compostela por Almanzor hace mil años." *En la España medieval* 21 (1998): 9–28.

Pierre Abélard, Pierre le Vénérable: Les courants philosophiques, littéraires et artistiques en occident au milieu du XIIe *siècle.* Colloques internationaux du Centre National de la Recherche Scientifique 546. Paris: E´ditions du Centre national de la recherche scientifique, 1975.

Prideaux, Humphrey. *The True Nature of the Imposture Fully Displayed in the Life of Mahomet with a Discourse Annexed, for the Vindicating of Christianity from This Charge; Offered to the Consideration of the Deists of the Present Age.* London, 1697.

Pringle, Denis. *The Churches of the Crusader Kingdom of Jerusalem: A Survey.* Vol. 2. Cambridge: Cambridge University Press, 1998.

Pryor, John H. "The *Eracles* and William of Tyre: An Interim Report." In *The Horns of Hattin*, ed. Kedar, 270–93.

Quéruel, Danielle, ed. *Splendeurs de la cour de Bourgogne.* Paris: Laffont, 1995.

Rashed, Rosdhi, et al. *Histoire des sciences arabes.* 3 vols. Paris: Seuil, 1997.

Réau, Louis. *Iconographie de l'Art chrétien* 3 (Paris: Presses universitaires de France, 1959): 341–44.

Regan, Geoffrey. *Saladin and the Fall of Jerusalem.* London: Croom Helm, 1987.

Repertorium fontium historiae medii aevi. Rome: Istituto storico italiano per il Medio Evo, 1962–.

Richard, Jean. "L'arrière-plan historique des deux cycles de la Croisade." In *Les épopées de la croisade*, ed. Bender, 6–16.

———. *Croisés, missionnaires, et voyageurs: Les perspectives orientales du monde latin médiéval.* London: Variorum, 1983.

———. "L'Extrême-Orient légendaire au Moyen-Age: Roi David et Prêtre Jean." *Annales d'Ethiopie* 2 (1957): 225–42.

———. "The Mongols and the Franks." *Journal of Asian History* 3 (1969): 45–57.

Riera i Sans, Jaume. "L invencio literaria de Sant Pere Pasqual." *Caplletra* 1 (1986): 45–60.

Riley-Smith, Jonathan. *The First Crusade and the Idea of Crusading.* Philadelphia: University of Pennsylvania Press, 1986.

Rotter, Ekkehard. *Abendland und Sarazenen: das okzidentale Araberbild und seine Entstehung im Frühmittelalter.* Berlin: Walter de Gruyter, 1986.

Rouche, Michel. *Clovis.* Paris: Fayard, 1996.

Russell, Norman. *Lives of the Desert Fathers.* Kalamazoo: Cistercian Studies, 1981.

Saiz Muñoz, Guadalupe. "Críticas contra el profeta Muhammad contenidas el la obra *El obispo de Jaén contre la seta Mahometana* de Pedro Pascual (Siglo XIII)." In *Homenaje al prof. Darío Cabanelas Rodríguez,* 477–90. Granada: Universidad de Granada, Departamento de Estudios Semiticos, 1987).

Salman, D. "Algazel et les Latins." *Archives d'histoire doctrinale et littéraire du Moyen Âge* 10 (1935–36): 103–27.

Santiago Otero, Horacio, ed. *Diálogo filosófico-religioso entre cristianismo, judaísmo, e islamismo durante la edad media en la península ibérica.* Turhoult: Brepols, 1994.

Scheffert-Boichorste, Paul. "Der Kaiserliche Notar und der Straßburger Viztum Burchard." *Zeitschrift für Geschichte des Oberrheins,* n.s. 4 (1889): 456–77. Reprinted in *Gesammelte Schriften von Paul Scheffert-Boichorste, Historischen Studien* 43:225–47.

Schimmel, Annemarie. *And Muhammad Is His Messenger: The Veneration of the Prophet in Islamic Piety.* Chapel Hill: University of North Carolina Press, 1985.

Sénac, Philippe. "Al-Mansûr et la reconquête." In *Guerre, pouvoirs, et idéologies*, ed. Deswarte and Sénac, 37–50.

Shahîd, Irfan. *Rome and the Arabs: A Prolegomenon to the Study of Byzantium and the Arabs.* Washington: Dumbarton Oaks, 1984.

Sidelko, Paul. "The Condemnation of Roger Bacon." *Journal of Medieval History* 22 (1996): 69–81.

Simon, Larry ed. *Iberia and the Mediterranean World of the Middle Ages: Studies in Honor of Robert I. Burns.* Leiden: Brill, 1995.

Smith, Jane, and Yvonne Haddad, *The Islamic Understanding of Death and Resurrection.* Albany: SUNY Press, 1981.

Southern, Richard. *Western Views of Islam in the Middle Ages.* Cambridge, Mass.: Harvard University Press, 1962.

Spiegel, Gabrielle. *Romancing the Past: the Rise of Vernacular Prose Historiography in Thirteenth-Century France.* Berkeley: University of California Press, 1993.

Stephanus, H. *Thesaurus graecae linguae.* Paris: Firmin Didot, 1848–54.

Stroll, Mary. *Symbols as Power: The Papacy Following the Investiture Contest.* Leiden: Brill, 1991.

Stone, Edward N. *Three Old French Chronicles of the Crusades.* Seattle: University of Washington Press, 1939.

Stones, Allison. "Sacred and Profane Art: Secular and Liturgical Book-Illumination in the Thirteenth Century." In *The Epic in Medieval Society: Aesthetic and Moral Values*, ed. H. Scholler, 100–112, esp. 106–7. Tübingen, 1977

———. "Secular Manuscript Illumination in France." In *Medieval Manuscripts and Textual Criticism*, ed. C. Kleinhenz, 83–102. Chapel Hill: University of North Carolina Press, 1976.

Sumberg, Lewis. "Au confluent de l'histoire et du mythe: la *Chanson d'Antioche*, chronique en vers de la première Croisade." In *Les Épopées de la croisade*, ed. Karl-Heinz Bender, 58–65.

Tabulae codicum manuscriptorum in Bibliotheca palatina Vindobonensi. Vienna: Academia Caesarea Vindobonensis, 1864, 1966.

Thomas, Rudolf. "Die Persönlichkeit Peter Abaelards im *Dialogus inter Philosophum, Iudaeum et Christianum* und in den *Epistulae* des Petrus Venerabilis: Widerspruch oder Übereinstimmung?" In *Pierre Abélard, Pierre le Vénérable*, 255–69.

Tolan, John. "Du sage arabe au Sarrasin irrationnel: vers une idéologie de la supériorité occidentale." In *Culture arabe et culture européenne*, ed. Clément, Pondevie and Tolan, 189–201.

———. "Mahomet et L'Antéchrist dans l'Espagne du IXe siècle." *Wodan: Greifswalder Beiträge zum Mittelalter* 68 (1997): 167–80.

———. "Las traducciones y la ideología de reconquista: Marcos de Toledo." In *Musulmanes y cristianos en Hispania*, ed. Barcelo and Martínez Gázquez, 79–85.

———. *Petrus Alfonsi and His Medieval Readers.* Gainesville: University Press of Florida, 1993.

———. "Réactions chrétiennes aux conquêtes musulmanes: étude comparée des auteurs chrétiens de Syrie et d'Espagne." *Cahiers de civilisation médiévale* 44 (2001): 349–67.

———. "Reading God's Will in the Stars: Petrus Alfonsi and Raymond de Marseille Defend The New Arabic Astrology." *Revista Española de Filosofía Medieval* 7 (2000): 13–30.

———. *Le saint chez le sultan: La rencontre de François d'Assise et de l'islam, Huit siècles d'interprétation.* Paris: Seuil, 2007.

———. *Saracens: Islam in the Medieval European Imagination.* New York: Columbia University Press, 2002.

———, ed. *Medieval Christian Perceptions of Islam: A Book of Essays.* New York: Garland, 1994; London: Routledge, 2000.

Torrell, Jean-Pierre. "La notion de prophétie et la méthode apologétique dans le *Contra Saracenos* de Pierre le Vénérable." *Studia Monastica* 18 (1975): 257–82.

Torrell, Jean-Pierre, and Denise Bouthillier. *Pierre le Ve´ne´rable et sa vision du monde.* Leuven: Spicilegium Sacrum Lovaniense, 1986.

Torres-Balbás, Leopoldo. *La Mezquita de Córdoba y las ruinas de Madinat Al-Zahra.* Madrid: Plus-Ultra, 1952.

Tristram, E. W. *English Medieval Wall Painting,* vol. 2:, *The Thirteenth Century.* Oxford: Oxford University Press, 1950.

Tyerman, Christopher. *England and the Crusades, 1095–1588.* Chicago: University of Chicago Press, 1988.

van Koningsveld, Peter Sjoerd. "La Apología de Al-Kindî en la España del siglo XII: Huellas toledanas de un 'animal disputax'" in *Estudios sobre Alfonso VI y la reconquista de Toledo. Actas del II congreso Internacional de Estudios Mozárabes* 1 (Toledo: Instituto de Estudios Visigoto-Mozarabes, 1986): 107–29.

van Koningsveld, Peter Sjoerd, and G. A. Wiegers. "The Polemical Works of Muhammad al-Qaysî (fl.1309) and Their Circulation in Arabic and Aljamiado among the Mudejars in the Fourteenth Century." *Al-Qanara: Revista de estudios árabes* 15 (1994): 163–99.

Van Riet, Solomon. "The Impact of Avicenna's Philosophical Works in the West." *Encyclopaedia Iranica* (London: Routledge, 1989), 3:104–7.

Vanoli, Alessandro. "Immagini dell"Altro' nelle fonti arabo-spagnole." In *Mediterraneo medievali: Cristiani, musulmani et eretici tra Europa e Oltremare,* ed. M. Meschini, 29–50. Milan: Vita e Pensiero, 2001.

Vaughan, Richard. *Matthew Paris.* Cambridge: Cambridge University Press, 1958.

von den Steinen, Wolfram. "Literarische Anfänge in Basel." *Basler Zeitschrift für Gedichte und Altertumskunde* 32 (1933): 239–304.

———. "Les sujets d'inspiration chez les poètes latins du XIIe siècle." *Cahiers de civilization médiévale* 9 (1966): 165–75, 363–83.

Von Moos, Peter. "Les collations d'Abélard et la 'question juive' au XIIème siecle." *Journal des Savants* (1999): 449–89.

Ward, Benedicta. *Miracles and the Medieval Mind.* Philadelphia: University of Pennsylvania Press, 1987.

Webb, Diana M. "The Truth about Constantine: History, Hagiography, and Confusion." In *Religion and Humanism: Papers Read at the Eighteenth Summer Meeting and Nine-*

teenth Winter Meeting of the Ecclesiastical History Society, ed. Keith Robbins, 85–102. Oxford: Blackwell, 1981.

Wippel, John. "The Condemnations of 1270 and 1277 at Paris." *Journal of Medieval and Renaissance Studies* 7 (1977): 169–201.

Wolf, Kenneth. *Christian Martyrs in Muslim Spain*. Cambridge: Cambridge University Press, 1988.

———. "Christian Views of Islam in Early Medieval Spain." In *Medieval Christian Perceptions of Islam*, ed. Tolan, 85–108.

———. "The Earliest Latin Lives of Muhammad." In *Conversion and Continuity*, ed. Gervers and Bikhazi, 89–101.

———. "Muhammad as Antichrist in Ninth-Century Córdoba." In *Christians, Muslims, and Jews*, ed. Meyerson and English, 3–19.

Wollstonecraft, Mary. *Vindication of the Rights of Woman*. New York: Humboldt, 1891.

Wood, Ian. "Gregory of Tours and Clovis." *Revue belge de philologie et d'histoire* 63 (1985): 249–72.

Worstbruck, F. "Burchard von Straßburg." *Die Deutsche Literatur des Mittelalters: Verfasserlexicon* (Berlin and New York, 1978), 1:118–19.

Zanetti, Ugo. "Matarieh, la Sainte Famille et les baumiers." *Analecta Bollandiana* 111 (1993): 21–68.

Zeibi, Abdulmajid. "Saladin de l'histoire à la légende (XIIème- XVème siècles)." Université de Grenoble III Stendhal: Thèse de doctorat nouveau régime, 1990.

Zerbi, Piero. "Remarques sur l'*Epistola 98* de Pierre le Vénérable." In *Pierre Abélard, Pierre le Vénérable*, 215–34.

———. "San Bernardo di Chiaravalle e il concilio de Sens." In *Studi su S. Bernardo di Chiaravalle*, 49–73. Rome: Editiones cistercienses, 1975.

Zilio-Grandi, Ida. "La Vierge Marie dans le Coran." *Revue de l'histoire des religions* 214 (1997): 57–103.

Credits

The chapters in this book were originally published in the sources below:

Chapter 1: "Antihagiography: Embrico of Mainz's *Vita Mahumeti*," *Journal of Medieval History* 22 (1996): 25–41.

Chapter 2: In French, as "Un cadavre mutilé: le déchirement polémique de Mahomet," *Le Moyen Âge* 104 (1998): 53–72.

Chapter 3: "Rhetoric, Polemics, and the Art of Hostile Biography: Portraying Muhammad in Thirteenth-Century Christian Spain," in *Pensamiento hispano medieval: homenaje a Horacio Santiago Otero*, edited by José María Soto Rábanos (Madrid: Consejo Superior de Investigaciones Científicas, 1998), 1497–1511.

Chapter 4: "Peter the Venerable on the "Diabolical Heresy of the Saracens," in *The Devil, Heresy, and Witchcraft in the Middle Ages: Essays in Honor of Jeffrey B. Russell*, edited by Alberto Ferreiro (Leiden: Brill, 1998), 345–67.

Chapter 5: In French, as "Le Baptême du Roi 'Païen' dans les Épopées de la Croisade," *Revue de l'Histoire des Religions* 217 (2000): 707–31.

Chapter 6: "Images of the Other: Europe and the Muslim World before 1700," *Cairo Papers on Social Science* 19, no. 2 (Summer 1996): 7–38.

Chapter 7: In French, as "*Veneratio Sarracenorum*: dévotion commune entre musulmans et chrétiens selon Burchard de Strasbourg, ambassadeur de Frédéric Barberousse auprès de Saladin (v. 1175)," in *Chrétiens et musulmans en méditerranée médiévale (VIIIe-XIIIe siècle): échanges et contacts*, edited by N. Prouteau and P. Sénac (Poitiers: Centre d'Études Supérieures de Civilisation Médiévale, 2003), 185–95.

Chapter 8: "Saracen Philosophers Secretly Deride Islam," *Medieval Encounters: Jewish, Christian, and Muslim Culture in Confluence and Dialogue*," 8 (2002): 185–208.

Chapter 9: In French as "Barrières de haine et de mépris : la polémique anti-islamique de Pedro Pascual," in *Identidad y representación de la frontera en la España medieval (siglos XI–XIV)*, edited by C. de Ayala, P. Josserand and P. Buresi (Madrid: Casa de Velázquez, 2001), 253–66.

Chapter 10: In French, as "Affreux vacarme: sons de cloches et voix de muezzins dans la polémique interconfessionnelle en péninsule ibérique," in *Pouvoir, guerre et idéologie autour de l'an mil en péninsule ibérique* (Poitiers: Centre d'Études Supérieures de Civilisation Médiévale, 2004).

Index

The Arabic article al- is not taken into account for alphabetization.

John V. Tolan, professor of medieval history at the University of Nantes, France, is the author of numerous articles and books in medieval history and cultural studies, including *Petrus Alfonsi and His Medieval Readers*, *Saracens: Islam in the Medieval European Imagination*, and *Saint Francis and the Sultan: The Curious History of a Christian-Muslim Encounter.* He is also the coauthor of *Europe and the Islamic World.* He currently is director of a major project funded by the European Research Council, "RELMIN: The legal status of religious minorities in the Euro-Mediterranean world (5th-15th centuries)" (www.relmin.eu).

www.ingramcontent.com/pod-product-compliance
Lightning Source LLC
Chambersburg PA
CBHW020835160426
43192CB00007B/658
9780813044675